Ethics of Tibet

Bibliotheca Indo-Buddhica Series No. 108

Ethics of Tibet

Bodhisattva Section of Tsong-Kha-Pa's Lam Rim Chen Mo

Translated from the Tibetan original by

Alex Wayman

Foreword by the Dalai Lama

SRI SATGURU PUBLICATIONS
A DIVISION OF
INDIAN BOOKS CENTRE
DELHI-INDIA

Sri Satguru Publications
A Division of
Indian Books Centre
24/4, Shakti Nagar, Near Dena Bank,
Delhi-110007
(INDIA)

ISBN 81-7030-324-9

Printed at :
D.K. Fine Art Press,
Delhi

Printed in India

Contents

THE DALAI LAMA

FOREWORD

Of the many works of the Tibetan master Tsong-kha-pa, few compare in terms of popularity and breadth of influence with his *Great Exposition of the Stages of the Path, (Lam-rim Chen-mo)* which has been treasured by practitioners and scholars alike for centuries. What distinguishes it as one of the principal texts of Mahayana Buddhism is its scope and clarity. It expounds the entire path, from the way one should rely on a spiritual teacher, which is the very root, right up to the attainment of complete Buddhahood, which is the final fruit. The various stages of the path are presented so clearly and systematically that they can be easily understood and are inspiring to put into practice.

The heart of Mahayana training is the altruistic aspiration for enlightenment, the practice of the six perfections, and so forth, characteristic of a Bodhisattva. In addition to its clarity, Tsong-kha-pa's presentation of this topic is inspiring due to its sheer authority, for he draws not only on the works of the great Indian pioneers such as Nagarjuna, Asanga, Shantideva and Kamalashila, but also incorporates advice from the mind training tradition of the early Kadampa masters of Tibet.

This English translation of the section concerning the practice of a Bodhisattva, specifically the first five perfections, is welcome. Nowadays there are many people, who although they do not read Tibetan, have an abiding interest in these instructions.

I admire the worthy intentions of the translator and pray that those who seek actually to engage in this inestimable mode of training will meet with complete success.

Tenzin Gyatso

July 30, 1990

Introduction

It is a keen pleasure for the translator to present this Bodhisattva section of the *Lam rim chen mo* by Tsong-kha-pa (1357–1419, A.D.) who finished this great work on the Buddhist path in 1402 A.D. in the medium of the Tibetan language. The Bodhisattva section is a remarkable exposition of Buddhist ethics—an exemplary piece of Tibetan writing in the "golden age" of Tibetan culture. It is a kind of gem, deserving of every intelligent effort to make it shine in the English language as it does in its original Tibetan version.

The Bodhisattva section comes just prior to the last two parts of the *Lam rim chen mo,* which the present translator published (1978) under the title *Calming the Mind and Discerning the Real.*[1] It comes as the third of three sections of respective teaching to three different kinds of persons (*infra.*) delineated in the *Bodhipathapradīpa* (Light on the Path to Enlightenment) by Atīśa. Atīśa's path lineage, as it comes down to Tsong-kha-pa, combines the practice theory of the famous Buddhist masters, Nāgārjuna and Asaṅga. A way in which these two kinds of lineage present themselves has already been shown in the book *Calming the Mind and Discerning the Real.* The Bodhisattva section shows this combination in a different way (see, below, "The Tibetan author's authorities"). Since the teaching is differentiated for each of the three kinds of persons, the teaching directed to the Bodhisattva is complete in itself. Besides, Tsong-kha-pa's Bodhisattva exposition is so sufficiently detailed—indeed well-prepared—that with inevitable supporting data it can constitute a solid and important volume, even though the preceding part of the *Lam rim chen mo* had not been rendered into publishable English.

There are already in Western languages a number of works dealing with the Buddhist theory of the Bodhisattva. Tsong-kha-pa's treatment should be acknowledged as a significant advance over the comparable material in the classical study by Har Dayal, *The Bodhisattva Doctrine,* which by its very title would not admit that this is a *practice*. Of course, the translations of Śāntideva's *Śikṣāsamuccaya* and *Bodhicaryāvatāra,* and more recently Ārya-Śūra's *Pāramitāsamāsa,* give the reader an idea of this practice.[2] Even so, Tsong-kha-pa's contribution will doubtless cast light on these works in an inimitable fashion. The Bodhisattva section—difficult to translate — should demonstrate the maturity of Tibetan writing on religious topics, especially on ethics, with its subtle distinctions. I may even dare predict that it will stand the test of time as a kind of classic.

This part of the *Lam rim chen mo* represents for the translator a long-time preoccupation and objective. The first draft rendition of the section was made during a year in the late 1950's, but not seriously attended to until the end of the 1970's after the publication of the last two parts, as mentioned above. Then I completely revised my early draft, especially bearing down on the citations, since most of them had extant Sanskrit. Because of various baffling passages, I sought and received help from the American Institute of Indian Studies for research in India during the period Dec. 20, 1981 to Jan. 19, 1982, in Dharamsala, Himachal Pradesh. During the various meetings there, the learned Geshe Lobsang Gyatso, Director of the Tibetan School of Dialectics, helped solve certain knotty problems that I pointed out to him. A specialist in Tibetan medicine, Lobsang Rapgay, interpreted for the Geshe and also made suggestions for the translation starting from its beginning. When in Spring 1988 the Ganden Foundation of New York City brought Geshe Lobsang Gyatso to New York for a series of lectures, I was able to attend two of them. I was reminded of my plan about the Bodhisattva section, from which I had been diverted by other commitments and numerous requests for articles in the intervening years. Thereupon I was privileged to have the precious help of my colleague Lozang Jampal who has gone through the whole translation making numerous suggestions for improvement. I had traced out the original

Sanskrit for most of Tsong-kha-pa's citations. Much has gone into placing the Bodhisattva section before the reader.

Three Different Kinds of Persons

The first part of the *Lam rim chem mo* dealing with the three orders of persons expands upon the brief but trenchant teachings of Atiśa's *Bodhipathapradīpa*. The relevant verses (nos. 2 – 5) should be given here:[3]

> Three (religious degrees of) persons should be known—as lesser, middling, and superior. Their characteristics will be clarified; their differentiation delineated.
>
> Whoever, by whatever means, pursues only one's own aim in just the pleasures of this world, that one is known as the lesser person.
>
> Whoever, turning one's back on the pleasures of phenomenal existence, and averting oneself from sinful actions, pursues only one's own quiescence, that one is known as the middling person.
>
> Whoever, through the suffering belonging to one's own stream of consciousness, completely desires the right cessation of all the suffering of others—that person is superior.

It follows that there is a different kind of teaching for each of these three kinds of persons. The four persuasions which are treated at the end of this Bodhisattva section must change interpretation for the kind of person. The four are Giving, Pleasant speech, Aim inducement, and Common pursuits. Evidently to start with the first kind of person, Tsong-kha-pa cites *Sūtrālaṃkāra* (XVI, 74):

> By the first [Giving], one becomes a fit candidate. By the second [Pleasant speech], one has faith. By the third [Aim inducement], one practices. By the fourth [Common pursuits], one applies.

The teaching is clearly intended for both men and women. Buddhist scriptures refer to "sons of the family" and "daughters of the family." Accordingly, the translator has tried to avoid the male pronoun in passages of general instruction, and where the text itself does not assign, for example, a male value, to the pronouns.

Mahāyāna literature also speaks of three kinds of persons, calling them Śrāvaka, Pratyekabuddha, and Bodhisattva. While Atīśa's descriptions in the above-cited verses do not directly apply to these names, it does appear that the aim of this Path lineage is to so teach the first kind of person in those verses that one will become a Śrāvaka; the second kind will become a Pratyekabuddha; the third kind will become a Bodhisattva.

Besides the specialized instructions to those three kinds of persons, there is a common or shared instruction. For the latter, Tsong-kha-pa, in his treatment of the first kind of person ("lesser"), cites Candrakīrti's *Madhyamakāvatāra* (II,7) regarding the common applicability of the ten paths of virtuous *karma*:[4]

> so so'i skye bo rnams dang gsung skyes dang
> rang byang chub la bdag nyid nges rnams dang
> rgyal sras rnams kyi nges par legs pa dang
> mngon mtho'i rgyu na tshul khrims las gzhan med

> For ordinary persons [*pṛthagjana*]; for those [i.e. Śrāvakas] born from [the Buddha's] speech; for those self-determined toward the enlightenment of the Pratyekabuddha; for the excellence of the children [i.e. Bodhisattvas] of the Jina, there is no cause of a good result other than morality.

The ten virtuous paths are the ten kinds of refraining from unvirtuous actions, namely, three of body — killing sentient beings, stealing, wrong sexual conduct; four of speech — lying, harsh words, slander, chatter; three of mind — covetousness, ill will, deviant views.

Regarding the three kinds of path persons taken individually, a Mahāyāna scripture called *Ajātaśatrukaukṛttyavinodana*,[5] utilized in the Derge ed., Mdo sde, Vol. Tsha, has revealing information. At Tsha, f. 241b – 2,3, the scripture mentions that there are three groups (*piṭaka*), namely, the Śrāvaka, Pratyekabuddha, and Bodhisattva. In explanation it states:

rigs kyi bu dag de la nyan thos kyi sde snod ni pha rol gyi sgra'i rjes su 'brang bas thob pa'o
rang sangs rgyas kyi sde snod ni rten cing 'brel par 'byung pa rtogs pa'i phyir rgyu zad par rtogs pa'o
rigs kyi bu dag byang chub sems dpa'i sde snod ni chos tshad med pa rtogs shing rang byung ba'i ye shes dang 'thun pa'o

Children of the family, among them the group [*piṭaka*] of the Śrāvakas has the receipt by following the speeches of others. The group of the Pratyekabuddhas completely comprehends the causes by comprehending Dependent Origination. Children of the family, the group of the Bodhisattvas is consistent with the self-originated wisdom, comprehending the immeasurable Dharma.

At Tsha, f. 241b–6,7, the scripture mentions that there are three practices associated with these groups:

rigs kyi bu dag de la nyan thos kyi bslab pa ni phyogs gcig pa bdag gi bsam pa'i rgyud snang ba'i mtshan nyid do
rang sangs rgyas kyi bslab pa ni nan tan bar ma dang ldan zhing snying rje chen po dang bral ba'o
rigs kyi bu dag byang chub sems dpa'i bslab pa ni tshad med pa'i rjes su song ba
snying rje chen pos zin pa'o

Children of the family, the practice of the Śrāvakas is characterized as the appearance in their streams of consciousness of their own expectations of a single direction. The practice of the Pratyekabuddhas has interruptions in endeavor and lacks great compassion. Children of the family, the practice of the Bodhisattvas has immeasurable approaching and is controlled by great compassion.

Tsong-kha-pa has various remarks about Mahāyāna, incorporating many avenues and approaches, and thus he contrasts with the Śrāvaka emphasis on a single direction.[6] Tsong-kha-pa's earlier section on the middling person does include the explanation of Dependent Origination, and so implicates the Pratyekabuddha. Besides, when the Pratyekabuddha is pointed to as lacking 'great compassion,' this does not amount to denying compassion in either the Śrāvaka or the Pratyekabuddha. This is because Tsong-kha-pa's large treatment of generating the Thought of Enlightenment clarifies that 'great compassion' is the kind which the Bodhisattva meditates upon to expand and continue at all times and in all postures, whether standing, lying down, etc.

The Tibetan Author's Authorities

Tsong-kha-pa's main authority for the Bodhisattva section is the corpus of canonical works that are agreed upon in this Path tradition. To be included in the Mādhyamika, descendant from Nāgārjuna, is Nāgārjuna's own *Ratnāvalī* (partly available in Sanskrit), Śāntideva's *Śikṣāsamuccaya* and *Bodhicaryāvatāra;* Kamalaśīla's three *Bhāvanākrama* (BK). In the Yogācāra, there are two works in Asaṅga's tradition—the *Mahāyāna-Sūtrālaṃkāra* and the *Bodhisattvabhūmi*. Ārya-Śūra's *Pāramitāsamāsa* and Candragomin's *Śiṣyalekha* may well go with both the Nāgārjuna and the Asaṅga traditions. Fortunately, except for BK Two, the other treatises mentioned are available in edited Sanskrit.

Tsong-kha-pa also accepts as authoritative certain sayings of older teachers of Tibet. Geshe Lobsang Gyatso mentioned that various of these personages, Po-to-ba and Śa-ra-ba in particular, were from a Tibetan province called Kongpo, which is East of Lhasa. There are plausible reasons for Tsong-kha-pa to include these sayings. He could include them to honor the transmitters of the Path lineage from Atīśa. The handed-down sayings do add to the author's powerful statement of Bodhisattva practice, and do serve the end of making this section as appealing as possible and thus successful as a work of literature. But perhaps the most important reason for including them is to suggest how the Tibetans grappled with these teachings, trying to take them to heart; and so it was not just a matter of what was in the Buddhist texts called the Dharma, but that the Tibetans tried to practice accordingly, and then ran into various problems which the sayings allude to.

Tsong-kha-pa also stressed chapters or works on Buddhist ethics as his special concern. Thus, he wrote a commentary on the morality chapter (*śīlapaṭala*) of the *Bodhisattvabhūmi* — the *Byang chub gzhung lam*, which he refers to three times in the present Bodhisattva section.[7] He wrote a work on the Vinaya novice, the *Gnam lce ldeng ma*, and a treatise on Bhikṣu practices, the *Gnam lce ldeng mar grags pa*. He also made a synopsis of Guṇaprabha's *Vinayasūtra*. He wrote a commentary on the *Gurupañcāśikā* (Fifty verses on the Guru), the *Slob ma'i re ba kun skong*, and a treatise on Vajrayāna ethics, the *Dngos grub kyi snye ma*. In the *Lam rim chen mo* itself, the first two sections devoted to the "lesser person" and the "middling person" are very much colored by ethical expositions, as is this whole Bodhisattva section. There is little doubt that the author has expressed himself on ethical issues energetically and at length. These ethical matters involve past Tibetan arguments going back to the first period of Tibetan Buddhism.[8]

The Doctrinal Foundation

The Tibetan author presents the Bodhisattva practice in two parts. In terms of the Tashilunpo edition of the *Lam rim chen mo*, the entire section on Bodhisattva practice ('Precepts for the Great Person') goes from f. 167b–2 to 282a–3. Part I of the section, starting at 167b–2, is devoted to the Thought of Enlightenment (*bodhicitta*), and Part II, starting at 214b–5, to the Stages of Instruction (the six Perfections and the four Persuasions). The exposition should agree with the Path lineage brought into Tibet by Atīśa (entered Tibet in 1042 A.D.) — combining the teachings descended from Nāgārjuna (c. 100–200 A.D.) and Asaṅga (c. 375–430).

The part from Asaṅga's tradition is in a textual sense the treatises *Sūtrālaṃkāra* and *Bodhisattvabhūmi*. These in turn depend upon a preceding literature called *Bodhisattvapiṭaka*, especially the *Bodhisattvapiṭaka-sūtra* and the *Akṣayamatinirdeśa-sūtra*.[9] The former of these contains on a *sūtra* level (part of the Ratnakūṭa collection of Mahāyāna scriptures) a discussion of the Thought of Enlightenment, the six Perfections, and finally the four Persuasions, which is the structure of the present Bodhisattva section of the *Lam rim chen mo*.[10] Aside from this structural resemblance, the *sūtra* discussion — a compilation of about 100 A.D. — has little in common with the actual content of Tsong-kha-pa's section. The reason for this striking difference in content is that the primitive exposition of this Bodhisattva practice was undoubtedly assailed by the more conservative wing of Buddhism and could not defend itself. Speaking briefly, the subsequent rewriting of this material gradually forged a more convincing front. Before it could get into the appearance of the *Lam rim chen mo*, the Bodhisattva theory had to put on a more secure footing by a movement headed by Nāgārjuna.

Nāgārjuna during his long life spanning the second century, A.D., appears to have had three careers. First, as a young teacher at Nālandā he engaged in many debates with the Abhidharmists, and these activities culminated around 150 A.D. with his famous Madhyamaka works such as the *Madhyamaka-kārikā* and the *Vigrahavyāvartinī*. Next he seems to have become head of a large Buddhist establishment in far Northwest India, guiding the new movement which would become known as the 'Great Vehicle,' especially with the production of a kind of scripture called *Prajñāpāramitā*, starting with the '8,000' one — for which activities his life would become regarded with awe and legends would grow up around him. Then in the last quarter of the second century, being invited to South India by a Śatavāhana king—and probably back to his birthplace — he promoted Buddhist activities here with the evidence of two letters to the king, the well-known *Suhṛllekha* and the *Ratnāvalī*.[11] In the second of these, one of the chapters presents the system of ten Bodhisattva stages with names that would be the basis of the Mahāyāna scripture *Daśabhūmika* stressing the need for the gradual path to Buddhahood, while the *Prajñāpāramitā* scriptures taught the enlightenment in a single moment that culminates the gradual path. Both these scriptural positions are basic to the Bodhisattva section of the *Lam rim chen mo*. It was this Nāgārjuna lineage which, combined with the *Bodhisattvapiṭaka* structure that was to be elaborated in Asaṅga's school, leads directly to the presentation in the present Bodhisattva section.

The *Daśabhūmika-sūtra* allots a Perfection prominence to each Bodhisattva stage in their regular order, with the other five (of the six Perfections) subordinated. This system is presented within the exposition of *dāna-pāramitā* (the Perfection of Giving) in Tsong-kha-pa's work. No attempt is made to show how the fractional system of the Perfections is worked out for the last four of the ten Bodhisattva stages.

In short, the main exposition of the Bodhisattva section follows the lead of Asaṅga's tradition, but there is no doubt that the tradition of the *Ratnāvalī* and the *Daśabhūmika-sūtra* is also insisted upon. Kamalaśīla's three *Bhāvanākrama* and Śāntideva's two treatises are of the highest importance to Tsong-kha-pa.

As to the *Abhisamayālaṃkāra*'s five paths, Tsong-kha-pa alludes to one of them, the 'stage of praxis' (*prayoga-mārga*), during his discussion of the 'Perfection of Forbearance' (*kṣānti-pāramitā*), but only when treating the theories of some scholars about "destroying the roots of virtue." Hence, this kind of *Prajñāpāramitā* exegesis is not involved in the formulation of the Bodhisattva section.

The Thought of Enlightenment

The theory of a Bodhisattva taking on the Thought of Enlightenment contrasts with the old ideal of getting liberated, for which the words *mokṣa* and *nirvāṇa* were employed. Historically, it was a stress on the 'Jewel of the Buddha' rather than the Arhat ideal which was the finest fruit of the Buddhist 'Jewel of the Sāṃgha.' In the old days, it was the Mahāsāṃghika sect which gradually built up the theory of the Bodhisattva, modelled after the life and theoretical former lives of Gautama Buddha. Perhaps the scripture *Bodhisattvapiṭaka-sūtra*, which is a rambling, loosely knit text, constitutes the ultimate form of this effort by the Mahāsāṃghikas, and came to this form around 100 A.D. But then it was taken out of the hands of the Mahāsāṃghika when this scripture was redone in the form of the *Akṣayamatinirdeśa-sūtra* in the second half of the second cent. A.D. It was this latter scripture which was the scriptural base of the Bodhisattva theory inherited by Asaṅga later on, to use for his Mahāyāna treatises.

In Tsong-kha-pa's subsection "The Teaching that Buddhahood is not accomplished by practicing the means or insight in isolation" he mentions that Kamalaśīla has well set forth the two kinds of 'Thought of Enlightenment,' the conventional (*saṃvṛti*) and the absolute (*paramārtha*) kinds. The basic discussion is in Kamalaśīla's *Bhāvanākrama Two*, while a two kinds are also in his *Bhāvanākrama One*. Thus in *BK Two* at PTT Vol. 102 (Tibetan edition), p. 31 – 3 – 2, ff., Kamalaśīla states for the 'conventional Thought of Enlightenment' that one with compassion commiserates with suffering humanity and initially generates the mind of enlightenment thinking that as a Buddha he could help sentient beings. Afterwards he should attain the 'absolute' Thought of Enlightenment, which is supramundane, free from elaboration, immaculate, and so on. *BK One* in G. Tucci's edition says that *bodhicitta* is of two kinds, the mind of aspiration (*praṇidhicitta*) and the mind of entrance (*prasthānacitta*). *BK One* defines the first kind, 'mind of aspiration' as follows: "The initial goal-oriented idea, 'May I become a Buddha for the benefit of all living beings.'" And defines the second kind 'mind of entrance' as follows: "The subsequent engagement in the collections (of merit and knowledge) while holding the vow (*saṃvara*)." These latter two could be counted as 'conventional Mind of Enlightenment.' The contrast between the 'conventional' and the 'absolute' kinds of Mind of Enlightenment is, as mentioned by my colleague Lozang Jamspal, to regard them as respectively 'contrived' and 'spontaneous.' The absolute kind is enlightenment (*bodhi*), as when the *Aṣṭasāhasrikā Prajñāpāramitā* in its beginning refers to it as 'non-*citta*,' namely, changeless and unconstructed; spontaneous because reached and non-contrived.

Given the 'Thought of Enlightenment,' it is taught that the Bodhisattva shares with the Śrāvaka and the Pratyekabuddha the removal of the 'hindrance of defilement' (*kleśa-āvaraṇa*) and the experience of Voidness, but also that the motives differ and that the Bodhisattva is doing it in the course of his career while practicing the six Perfections and the four Persuasions. And in terms of the ten-stage theory, upon entering the Eighth Stage the Bodhisattva has overcome the 'hindrance of defilement,' but still has to eliminate the 'defilement of the knowable' (*jñeya-āvaraṇa*), which will be noticed below as the 'discursive thought' of the three spheres (*trimaṇḍala*). This can also be referred to as 'purification of the three spheres.' And this is the course toward enlightenment.

The Six Perfections

The second part of the Bodhisattva section accordingly is devoted to the Bodhisattva's career with a double aim—the practice of the six Perfections as his own aim, and the practice of the four Persuasions as the aim of others.

The foregoing helps explain why the Perfections of Giving (*dāna-pāramitā*) is the first of the six and is given so much space for its development. As easily observed, 'giving' enters strongly into the four Persuasions, and while it was employed metaphorically it is the example for the 'three spheres' (*trimaṇḍala*), the giver, the gift, and the recipient. This Perfection is the topic of probably the most famous of the 'birth stories' (*jātaka*), and the first ten of the *Jātakamālā* are of this type. Among the most well-known ones are the King Viśvamtara who gave everything away, and King Śibi who in one version gave his eyes to the blind beggar and in another version gave his flesh to the hawk, while both the askers were Indra in diguise.

The second Perfection, Morality (*śīla*), has been pointed to as a special interest of Tsong-kha-pa's; and shows the continuity into Mahāyāna Buddhism of the old Buddhist stress on morality. Here is the tenfold path of *karma*, meaning the ten previously exposed above. Morality will bring one to heaven, but it is taught that there is a return, after a long interim, from heaven. Appealing to the *Bodhisattvabhūmi*, the author insists that the Bodhisattva, whether home-based or a monk in the religious life, must have the Prātimokṣa-vow (the Vinaya morality) as a basis for the Bodhisattva vow. Furthermore, in Tsong-kha-pa's tantric reform, it is necessary to have those two as a preliminary for the birth of the Mantra vow.

The next Perfection is *kṣānti*, rendered 'forbearance.' The injunction here especially is against the holding of anger at imagined or actual mistreatment. This Perfection makes it difficult for the performer to enter into the usual kind of debate, where the parties frequently become incensed at each other. To hold this Perfection is said to be the best austerity.

The rendition 'Perfection of Striving' is adopted for the expression *vīrya-pāramitā*, based on the definition in the *Caryāvatāra* (VII, 2a) which Tsong-kha-pa cites for the 'actuality' (Asaṅga's term *svabhāva* in the *Bodhisattvabhūmi* when defining the individual *pāramitā*-s) of *vīrya*. Long ago I noticed this definition and accordingly favored the rendition 'striving.'

For the last two of the six Perfections, namely, 'meditation' (*dhyāna*) and 'insight' (*prajñā*), the author's treatment is replete with interesting and important information. He invites the reader to read the expanded versions of these two in the last two sections of the *Lam rim chen mo*, which show respectively the steps of practice for 'meditation' and 'insight.' The present translator published these two lengthy sections in the book *Calming the Mind and Discerning the Real*.

Under the 'insight perfection,' Tsong-kha-pa mentions that the other five perfections in the absence of 'insight' are like a missing eye, and for this he cites the *Saṃcaya-gāthā* (VII,1).

The Mahāyāna

The term *yāna* is translated into Tibetan as *theg pa*, which means a 'vehicle' or 'carriage,' so there should be no objection to rendering the term *mahāyāna* as 'great vehicle.' The scriptures referred to as *Mahāyāna-sūtra* (an expression which came into use circa 200 A.D.) appear to agree in presenting the career of a person called the 'Bodhisattva.' Yet it is certain that the concept of a Bodhisattva and the attribution of certain practices to such a person, considerably antedate the use of the expression 'Mahāyāna' or 'Mahāyāna-sūtra.'

For scriptural references to 'Mahāyāna,' I have first consulted the *Bodhisattvapiṭaka-sūtra*, which in the Peking Kanjur canon starts in Vol. Dzi and ends in Vol. Wi (in the Ratnakūṭa group). In PTT, Vol. 22, p. 252–2–1, there is the explanation of the term 'bodhisattva' but without the term 'mahāyāna,' as follows: "The one possessing the aspiration of a Bodhisattva and the thought of enlightenment of such sort is called 'Bodhisattva'" (byang chub sems dpa' bsam pa dang / byang chub kyi sems de lta bu dang ldan pa ni / byang chub sems dpa' zhes bya bya'o). The only reference to 'Mahāyāna' that I have succeeded in finding in this large scripture is worth citing for its message, namely, near the scripture's end, PTT, Vol. 23, p. 89–2–8. Among the explanations for the 'Four Persuasions' (see the treatment in the present Bodhisattva section at its end), this scripture says for the fourth one: "*Common pursuits* means consignment to the Mahāyāna" (don 'thun pa ni theg pa chen po la bsngo ba'o). The scripture evidently intends that the Bodhisattva in "common pursuits" creates a Mahāyāna family. This may also be the intention in the Mahāyāna scripture *Śrī-Mālādevīsiṃhanāda* (translated by A. and H. Wayman with title *The Lion's Roar of Queen Śrīmālā*) of mentioning a *'bodhisattvagaṇa.'*

The *Aṣṭasāhasrikā Prajñāpāramitā* in its first chapter devotes a section to the meaning of 'Great Vehicle.' At the end of the explanation, the scripture says that one cannot apperceive the Great Vehicle's beginning (*anta*), its end (*aparānta*), or its middle (*madhya*); that this vehicle is the same (*sama*); and so it is called 'Great Vehicle.' The term *sama* here is intriguing in the light of the *Bodhisattvapiṭaka-sūtra*'s explanation for the fourth Persuasion, for which the *Mahāyāna-Sūtrālaṃkāra*, XVI, 72, gives the Sanskrit term *samārthatā*, rendered above as *common pursuits*. So if the intention of the '8,000' scripture is that this Great Vehicle is the same for all beings in it, there is agreement with the *Bodhisattvapiṭaka-sūtra*.

Tsong-kha-pa starts his Bodhisattva section by bringing in the notion of the Great Vehicle, also called in citations 'Royal Vehicle' and 'ultimate vehicle,' and which is entered only by generating the Thought of Enlightenment. In the initial citation from *Pāramitāsamāsa* (VI, 65), the nature of this vehicle is stated to be "the single taste of benefit for others," so this may also be the intention of the term *sama* in the '8,000' scripture, namely, the *same taste* of benefit.

The Old Debate about 'Discursive Thought'

It appears that the Mahāyāna was welded in a hotbed of controversy. The contrasting views continued over the centuries, and many of these arguments were transferred to Tibet. Tsong-kha-pa especially uses his large subsection on requiring both 'means' (*upāya*) and 'insight' (*prajñā*), to present these disputed matters. We read there: "Hva-shang has (tried to) prove that position by quoting eighty sources of scriptures that praise 'by all means no discursive thought.'" What is meant is that in the c. 792 A.D. debate between the Chinese party, headed by Hva-Shang Mahāyāna, and the Indian party, headed by Kamalaśīla—it is the position of the Chinese party in the dispute that enlightenment is an instantaneous matter upon realizing the pure mind within when free from all discursive thought. Since this is realized within, what is the use of Giving, the Perfection, which involves outside beings? Similarly, morality, to accord with the norms of society, is immaterial to such a realization. This of course does not implicate stinginess or immorality among partisans of such a view: it is rather that such externally directed activities are deemed to be irrelevant to the nature of enlightenment.

Tsong-kha-pa's position is overwhelmingly in support of Kamalaśīla's three *Bhāvanākrama*. It is fair to state that the Tibetan author, due to his extensive learning, due to his deep understanding, and due to his mastery of writing in his own Tibetan language, has advanced Kamalaśīla's arguments. Indeed, the Tibetan author obviously condemns the Chinese party's viewpoint in no uncertain terms, and by implication thereby rejects certain contemporary theories of other Tibetan sects. Tsong-kha-pa does not mention that the opposing position shows a deficient education in the use of grammar and the meaning of words, although this appears to be the case.

That is to say, when such an expression as *amanasikāra* occurs in these texts — it did! — a reader might think it means "no *manasikāra* (attention to something)." But the Sanskrit negation a/an- is susceptible of six different interpretations according to the Sanskrit grammarians. For example, the expression *akāka* does not mean 'no crow,' but 'not a crow,' i.e. any bird (or other creature) that is not a crow. The expression *adharma* (contrasting with *dharma*) does not mean 'no *dharma*' but 'bad *dharma*.' And in the '8,000' scripture, the term *acitta*, as was previously mentioned, does not mean 'no mind' (at all), but 'no thinking' (in that case). Indeed, every case of 'thinking' can be called 'not thinking' since one cannot think of something without failing to think of many other things. While this should seem obvious, one would be naive to believe that the debators of such issues are aware of the 'obvious.' In fact, it is precisely such a situation that is present in the debate about 'discursive thought,' since in these texts 'no discursive thought' implies 'discursive thought.'

When in that mentioned subsection Tsong-kha-pa discusses three *sūtra* passages and shows how they are misunderstood, the bare fact is that they are indeed misunderstood (whether or not the persons so misunderstanding are poorly educated). Among those three as cited in *Bhāvanākrama Three*, fortunately the Sanskrit is given for an unnamed *sūtra* at Tucci's edition, p. 22.18 to 23.1. Then, it is a second citation, p. 23.6–10 that Tsong-kha-pa reports as the *Triskandhaka*, a Mahāyāna scripture that in the Derge Kanjur is in Mdo sde, Vol. Ya. The third passage is the *Brahmaparipṛcchā* with the Sanskrit at p. 24.1–2. Tsong-kha-pa's longest discussion is of the second one, the *Triskandhaka*. From his treatment, one may interpret this title *triskandhaka* as equivalent in meaning to the term *trimaṇḍala*, previously mentioned as meaning the giver, the gift, and the recipient—whether concretely or metaphorically. Near the end of the Bodhisattva section is a citation credited to Maitreya (i.e. one of the five books of Maitreya according to the Tibetan tradition, the *Byams sde lnga*), which I located in the *Uttaratantra* (*Ratnagotravibhāga*), V, 14 – 15, of which k. 14 is the following according to the Tibetan translation:

> We claim that the discursive thought (*vikalpa*) of the three spheres (*trimaṇḍala*) is the hindrance of the knowable (*jñeyāvaraṇa*).// We claim that the discursive thought of stinginess and so on, is the hindrance of defilement (*kleśāvaraṇa*).

According to the theory of the gradual path exposed in such a scripture as the *Daśabhūmika,* one must first get rid of defilement, by getting 'no discursive thought' namely, of stinginess, etc. And yet with this 'no discursive thought' one still has 'discursive thought,' namely, of the 'three spheres.' It is true that one must also get rid of this kind of discursive thought in order to be 'enlightened.' However, the partisans of 'no discursive thought (at all)' do not explain it this way, but claim there is an 'instantaneous' enlightenment which does not require the gradual path. Certainly, according to Indian Buddhism one must follow this gradual path in order to reach the 'instantaneous enlightenment' at its culmination. Therefore, the position of the Chinese party in the dispute might be correct (but we need not concede this) as a non-Buddhist system — it is certainly not correct as a Buddhist system.

Besides, that enlightenment consists in attaining the pure mind within free from discursive thought is denied in the content of the five dreams of Gautama that portended his enlightenment — the five that are in Pāli in the Aṅguttara-nikāya, Vol. III; in the *Mahāvastu,* Vol. II, and that are in the Mahāyāna Buddhist biography of the Buddha, the *Lalitavistara*. It can quickly be determined by reading these five dreams in any of those three versions that the portent of enlightenment involves reaching out to the receptacle world (the *bhājana-loka*) and to the sentient world (the *sattva-loka*). Hence, these dreams show the overcoming of the 'hindrance of the knowable.' Thus, the Buddhist solution for the enlightenment preparation involves going outside of oneself, not a retreat within. It is true though that the prescription for getting rid of defilement — since this is a personal matter — does require getting rid of this kind of discursive thought, with the aim of liberation, but not of enlightenment.

Besides, the topic should not be left without a pointing out that both the Eightfold Noble Path of early Buddhism and the Three Instructions (*triśikṣā*) insisted upon in this Bodhisattva section accept that there is a good kind of discursive thought, as when one thinks, "This act won't do; the other act is better." This of course as long as one stays in the scope of Buddhism. This is not to deny that some persons might prefer otherwise, but then why claim that the 'otherwise' is Buddhism?

Tsong-kha-pa's Autobiographical Sketch

As to Tsong-kha-pa's own biography, I presented a brief version in the introduction to my translation *Calming the Mind and Discerning the Real*. Besides, a book of selections entitled *Life & Teachings of Tsong Khapa* was published at Dharamsala; from which the reader can derive more information.[12] This latter work contains a translation of Tsong-kha-pa's *Mdun legs ma*, a kind of autobiographical text. Since I also published a translation of this text within my article in *IIJ*, 1972, it seems proper to reprint it here. The original translation was made with the help of Gonsar Rinpoche, when I was in Dharamsala in 1970 (now he is the head of the Tibetan center at Vevey, Switzerland). My colleague Lozang Jamspal suggested to me the rendering 'Thank you' in the verse refrain. Here I omit the Tibetan which was presented in transcription in the *IIJ* article:

> Om. May there be happiness and good fortune! I worship at the feet of the kindly guru and Venerable Treasure of Wisdom, who are the roots of happiness and good fortune, the eyes viewing the world, heaven and the way of release; and the plane of utmost rest in the tiring journey through *saṃsāra*.
>
> It is said that the time of meager effort is best for collecting magnanimity and for sympathetic joy with [others'] virtue. In particular, the Victor said that when one generates the great joy free from pride in one's former virtue, the former virtue develops ever higher. In order to fulfill the meaning of that saying, and besides to repeatedly observe other stipulations, it is good to generate in the following way the joy of thee, O Mind. In the beginning frequently seek broad practice. In the middle have all the texts arise as counsel. In the end take them to heart all day and night; and consign them [to others] for the sake of spreading the Teaching. Contemplating this method, it is indeed an auspicious preparation. Thank you very much, O Venerable Treasure of Wisdom!
>
> Not having dispelled by the lamp of right practice the confusing darkness regarding abandonment and acceptance, one

does not know the way; in this case it is useless to say one can have entrance into the supreme City of Liberation! On that account, I was not satisfied with occasional consultation and rough application to the teachings of Maitreya-nātha and of those persons famed as the six ornaments and two best of India, but exerted myself in fine detail on all [of those teachings]. Contemplating this method, it is indeed an auspicious preparation. Thank you very much, O Venerable Treasure of Wisdom!

In particular, by looking in this direction, I again and again exerted myself with many efforts in the difficult spots of texts that have right principles, thus constituting the single gateway to a foundation for concrete reality. Contemplating this method, it is indeed an auspicious preparation. Thank you very much, O Venerable Treasure of Wisdom!

Even though I had often stayed on the texts of Sūtra and Tantra, when I practiced and told their deep meaning, I found that I had not advanced much from that kind of theory which has no studying let alone understanding. So I studied all the essentials of Nāgārjuna's textual school that lead in perfect theory through the path of fine principles to the opening of the Deep; and my doubts were cleared up. Contemplating this method, it is indeed an auspicious preparation. Thank you very much, O Venerable Treasure of Wisdom!

Now, for guidance to Complete Buddhahood, there are both the profound Diamond Vehicle and Pāramitā Vehicle. It is well known that the Mantra path far surpasses the Pāramitā path, like the sun and moon. Some respect this as a true word, but do not try to find out what the Diamond Vehicle is, while posing as wise men. If in such manner they are wise men, who then are the more stupid ones? It is most surprising that one should cast aside this sort of highest path so difficult to encounter. Therefore, I entered and exercised myself with many endeavors in that Deep which is the highest vehicle of the Jina and even more rare than a Buddha and which is the treasure of the two occult successes. Contemplating this method, it is indeed an auspicious preparation. Thank you very much, O Venerable Treasure of Wisdom!

When one, not knowing the way of the path of the three lower Tantras, concludes that the Anuttarayoga-tantra is the chief of the Tantra divisions, that is no more than a vow. Upon observing that, I engaged myself at length on the general and special Tantras belonging to the three families of the Kriyā-tantra, including the *Sāmānyavidhinām guhyatantra*, the *Susiddhi*, the *Subāhuparipṛcchā*, and the *Dhyānottara*. Contemplating this method, it is indeed an auspicious preparation. Thank you very much, O Venerable Treasure of Wisdom!

I then reached certitude in the parts of the Caryā-tantra, the second class of Tantra, by exercising in [and well understanding] the *Mahāvairocanābhisaṃbodhi*, the chief Tantra of this division. Contemplating this method, it is indeed an auspicious preparation. Thank you very much, O Venerable Treasure of Wisdom!

I exercised in the third Tantra division, the Yoga-tantra, with the chief works, the *Śrītattvasaṃgraha;* its Explanatory Tantra, the *Vajraśekhara*, and so on, and experienced keen enthusiasm for the Yoga-tantra. Contemplating this method, it is indeed an auspicious preparation. Thank you very much, O Venerable Treasure of Wisdom!

I exercised myself in the fourth Tantra division, the Anuttarayoga-tantra, which has texts celebrated like the sun and the moon to the learned men of India, namely, the *Guhyasamāja* of the Father Tantra, the *Hevajra* and *Srī-Cakrasaṃvara* of the Mother Tantra, their Explanatory Tantras, and so on, the great way-layer *Kālacakratantra* and its clarification the *Vimalaprabhā* which have ways of explanation differing from other Sūtras and Tantras. Contemplating this method, it is indeed an auspicious preparation. Thank you very much, O Venerable Treasure of Wisdom!

The first phase, seeking broad practice, was completed.

Then I prayed and persevered in all the set of reasons, so as to get the textual matter to arise [in my mind] as counsel. This I did by steadfast faith with protracted fierce energy toward Mañjughoṣa, who best dispels the darkness of cognition in the candidates. Contemplating this method, it is indeed an auspicious preparation. Thank you very much, O Venerable Treasure of Wisdom!

By such endeavor, I obtained uncommon certainty in the Stages of the Path to Enlightenment descended in sequence from Nāgārjuna and Asaṅga, whereupon the most profound of texts, the Pāramitā, arose as counsel. Contemplating this method, it is indeed an auspicious preparation. Thank you very much, O Venerable Treasure of Wisdom!

Now, in this Northern land, there are many, trained and untrained in the texts of logic, asserting in unison that this *"sūtra"* [by Dignāga] and the Seven Treatises [by Dharmakīrti] contain no stages to take to heart that lead to enlightenment. I found this to be an important saying lacking principle, because I respect as authoritative Mañjughoṣa's gracious prophecy to Dignāga that his composition actually would be in the future an "eye" for all living beings. Upon pondering along these lines, [I decided] that the meaning of the introductory prayer of the *Pramāṇasamuccaya* when it termed the Lord *pramāṇabhūta* [[our] authority] was that He pursued the goal of liberation by the forward and the reverse orders, proving logically. Since I had gained profound certainty that the Teaching from Him and of Him is the entering ford for those desiring liberation, I found a great joy in the fact that the essentials of the two paths, Hīnayāna and Mahāyāna, issue from this logical method. Contemplating this method, it is indeed an auspicious preparation. Thank you very much, O Venerable Treasure of Wisdom!

Then I worked methodically on the two fine compositions—the *Bodhisattvabhūmi* and the *Sūtrālaṃkāra*, correlating them, and all the texts of Maitreya the Dharmaswamin and his followers arose [in my mind] as counsel to take to heart. Contemplating this method, it is indeed an auspicious preparation. Thank you very much, O Venerable Treasure of Wisdom!

Especially by depending on the *Śikṣāsamuccaya* which bestows [on everybody] certainty in all the essentials of the path according to a sequence prepared from the scriptures broad and profound, I have seen the meaning of the many superb texts of the Nāgārjuna school, such as the *Sūtrasamuccaya*, and thus have observed the steps to take to heart. Contemplating this method, it is indeed an auspicious preparation. Thank you very much, O Venerable Treasure of Wisdom!

Then I relied on the well-expressed precepts by Buddhaguhya [in his commentaries] on the *Dhyānottara* and the *Mahāvairocanābhisambodhi*, and all the essentials of the path arose [in my mind] in the manner of counsel. Contemplating this method, it is indeed an auspicious preparation. Thank you very much, O Venerable Treasure of Wisdom!

When I had taken notice of the essentials of the path of *Śrītattvasaṃgraha* comprised by the three samādhis, it was difficult to comprehend the method of meditating on the profound meaning of even a small part of that path. But the great Pandit Buddhaguhya systematically explained, by combining them together, the Basic Tantra, Explanatory Tantra, and Part-wise Similar Tantra. The way in which he explained the meditative sequence of the profound stipulated procedures belonging to the three [lower] Tantra divisions dispelled the darkness of my cognition. Contemplating this method, it is indeed an auspicious preparation. Thank you very much, O Venerable Treasure of Wisdom!

The glorious Anuttara Tantras are the ultimate of all the well-expressed Teaching of the Muni; and among them the most profound is the *Śrī-Guhyasamājatantra*. That is stated by the illustrious speaker Nāgārjuna. The essentials of the path in the Basic Tantra are placed with the seal of six alternatives and four ways. Hence they are said to be known from the guru's oral instruction by following the Explanatory Tantra. Having grasped that method as essential, I long engaged myself with such fundamental works as the *Caryāmelāpaka* which compresses the ultimate of oral instruction as well as with minor matters of the Ārya cycle of the *Samāja*. Then the Basic Tantra was made clear like a fire lamp. Taking recourse to it, I exercised with great endeavor on the five great Explanatory Tantras and on good [commentarial] compositions. Having exercised, I obtained all the essentials constituting generalities of the two stages [of generation and completion], and in particular, the essentials of the Stage of Completion. Contemplating this method, it is indeed an auspicious preparation. Thank you very much, O Venerable Treasure of Wisdom!

By dint of that [effort], the essentials of many other Tantras, such as *Cakrasaṃvara*, *Hevajra*, *Kālacakra*, arose [in my mind] as counsel. Since I have explained them elsewhere, here there is just a doorway to the discriminating person. Contemplating this method, it is indeed an auspicious preparation. Thank you very much, O Venerable Treasure of Wisdom!

The second phase, the arising of all manner of texts as counsel, was completed.

When becoming in that way a treasure of counsel, I exercised with engagement on the path that is full of the concise essentials, namely the two kinds of stages—those of the shared path of the two Vehicles [i.e. as in the *Lam rim chen mo*] and of the unshared path of the two Vehicles [i.e. as in the *Sngags rim chen mo*]. Contemplating this method, it is indeed an auspicious preparation. Thank you very much, O Venerable Treasure of Wisdom!

The Ganges streams full of the fervent aspirations of the Jina and His spiritual children are said to be included within the fervent aspirations of the illustrious Dharma gathering. In return, to whatever extent is my collected root of virtue I consign it all for the sake of spreading the Teaching of the Sage [Muni]. Contemplating this method, it is indeed an auspicious preparation. Thank you very much, O Venerable Treasure of Wisdom!

The third phase, taking into experience throughout day and night, and consignment of all for the sake of spreading the Teaching, was completed.

I have written this personal narration, so as to greatly increase my own virtue, and so as to teach methodically and errorlessly the entrance gate to many fortunate persons of discrimination. By reason of the collection of virtues obtained, and by reason of this sequence, may all living beings take the incomparable vow of the Sage and enter the path which pleases the Victor.

Thus this explanation limited to aphoristic form of his own narration is composed at Dge ldan rnam par rgyal ba'i gling of 'Brog ri bo by the bhikshu who heard many things, Śar Tsong kha pa Blo bzang grags pa'i dpal.

Just a few notes on the above: The six ornaments are Āryadeva, Vasubandhu, Dignāga, Dharmakīrti, Guṇaprabha and Śākyaprabha; and the two best are Nāgārjuna and Asaṅga; per the usual solution.[13] The expression "looking in this direction" (Tib. *tshu rol mthong*) has Sanskrit *arvāg-darśana*, and goes with the author's first phase, practicing the texts, while looking toward conventional things in the sense of conventional truth. The second phase is the arising of texts as counsel. In the case of "proving logically," the Viennese scholar Steinkellner has pointed out that the "forward" and the "reverse" orders go with the *Pramāṇavārttika*, Siddhi chapter.[14] Also, the present writer has shown that "Part-wise Similar Tantra" is one that goes with one or more sections of the basic Yoga-tantra.[15] The six alternatives and the four ways are set forth in Wayman's work on the *Guhyasamājatantra*.[16] The third level, making it one's own life, is here the taking of it into experience in day and night, and consignment of all of it—to other sentient beings, or to the goal of enlightenment.[17]

One might think from 'uncommon experiences' related in Mkhas-grub-rje's 'secret biography' (Tsong-kha-pa's collected works, Vol. One, Ka, the *Rin-po-che'i snye ma*), that these begin with the second phase, when Tsong-kha-pa evoked the Bodhisattva Mañjughoṣa. In this secret biography there is mention of various deities and deity groups that he imaginatively evoked. However, a close study of Tsong-kha-pa's biography should reveal that he had 'uncommon experiences' starting as a child. It is also held that a certain mountain deity accompanied him when he first left his birthplace for Central Tibet; this deity is called Dge bsnyen Phying dkar ba.[18]

It is of interest to observe that such experiences did not make of Tsong-kha-pa a 'visionary' in the Western sense, with a mystical language difficult to penetrate. If this Bodhisattva section is properly translated—and the present translator has tried his best to do this—the reader should find throughout a cogency of expression, that the author has through some kind of alchemy exposed this enormously complicated and richly defined system in a manner that appeals to our understanding, that somehow gets across to us—whether or not we are motivated to follow the path which he has clarified so skillfully and sensitively.

If after the previously mentioned help from learned Tibetans on difficult points of this Bodhisattva section, and all the present translator's labors, there should still be some imperfections, the reader deserves our apology. This is because when properly translated this Bodhisattva section of the *Lam rim chen mo* is a classic of Tibetan literature and a treasure of ethics.

Part I

Precepts for the Great Person

I bow reverently at the feet of the saintly ones of great compassion.

As a consequence of contemplating that way uninterruptedly for a long time on the diversity of disadvantages of the cyclical flow *(saṃsāra)*, one views all of phenomenal life as a fire-pool.[1] The one whose mind is pressured with the desire to gain the liberation consisting in the pacification of defilements (*kleśa*) and suffering (*duḥkha*) may attain the liberation which frees that one from the cyclical flow by one's practicing the three precious subjects of instruction (*triśikṣā*)[2] and which is not like the return from the glory of heaven.[3]

Nevertheless, there is a one-sidedness of ending the faults and gaining of merit, so that one's own aim is not fulfilled,[4] and therefore one hardly fulfills the aims of others. At last, by urging of the Buddha, one must enter the Great Vehicle. Hence, it is right for those with intelligence to enter the Great Vehicle from the very beginning, just as is said in the *Pāramitāsamāsa* (VI, 65):

> Having at the very outset discarded the pair of vehicles [i.e. Śrāvaka and Pratyekabuddha], that are impotent in the method of accomplishing the aim of the world, with one's path pointed out by compassion, one must resort to the royal vehicle of the Munis, the nature of which is the single taste of benefit for others.

And (VI, 67):

> Contemplating pleasures and pains as the stuff of dreams and humanity as wretched through its fault of delusion, how could one trouble oneself with one's own aim, discarding one's proper task, which takes joy in the aims of others?

Thus, one's self seeing the living beings, as though falling into the ocean of phenomenal life, their steps in reeling gait, incapable of walking in the direction free from the danger, because of the closing of the eye of insight (*prajñā*) which discriminates accepting and rejecting, it is not right for those in the lineage of the Jina to lack compassion toward others and to not exert themselves for their aim. The *Pāramitāsamāsa* (VI, 73) says this:

> Of what man in the royal lineage of the Jina, intent on fulfilling the aim of the world, would there not be a mind with tender compassion toward those who are stumbling, their insight-eye closed, or not in him a resolute striving towards extinction of their fault of delusion.

Indeed, the joy and glory of humans, as well as the skill of humans, are the principle of carrying the burden of others' aim, because staying only in one's own aim is shared with the animals. For that reason, the character of the great ones is limited to the benefit and happiness of others. The *Śiṣyalekha* (k. 100 – 101) says this:

> Also, the animal only works for itself on the easily-obtained food of grass; or, oppressed by fierce thirst, drinks the water found fortuitously. But whatever person here exerts oneself to work for the sake of others, has one's own glory [*tejas*].[5] Indeed, this happiness is human.

> The sun, while illuminating, wanders with unwearied steeds.
> Earth, whose burdens are uncounted, always supports the world.
> No own-aim at all: this is the underlying nature of the great ones.
> They are solely absorbed in the benefit and happiness of the worldlings.

Thus, seeing the living beings oppressed by suffering, the one who is occupied for their sake, is called the 'human' (*puruṣa*) and also the 'skillful one' (*sukṛtin*). The same work says (k. 102):

> Beholding the world, its destiny enveloped in a confusion of murky whorls of smoky nescience, falling powerless into the blazing fire of suffering—whoever exert themselves as if the blaze of the spreading fire had occupied their head and was dragging it off, those are the wondrous persons, those are here the skillful ones.

For that reason, when one sees, hears, remembers, and contacts the great path which is the source of all the good things for one's self and others, which is the medicine casting out all the weaknesses, and which is walked by all skillful men—it becomes the healer of all the living beings. While one's own aim is not incomplete by engaging in the aim of others (*per se*), this is the great skillful means for accomplishing (his own aim) incidentally.[6] He should think, "I have entered the Great Vehicle which has (that skillful means). O, I have discovered a wondrous profit," and so thinking should enter this best of vehicles with whatever his human capacity.

Furthermore, the *Pāramitāsamāsa* (VI, 69) states:

> This ultimate vehicle purifies insight, for the omniscience of the Munis having it as source, becomes, so to say, the eye of the world, like the light springing from the surface of the solar disk.

Thus the one who seeks through various avenues the good qualities of the Great Vehicle should generate reverence captivating the mind, and enter it.

Now, there are three sections to the mental practice in the stages of the path of the great person: teaching that only the generation of the thought (of enlightenment) is the door of entrance to the Great Vehicle; the method of generating that thought; the method of practicing the career after having generated the thought.

Teaching that Only the Generation of the Thought is the Door of Entrance

Now, if there is the purpose to enter the Great Vehicle, through which door does one enter? In this regard, the Victor (*jina*) has promulgated two (vehicles) — The Great Vehicle of the Perfections (*pāramitā*) and the Great Vehicle of the Mantras (i.e. Vajrayāna, the 'Diamond Vehicle'); and apart from these, there is no Great Vehicle. However, whichever one of these two one enters, the door of entrance is only the Thought of Enlightenment (*bodhicitta*). At the time that (thought) is born in the stream of consciousness, no matter what else is not born, one has entered the Great Vehicle. However, at the time when one is separated from that (thought), whatever good qualities there be of comprehending voidness, and so forth, one falls into the stage of the Śrāvaka and so forth, and loses the Great Vehicle. This is often stated in many texts of the Great Vehicle, and is also proved by logic.[7] Therefore, even when entering the Great Vehicle for the first time, one is situated in it merely by generating that thought; and also if at a later time one would exit from the Great Vehicle, the leaving consists merely in abandoning that (thought). In short, one follows after, or turns away from, the Great Vehicle respectively by the presence or absence of that thought (of enlightenment).

Furthermore, the *Caryāvatāra* states (I, 9a–c):

> The very instant the miserable one, chained in the prison of gestation, gives birth to the Thought of Enlightenment, he is proclaimed 'Son of the Sugata.'

And (III, 25c–d):

> Today I shall be born in the family of the Buddha. Now I am a son of the Buddha.

This sets forth that immediately upon arousing the thought, one becomes a son of the Victor. The *Ārya-Maitreya-Vimokṣa* says it this way:

> Verily, son of the family, even when broken the diamond-gem is distinguished above all others and overpowers a golden ornament, and does not lose the name of diamond-gem; it wards off all poverty. So also, son of the family, the diamond which is the generation of the Thought of Enlightenment, even though divorced from resolve and practice, overpowers the gold ornament which is the good qualities of all the Śrāvakas and Pratyekabuddhas, and does not lose the name of Thought of Enlightenment; it wards off the poverty of all rebirths.

This informs us that even when one is not instructed in proper conduct, if there is that Thought, one is a Bodhisattva. Furthermore, *nātha* Nāgārjuna says:

> If I and this world desire to attain the incomparable enlightenment, its foundation is the Mind of Enlightenment, firm like the King of Mountains (i.e. Meru).

Moreover, the *Vajrapāṇyabhiṣekatantra* explains:[8]

> "Great bodhisattva! This *maṇḍala* of the great mantra [Vehicle], which is so far-extended, so profound, so difficult to fathom, and more secret than the 'secret ones' [*guhyaka*] [i.e. the *yakṣas*]—this must not be shown to sinful beings." "Vajrapāṇi, you say this is a rarity. This having not been heard before, to whom of the sentient beings is it to be explained?" Vajrapāṇi replied, "Mañjuśrī, whoever enters the cultivation of the Thought of Enlightenment. And whenever their Thought of Enlightenment is completed, at that time, Mañjuśrī, those bodhisattvas who engage in the Bodhisattva practice by way of *mantra* will enter the *maṇḍala* of the Mantra [vehicle] and be initiated in the great knowledge. However, whatever ones have not completed their Thought of Enlightenment are not to enter. They are not even to be shown the *maṇḍala*. Nor are they to be taught the 'seals' [*mudrā*] or the incantations [*mantra*]."

Hence, it does not suffice to have as doctrine the doctrine of the Mahāyāna, but it is important that the person be enrolled as one of the Great Vehicle. Also, the possible activity in the Great Vehicle is dependent upon that very Thought of Enlightenment.

Therefore, if there is nothing else than the dawning of that Thought, the Great Vehicle is also like that. However, if that Thought is complete with characteristics, the Great Vehicle is also completely pure. Consequently, one should endeavour in it.

In regard to this, the *Gaṇḍavyūha* teaches:

> Son of the family, the Thought of Enlightenment is the seed, so to say, of all the Buddha natures.

And since one should gain certainty in this matter, I shall explain it. In this connection, water, manure, warmth, earth, and so forth, at the time of coming together (*tshogs*) with the seed of rice, constitute causes (*hetu*) of the shoot of rice; and at the time of coming together with the seed of wheat, peas, etc., also constitute causes of their shoot. Hence, those are the shared cause (*sādhārana-hetu*). It is not feasible for a barley seed to be the cause of a rice shoot, even with the coming together of whatever conditions (i.e. water, etc.). Hence it is the unshared cause of the shoot of barley; and given the water, manure, etc. incorporated by it, becomes the cause of the shoot of barley.

In the same way, the Thought of Enlightenment is the unshared cause, comparable to the seed among the causes of the shoot of Buddhahood; and the insight intuiting the voidness, similar to the water, manure, etc., is the shared cause of the three enlightenments.[9] For that reason, the *Uttaratantra* (I, 34a – b) states:

> Whose seed is the conviction in the superior vehicle; whose mother is the insight for giving birth to the Buddha natures.

Thus, the Thought of Enlightenment is like the father seed; and the insight intuiting non-self is like a mother. For example, a Tibetan father would not be able to give birth to Indian, Mongolian, and so forth, sons. The father is the surety cause of the son lineage. From a Tibetan mother there is born a diversity of sons, so it is a shared cause. Also, *nātha* Nāgārjuna says:

> You are the sole path of liberation, the sure support for the Buddhas, Pratyekabuddhas, and Śrāvakas. It is sure that there is no other.

Thus, praising Perfection of Insight (*prajña-pāramitā*), (the verse) shows that also the Śrāvakas and Pratyekabuddhas take recourse to it, and so *Prajñāpāramitā* is called the Mother. Hence, it is the Mother of the Sons, consisting in the two vehicles, great and small. For this reason, the insight which comprehends voidness does not distinguish the great and lesser vehicles. However, they are distinguished by the Thought of Enlightenment and by great magnanimity of conduct. The *Ratnāvalī* (IV, 90) says this:

> In the Vehicle of the Śrāvakas there is no mention of the vow of the Bodhisattva or of his consignment (to others) of his (bodhisattva) career. How, then, is one a Bodhisattva through that [vehicle]?

This shows that they are not distinguished by viewpoint (*darśana*), but are distinguished by career (*caryā*).

If in that way, even the insight which comprehends voidness is not the unshared path of the Great Vehicle, how much less would be the paths other than it! For that reason, when one does not practice while holding deeply the precept of the Thought of Enlightenment, but only remembers the words for the outset of a meditative session, when one endeavors with many exertions in each tiny part of the path, one has very weak sinews of the Dharma.[10]

In general, for the generation of a son, it is necessary to have the portions of both father and mother. Comparable to that, for the parts of the path to be complete, one must have the sides of means and insight complete. In particular, the chief means, which is the Thought of Enlightenment, and the chief insight, which is the comprehension of voidness, are stipulated. And if one aims at only liberation from the cyclical flow, not cultivating one of the two, he should not be mistaken regarding calming (the mind) and discerning (the real), which require one to cultivate the meaning of non-self and voidness. If one is pledged as one of the Great Vehicle, then he must exercise in the Thought of Enlightenment, just as was said by the venerable Maitreya (in the *Abhisamayālaṃkāra*, I, 10a–b):

> With insight, one does not stay in phenomenal life; with compassion, one is not fixed in quiescence.

Thus one should avoid by insight the fall on the one hand into cyclical flow, and should avoid by compassion on the other hand the fall into quiescence; because insight does not hinder a fall into quiescence, because the lower vehicle also has the extreme of not falling into the phenomenal world, and because the chief thing the Bodhisattva path should avoid is the extreme of falling into quiescence.

Therefore, one should hold in mind, according to the purport of the Victor, the wondrous words, "The offspring of the Victor, who is the authority, upon giving birth to this precious Thought in their stream of consciousness, give birth to a wondrous Path like this." But should not hold in mind the mere arising in the stream of consciousness of each tiny good quality that would delight a (spiritually) immature person. The *Caryāvatāra* (I, 25) says this:

> How does this excellent jewel of the sentient beings arise, which was not hitherto? That resolve for the aim of others, arises for the rest, not for one's own aim.

And (I, 30, b–d):

> Where is there a good pêrson equal to him? And where is there such a friend? And where is there like merit?

And (I, 36ab):

> I bow to their bodies wherein arise that best jewel of mind.

And because it says (III, 31cd):

> It extracts the butter essence as a result of churning the milk of the illustrious Doctrine,

which sets forth as best the precept which extracts the essence of the scripture.

Now, Śrī Atīśa adhered to the Mādhyamika view, and Suvarṇadvīpi (Tib. Gser-gling-pa) adhered to the Cittamātra view that (mental) images are true. Yet, relying (on the latter), (Atīśa) obtained the Thought of Enlightenment. Hence, in his career (or life) (Atīśa) held him as the most kind among his gurus. When a person who knows this, observes it as the essential of the scripture, there would be (for that person) a great understanding of the essentials of the path.

When exerting oneself in this respect, if there is a genuine arising (of the Thought of Enlightenment), giving even one morsel of food to a raven, it is encompassed by that (Thought of Enlightenment). This is counted as 'career of the Bodhisattva.' However, if that is lacking, even the giving, replete with the jewels of the three thousand (worlds), does not constitute entrance into the 'career of the Bodhisattva.' By the same token, (the Perfections) morality up through insight, and the (tantric) contemplation of the gods and the contemplation of the 'veins' (*nāḍī*), the 'winds' (*vāyu*), the 'drop' (*bindu*), and so forth, do not (*per se*), constitute entrance into the 'career of the Bodhisattva.'

As is expressed in the world by the example of sharpening the sickle and of cutting the grass, when one has not undergone this essential, the precious Thought, however long this one endeavors in the practice of virtue, it is like cutting the grass with a blunt sickle: there is no cutting (i.e. succeeding) at all. But if one has undergone the essential, this Thought, it is as if for the time being one does not cut but sharpens the sickle; and when it has become keen, thereupon this one cuts, with the result that with little (effort) one ends by cutting much. It is because one is able with ease in each instant to eliminate the obscurations and to accumulate the collections (of merit and knowledge) and (because) for as long as one holds (the Thought) even the little virtue one will make big, and if it be exhausted one will revive it. The *Caryāvatāra* (I, 6b–d) says this:

> Not having the Thought of Enlightenment, what other virtue would vanquish that irresistible great power of sin?

And (I, 14ab):

> Like the fire due at the end of the world period (*yuga*) it consumes the great sins in an instant.

And (I, 21–22):

> Thinking, "I shall relieve the head distress of the sentient beings," the resolve of benefit is held with immeasurable merit. What is there to say of the one who wishes to dispel the immeasurable distress of each one and who wishes to bestow on every single sentient being immeasurable good quality?

And (I, 12):

> Like a plantain-tree, all other virtues, upon producing fruit, are exhausted; but the tree of enlightenment thought forever fructifies and is not exhausted, but grows ever larger.

The Method of Generating that Thought

This has four divisions: how it is generated by taking recourse to what cause; the stages of exercising the Thought of Enlightenment; the standard of generation; the method of taking it ritually.

How it is generated by taking recourse to what cause

This has three parts.
1) the method of generation through four conditions.

a) One generates the Thought, thinking, "Inconceivable is the (magical) power of the Buddhas or Bodhisattvas. Whether it was observed by me, or heard with trust, I shall take recourse to hearing, for wherever enlightenment is located and entered, it is of great (magical) power."

b) One generates the Thought, although such an observation or hearing be lacking, by having conviction in the wisdom of the Buddha at the time of practicing the scriptural collection that has its inception through the (Buddha's) incomparable enlightenment.

c) One generates the Thought, although without (the chance for) hearing the doctrine, thinking, "I notice that the sublime doctrine of the Bodhisattvas is in decline. Since the one dwelling in such a doctrine may dispel the suffering of sentient beings, in order that I may dwell for a long time in the doctrine of the Bodhisattvas, surely I should generate the Thought."

d) One generates the Thought, although not observing the doctrine in decline, but observing the difficulty of generating the Thought, thinking, "At this time, a bad time with a preponderance of delusion, of no shame or conscience, of envy, greed, and the like, if it is difficult to find a generation of the Śrāvaka-or-Pratyekabuddha (kind) of Thought, how much more (difficult) a generation of the incomparable Thought of Enlightenment!" If meanwhile I generate the Thought, at another time it will arise that way."

Those are the four generations of the Thought. The method of generating the Thought is saying, "I shall render the mind generated into the great enlightenment." Thereby arises the desire to achieve the enlightenment.

In regard to the condition (*pratyaya*) by which it happens, the first is through thinking, "Having seen or heard the amazing magical performances, my wonder has arisen. Such an enlightenment as that I shall obtain." The second is hearing the good qualities of the Buddha from speakers of the Dharma, so that initial faith is produced, and thereupon the desire to obtain those (good qualities) is produced. The third is when one does not tolerate the decline in teaching of the Great Vehicle, and generates the desire to attain the knowledge of a Buddha. In regard to this, if the teaching has not declined, there is the view to ward off the suffering of the sentient beings, so one aims to dispel the suffering. However, not tolerating the decline of teaching is the chief condition (*pratyaya*) for generating the Thought. Otherwise, as it is explained and repeated below, one generates it by recourse to compassion. The fourth is when one observes the rarity of that Thought of great purpose; and urged on chiefly by that, gets the desire to attain Buddhahood. This generation of the Thought is laid out by way of getting the desire to attain enlightenment, but it is not laid out by way of there being a high goal.

If one does not desire to attain Buddhahood by way of applying faith in the good qualities of the Buddha, one does not ward off the mentality that is content with accomplishing one's own aim and quiescence alone. And when one observes the purpose of the aim of others by way of applying friendliness and compassion, one desires to attain Buddhahood, so is able to accomplish the aim of others and to ward off the contentment with quiescence alone. This is because one is not able to ward it off with the former contentment; and because there is no other agent for avoiding it. Furthermore, it is not the case that there is no need to ward off the mentality that is content with accomplishing one's own aim and quiescence alone; because there is no perfection of one's own aim since one is not free from the one-sidedness of elimination and comprehension in the lower vehicle which only liberates from the cyclical flow; also because, although these liberate one from the trouble of phenomenal life, they do not liberate from the trouble of quiescence; and because the perfection of one's own aim is said to be the Buddha's Dharmakāya.[12] Therefore, even when applying faith in the good qualities of the Buddha, observe the aims of others! Also, in order to accomplish one's own aim, the goal of Buddhahood is necessary, seeing that this is a weighty condition for not backsliding to the lower vehicle.

In regard to the first two generations of Thought as previously explained, they are not drawn by friendliness and compassion. Rather they are drawn by just observing the good qualities of the Buddha's *rūpakāya* and *dharmakāya* according to the scriptures and other exegetical treatises. There appear many explanations about generation of the Thought along with the desire to attain Buddhahood; and there is also stated the generation of the Thought with the vow of installing all sentient beings in Buddhahood. One should regard each of these two (motives for generating the Thought) the same as concerns the generation of the Thought *per se*. However, as to generating the Thought with full complement of characteristics, it does not suffice to have only the desire to attain Buddhahood, drawn by seeing merely the requirement of others' aim: one should also have the desire to attain by observing that one's own aim requires the goal of Buddhahood. This does not neglect the aim of others, because pursuing the aim of others is essential; so the *Abhisamayālaṃkāra* (I, 18ab):

> The generation of the Thought (*cittotpāda*) is for the sake of others (*parārtha*) and with the desire of right completed enlightenment,

which sets forth two 'aims' (*arthaka*), enlightenment (*bodhi*) and the sake of others (*parārtha*).

2) *generation from four causes*. This is the generation of the Thought through relying on the four [causes]; perfection of lineage, being governed by spiritual guides, compassion toward the sentient beings, zest in the ascetic practice while in the cyclical flow (*saṃsāra*).

3) *generation from four powers*. This is the generation through relying on the four [powers]: a) one's own power, which desires complete enlightenment by one's own power; b) the power of another, whereby he desires complete enlightenment by another's power; c) the power of the cause, which generates it merely by hearing in the present time the praises of the Buddha and Bodhisattvas when formerly the Great Vehicle had been made part of his nature; or d) the power of praxis, i.e. making part of one's nature for a long time the virtue of volition and so forth in taking recourse in this life to an illustrious person and in listening to the doctrine.

Furthermore, the *Bodhisattvabhūmi* explains that when relying on the eight causes and conditions (*hetu* and *pratyaya*) taken separately or not combined, if one generates it from the power a) of one's self and c) of the cause, it is steady; and that, in contrast, when relying on those causes and conditions, if one generates it from the power b) of another and d) of praxis, it is not steady.

Having thus well understood the approaching decline of the general teaching and of the teaching of the Great Vehicle, and understood now the time of degeneracy becoming even greater degeneracy, having been informed that the generation of the Thought from the bottom of one's heart is an exceeding rarity, one takes recourse to an illustrious friend. One endeavours in the praxis of listening and giving thought to the scriptural collection of the Great Vehicle. And not doing it by another's urging while lacking independence, by chasing after the irrelevant or by a custom. But one should do it at the basic stage of generating the Thought through tying resolve by means of one's own power, because all the practices of the Bodhisattvas must be based on this.

The Stages of Exercising the Thought of Enlightenment, Part I

There are two practices — that based on the precepts 'seven causes and effects' in the lineage from the great master (i.e. Atīśa), and that based on what comes from the texts of the *jinaputra* Śāntideva.

The seven causes and effects are as follows: complete Buddhahood arises from the Thought of Enlightenment; that Thought, from aspiration; that aspiration, from compassion; compassion, from love; love, from show of gratitude; gratitude, from mindfulness of kindness; mindfulness of kindness, from seeing as 'mother' — seven in all.

Here there are two sections: 1) the generation of certainty in the stages; 2) the essential of practicing in sequence.

1) *the generation of certainty in the stages*. This has two parts: a) teaching compassion as the basis of the Great Vehicle path; b) the method by which other causes and effects become the cause and effect of that.

a) *teaching compassion as the basis of the Great Vehicle path*. This has three phases.

a–1) *the initial principle* is as follows: If the mind is moved by great compassion, there arises the sure resolution for the sake of liberating all the sentient beings from cyclical flow; and if it is the lower compassion, one does not act that way, because carrying the burden of rescuing all the living beings depends on that (great compassion), and because if one does not carry that burden, he does not enter the Great Vehicle. Hence that compassion is the initial principle. Along those lines, the *Akṣayamatinirdeśa-sūtra* declares:

> Reverend Śāradvatīputra, furthermore the great compassion of the Bodhisattvas is inexhaustible. Why so? Because it is the animation. Reverend Śāradvatīputra, it is this way: just as the breathing in and out is the animation of the life organ, so also great compassion is the animation of the Bodhisattva who is rightly travelling in the Great Vehicle.

Besides, the *Gayāśīrṣa* states:

> What implant, Mañjuśrī, does the career of the Bodhisattvas have? What is its ground? Mañjuśrī replied, "Son of the gods, the career of the Bodhisattvas has great compassion as its implant; the sentient beings as its ground.

Thus, this covenant is the basis of undertaking the career, i.e. one foresees no accomplishment if one is not trained in the bountiful two collections (i.e. of merit and knowledge) and so undertakes the extensive collection that is difficult to amass.

a–2) *the intermediate principle* is as follows: Now, having generated in that way the Thought a single time, even if one has undertaken (the career), if one notices that the sentient beings commit numerous evil deeds, that it is very difficult to train them, that they are in great number and would need unfathomable time, one becomes fearful and falls into the lower vehicle. However, when one generates the great compassion not just one time, but repeatedly in ever greater amount, one disregards one's own happiness and does not tire of others' aim, so that with ease one completes the whole collection (of merit and knowledge). Along these lines, the *Bhāvanākrama One* states:

> Thus, moved by great compassion, the Bodhisattvas, disregarding themselves, for the sake of others' benefit exclusively, undertake the fatiguing occupation of accumulating the collection that is difficult to amass and takes a long time. As the *Ārya-Śraddhābalādhāna* says: "Here, for maturing all the sentient beings by compassion, there is no pain which they do not accept, and there is no pleasure which they do not reject." Thus, when one undertakes

the exceeding difficulty one completes the collection in not too long a time. Without doubt, one will attain the rank of omniscience. Consequently, the root of all the Buddha natures is just compassion.

a – 3) *the final principle* is as follows: Even at the time of acquiring the fruit of the Buddhas, one does not stay in quiescence as the lower vehicle does, but still seeks for the sake of the sentient beings in the extent of space, i.e. has the (magical) power of great compassion, because otherwise he is like the Śrāvakas. The *Bhāvanākrama Two* states:

> Governed by great compassion, the Buddha Bhagavats, while bearing all the perfection of their own aim, act while abiding up to the very limit of the sentient-being realm.

And:

> The cause of the "Nirvāṇa of no-fixed abode" (*apratiṣṭhita-nirvāṇa*) is great compassion itself.

For example, the harvest has as principles, first the seed, in the intermediate stage the water, and finally the maturation. Likewise the harvest of the Buddhas has compassion as the principle, i.e. in the beginning, the middle, and the end. This was told by *śrimat* Candrakīrti (*Madhyamakāvatāra*, I, 2):

> Whatever be the reason that compassion itself is asserted to be like the seed of this perfection, the harvest of the Jina; and like water for the rearing; [finally] like maturation, for dwelling in the enjoyment for a long time, for that reason I shall praise compassion first of all.

Taking account of the power of meaning, the *Dharmasaṃgīti* declares:

> The Bodhisattva, O Bhagavat, should not be made to train in too many natures. One nature, Bhagavat, should be well grasped and well understood by him, in which all the natures of the Buddha are, so to say, in the palm of his hand. And what is that? It is great

compassion. By great compassion, Bhagavat, all the Buddha natures are, so to say, in the palm of hand of the Bodhisattvas. Just as, Bhagavat, when the precious wheel of a universal monarch is going, all the army goes with it; so, Bhagavat, when the great compassion of a Bodhisattva is going, all the Buddha natures go with it. Just as, Bhagavat, when the life organ is present, the other organs are present; just so, Bhagavat, when great compassion is present, the other Bodhisattva natures are present.

If one obtains certainty in such a sublime essential of the path, which is proved with an infinitude of scriptures and reasons, then why does one not posit as the chief precept the compassion as the root of enlightenment-mind and its associated Dharma teaching? Now, Zang-sna Chung-ston-pa said, "When we request a precept from the master (i.e. Atīśa) he would say, Give up the worldly mentality and cultivate the Thought of Enlightenment; and would tell nothing more." Dge-bśes Ston-pa, having ridiculed these words ("and would tell nothing more"), said, "That is the essence of the precepts of Jo-bo (Atīśa), because he knows the core of the Dharma."

Furthermore, because just this obtaining of certainty is difficult, one must again and again collect (merit and knowledge), purify (defilement), peruse the scriptures of *Gaṇḍavyūha*, etc. and their commentaries, thus seeking firm certainty, just as said by the *śrīmat* Mātṛceṭa (his *Śatapañcāśatka*, k. 19):

> That seed of right, complete enlightenment, your jewel of mind, only you know its core, O hero! Other persons are in a far-off place [i.e. in a blundering state].

b) *the method by which other causes and effects become the cause and effect of that*. In this regard, the method giving rise to the causes from the mother recognition up to love, is in general just a desire that (someone) be free from suffering. Even though (that desire) be produced at the time of thinking again and again about the suffering of this sentient being, in order that such a mentality arise easily, strongly, and firmly, one must previously have the imagery of embracing this sentient being as one who gratifies and is much esteemed. (In worldly mentality,) when a kin is suffering, one cannot tolerate it; when an enemy suffers, one is glad; when suffering arises in the neutral (between enemy and kin), usually what happens is an indifference or neglect. Among them, there is the first (i.e. regarding the person who is suffering as a kin), because gratifying. Moreover, to whatever extent there is esteem, to that extent there is non-tolerance of the suffering; and to that extent does it (the non-tolerance) arise, because there is meager non-tolerance toward middling suffering when there is meager esteem, and there is great non-tolerance of even minor suffering when there is exceeding esteem. When seeing that an enemy is suffering, not only does one not get a desire to see him relieved, but has the attitude, "Might that (suffering) not be exhausted, but become even more intense, and he not get rid of it!" In this way, responding with dislike, the major or minor portion of dislike brings about a major or minor portion of gladness toward the occurrence of suffering. In the case of suffering of the neutrals (between enemies and kinsfolk), both the non-tolerance and the gladness toward it are lacking—a response with the lack of gratification or dislike.

If one acts that way, the cultivation of sentient beings as kinsfolk is for generating gratification. Now, the ultimate kin is the mother. Therefore, the three, mother-contemplative repetition, mindfulness of kindness, and show of return gratitude—are gratifying and productive of esteem. The love treating sentient beings affectionately like an only child, is the fruit of those three; and (in turn) generates compassion.

The love which desires an encounter with joy, and compassion, does not show a certainty of cause and result. Indeed, the three meditative objects, namely, mother recognition and so on, appear basic to both the love which wishes for encounter with joy as well as the compassion which wishes for liberation (of the sentient beings) from suffering. Hence, it is necessary to endeavor in these (three).

This cultivation of the sentient beings as kinsfolk is explained by the *ācārya* Candrakīrti, the reverend Candra(gomin), and the *ācārya* Kamalaśīla, to be the cause bringing about the generation of the Thought (of enlightenment).

The method for bringing to fruit the aspiration and generation of the Thought is as follows: If, by exercising the intellect sequentially in that way, compassión has arisen, one has gained the desire of attaining Buddhahood for the sake of the sentient beings. Now, suppose one thinks, "Although so much suffices, why does one do it in that case by using aspiration?" (In reply:) The boundless states of love and compassion imagining that the sentient beings are finding happiness and avoiding suffering occur also with the Śrāvakas and Pratyekabuddhas. But accepting as one's own burden to give happiness to, and rid suffering in all the sentient beings is only in the Great Vehicle. Therefore, one should generate the aspiration which is the superior resolve of fortitude. Hence, the idea, "May the sentient beings find happiness," and the idea, "May they be rid of suffering," do not suffice, but one should tie the heart to the burden of those ends and carry it by oneself. So one should distinguish those special things. The *Sāgaramati-paripṛcchā* says this:

> For example, Sāgaramati ["oceanic intellect"], a certain merchant-householder had one son, desired, loved, favorite, gratifying, without anything adverse to the sight. That boy, while playing in the mode of a child, fell into a cess-pit. Thereupon, the mother and kinsfolk of that boy saw that the boy had fallen into the cess-pit; and seeing that, sighed deeply, were sorrowful, and uttered lamentations, but they did not enter the cess-pit and bring out the boy. Then, the father of the boy, having approached, saw that his only son had fallen into that cess-pit. And seeing that, hastening swiftly, drawn near by his affection of aspiration for the only son, without nausea he descended into that cess-pit and brought out his only son. There, the cess-pit is a metaphor for the threefold realm; the boy, a metaphor for the sentient beings; the mother and kinsfolk [are the Śrāvakas and Pratyekabuddhas] who, seeing the sentient beings fallen into the cyclical flow, are sorrowful and utter lamentations, but are incapable of bringing them out; and the merchant-householder is a metaphor for the Bodhisattva.

his shows the meaning with metaphors; and sets forth that both e Śrāvakas and Pratyekabuddhas have a compassion like that aroused in a mother for the esteemed only child who had fallen into the cess-pit.

Therefore, relying on compassion, one should generate th aspiration of carrying the burden for rescuing the world. Bu when one gains the mentality of rescuing the sentient beings ir that way, such a situation of oneself is (still) incapable of accom plishing the aim of a single sentient being. And that is not all even if one attains the rank of the two Arhats,[13] there would b scarce hope for sentient beings; and even if one is able to accom plish his goal, liberation, it cannot install him in omniscience Hence, one should think, "Who is able to perfect for the uncount able sentient beings all their temporary and ultimate aims?" an so thinking, having recognized that only the Buddha has that ca pability, one should generate the desire to attain Buddhahood fo the sake of the sentient beings.

2) *the essential of practicing in sequence*. This has three parts: a the training in exerting oneself in the aim of others; b) the exer cise in exerting oneself in the Thought of Enlightenment; c) de termining the generation of the Thought as the fruit of the train ing.

a) *the training in exerting oneself in the aim of others*. This ha two parts: a–1) realizing evenness of thought toward the sentier beings; a–2) realizing them all as having a gratifying image.

a–1) *realizing evenness of thought toward the sentient beings*. A was previously explained in the sections on the lesser and th middling persons, here also, one is to take and to nourish the pr liminary and the other stages. Among them, at the outset on cuts out the one-sidedness of attraction to some beings and aver sion to others. That is, if one has not accomplished evenness thought in doing that, whether it be love or compassion that is ir volved, those come with one-sidedness. Since that does not hap pen when aiming without one-sidedness, one must cultivate in partiality (*upekṣā*).

Among the three kinds of impartiality, which are motivatio impartiality (*saṃskāra-upekṣā*), feeling impartiality (*vedan upekṣā*), and boundless impartiality (*apramāṇa-upekṣā*), the or here is the last. This one has two kinds, 1. the kind with image realizing non-defilement of attraction, aversion, etc. toward th sentient beings; and 2. the kind with evenness of one's mind through oneself being free from attraction and aversion toward sentient beings; and of these the one here is the latter.[14]

The easy way to manage this sequence of cultivation is first of all to take as one's meditative object a neutral person, who is neither beneficial nor harmful. Then one is to realize evenness of thought, dispelling attraction and aversion. Having realized evenness of thought in that case (i.e. of the neutral person), one realizes evenness of thought toward kinsfolk. Here, 'unevenness of thought' means either cutting off the (meditative) rank by means of attraction or aversion, or the unevenness (unbalance) by way of great or small attraction. Having become even in that case (i.e. toward kinsfolk), one cultivates evenness of thought toward enemies. Here, 'unevenness' means the aversion through seeing him as disagreeable in an aspect.

Having become even in that case (i.e. toward enemies), one cultivates evenness of thought toward all sentient beings. In that case, by what cultivation toward them is attraction and aversion eliminated? Two kinds are mentioned in *Bhāvanākrama Two:* 1. on the side of sentient beings, thinking, "Since all the sentient beings equally desire happiness and do not desire suffering, it is not proper to be close to some, providing them benefit, and to be distant from others, harming them." 2. on one's own side, thinking, "In beginningless cycles of life, there has been no sentient being who hundreds of times did not become kin of mine, so to whom is there to be attraction, and to whom aversion?" Furthermore, in regard to attraction toward kinsfolk, the *Candrottarā darikā paripṛcchā* is cited:

> In former times I killed all of you, and you in the past have hacked me to bits. All of you are mutual enemies and murderers. How can you have a thought of passion?

And as previously explained in the section on the fault of uncertainty, one is to contemplate in the manner in which all enemies and kinsfolk quickly change and pass away. Thereby, both aversion and attraction are warded off. Because one proceeds by assuming as basis the distinction of enemy and kin, there is no need to drop the differentiation of enemy and kin. Thus, using the reason that the enemies are kinsfolk, one can avoid the mentality which separates into classes by way of attraction and aversion.

a – 2) *realizing them all as having a gratifying image*. The *Bhāvanākrama Two* states:

> Moistening the mind continuum with the water of love, one renders it like ready earth. Then, if one sows the seed of compassion, it flourishes with ease. Thus, having applied with love, one is to rear the compassion.

Here, 'love' is having the gratifying image of seeing all the sentient beings as dear as a son. The cultivation of impartiality (*upekṣā*) smooths out the gulleys consisting in the unevenness through attraction and aversion. As if readying the field, one moistens with the water of love which views as gratifying. Thereupon, if one sows the viable seed of compassion, it is said that great compassion grows with ease. This (passage) conveys the essential points in an excellent manner. Here there are three topics:

1) *the mother contemplation*. "There is no beginning to cyclical flow, so my births have no beginning. In the continuity of birth and death in cyclical flow, there is no place where I have not been born and lived. Nor are there any who have not become my kinsfolk as mother, and so forth." As the *Bhūmivastu* cites: [15]

> [The Bhagavat said:] "It is difficult for me to see, given ever so long in the past, the place where you were not born, did not go about, and did not die. It is difficult for me to see, given ever so long in the past, a sentient being who did not come to be your father, or mother, or brother, or sister, or instructor [*ācārya*], or [monastery] abbot [*upādhyāya*], or master [*guru*] or *guru* representative ['stand-in'] [*gurusthānīya*]."

Furthermore, one should seek steadfast certainty in one's mother, thinking, "Furthermore, not only were they mothers in the beginningless past; but also will become mothers in the infinite future." Because when one so thinks, it is easy to arouse mindfulness of kindness, and so on; but when one does not so think, there is no basis for mindfulness of kindness, and so on.

2) *the mindfulness-of-kindness contemplation*. One should contemplate it according to what Po-to-ba maintained as the speedy production. Underlying the contemplation of all the beings as one's own mother, is the initial contemplation in regard to the mother of this life. One should think a single time, "I contemplate in front the clear image of my mother"; and should think, "The present time is not all: since beginningless life cycles the count of my mothers pass beyond all calculation. Thus in her time in the mother role she protected me against all harm, provided me with all benefit and happiness. In particular in this life also, the first thing I did was take a long period in her womb. Thereafter, in the time of rearing, my downy baby hair pressed against her warm flesh. Her ten fingers gave me recreation. She suckled me with the milk from her breast. With her mouth she fed me. My snivel she wiped from my mouth. Wiping away with her hand my filth, she succored me wearilessly by diverse means. Moreover, my own capacity falling short, she gave me food and drink in the time of hunger and thirst; clothes when I shivered; money when I was 'broke.' Even when those necessities were not found easily, nevertheless, mixing with sin, suffering, and evil reports, she served, rearing me to the utmost of her ability." Where there are such things as disease and pain in a son, she thinks, "Better I die than my son die; better I be sick than my son be sick; better I suffer than my son suffer." She chooses this course sincerely; then provides the means of dispelling (those things, suffering, etc.). In short, whether it be a benefit or a happiness it is performed through her measure of knowledge and measure of ability. So we should be 'one-pointed' in the methods by which the mother dispels harm and suffering.

When one contemplates this, the mentality that is mindful of kindness actually arises, not just as words. Then one should further contemplate that way, recognizing as mothers also one's father and other kinsfolk. Thereupon, one should contemplate also the neutrals, recognizing them as mothers. When one has aroused a like mentality toward kinsfolk, then one also contemplates the enemies, recognizing them as mothers. At the time one has aroused a like mentality toward them as one's mother, one recognizes all the sentient beings of the ten quarters as one's mother, contemplating as was done previously, spreading it out farther.

3) *the show-of-gratitude contemplation*. "To cast aside without respect those — my mothers, kindly, suffering, refugeless — besides being unrecognized because of birth, death, and transmigration — while I occupy myself with how to be liberated from the cyclical flow — there is no greater ingratitude." The *Śiṣyalekha* (k. 95) says this:

> If one liberates himself alone, casting aside his relations who pass into the ocean of cyclical flow [*saṃsāra*], appearing as fallen within a whirlpool, unrecognized [for kindness, *ārjavam*] because of birth, death, and transmigration — there is no greater ingratitude than that.

Hence one should think, "If it is not right even for wretches to be ungrateful, how is my conduct appropriate?," and should accept the burden of returning the kindness. The same work (k. 96–97) says:

> What wretch delights in neglecting those here, of whose breast milk one drank partaking of their love, while one a helpless infant rested in their lap, they who showed love, enduring many trials?
>
> What enemy delights in going off, abandoning those afflicted, suffering, refugeless ones here, in whose womb one took shape and obtained this opportunity, those who with affectionate mind cared for this person when weak?

And the *Guṇāparyantastotra* puts it this way:

> You termed "lacking my method" that person working for solitary liberation, who has abandoned the sentient beings whose minds have troubled resolve due to blinding nescience, and who, as fathers and sons, administer benefits with respect and love to that person. Consequently, you planted the fervent aspiration to liberate the "protectorless" world.

In that case, if one thinks, "What is the way to return the benefit?" (we respond): although a mother may obtain some joy and wealth in cyclical flow by herself, it is not the case that she is undeceived by all those. Hence, one should return the benefit, thinking, "Just as when formerly I experienced fierce wounds, wounded by the oppressive force of the defilement demons, they (the mothers) applied a stimulant of 'briny water' and so forth, and administered benefit with love (to me), so those who have natural suffering and then generate diverse sufferings I shall install in the joy of liberation and Nirvāṇa." The *Madhyamakahṛdaya* (of Bhavya) says this:

> Furthermore, just as when I formerly was oppressed by the defilement demons and those persons applied a stimulant to the wound, so when they have been afflicted with the illness of suffering and in other lives have benefitted [me] with love and respect, what benefit can I give [them] in return than Nirvāṇa [itself]!

Rather than the burden amounting to the ocean and Sumeru, the great burden is the unappreciated deed, and the appreciation of the deed is said to be the status celebrated by the wise. The *Nāgarājabherī-gāthā* says this:

> The ocean, Sumeru, and the earth are not my burden. However, the unappreciated deed — that is my great burden. Whatever men, without turmoil in their minds, appreciate the deed, feel the deed, and do not waste the deed—they are celebrated by the wise.

In short, suppose one's own mother is abnormal, deranged; blind and without a guide in her blind condition; as she goes ahead, stumbling each step, in fear of the yawning pits. If the mother cannot expect help from her son, from whom could she expect help? If a son has no responsibility to save a mother from danger, who would save her from it? Similarly, the sentient beings who are the mothers, their mental peace disturbed by the demons of defilement, cannot come to know by their own power. Thus deranged, they lack the eye which sees the path to heaven and *nirvāṇa;* and lack guides for the blind among their spiritual friends. By evil conduct in each moment, they create discord, so stumble (into the pits). One sees them wandering in general in cyclical flow and in particular in evil destinies. In that case, the mother would expect help from her son, and the son must deliver the mother. So reflecting, one should repay the kindness by delivering (others) from cyclical flow. The *Śikṣāsamuccaya* says this:

> Deranged with defilement, blind with delusion, stumbling at each new step on a path with many holes, both another and myself are always miserable. Because the sin of the living beings is the same.

This shows that when one looks at it that way, it is not right to seek the faults in others; and one should accept as wonderful every evidence of their good qualities. However, also here it is proper to practice the method of commiseration.

b) *the exercise in exerting oneself toward the Thought of Enlightenment*. There are three features to the essential of generating that mentality (the three being love, compassion, and aspiration).

b – 1) *the cultivation of love (maitrī)*. The meditative object (*ālambana*) of love is the unhappy sentient being. The mental aspect (*ākāra*) is thinking, "It would be nice for that one to meet with happiness"; thinking, "May that one meet with happiness"; and thinking, "I must make that one meet with happiness." The benefit (*anuśaṃsa*) is told in the *Samādhirāja-sūtra* (Chap. 32, k. 277):

> However many the offerings of all sorts and uncountable one may make continuously to the best of persons in fields by the myriads, the millions, and the billions, these cannot come up to the extent [in merit] of a loving thought.

This sets forth that the essential is so far-reaching that its merit surpasses the continual performance of offerings in fields (*kṣetra*) up to the highest of objects. Also, the *Mañjuśrībuddhakṣetraguṇavyūha* explains:

> At the Northeast junction, there is a world realm of the Buddha, King of Maheśvaras, called thousandfold adornments. Just as a monk is happy to enter cessation in that place, so the sentient beings are happy. Suppose he practices there the pure life for a hundred thousand myriad of years. In this field, if one realizes the thought of love for all the sentient beings even in the mere time of snapping the fingers, the merit of this far exceeds that of the former. How much more does it exceed when one stays realizing that (thought) many times during day and night!

Furthermore, the *Ratnāvalī* (III, 84–86) puts it this way:

> The offering three times a day on 300 colored dishes cannot equal the merit of just one moment's time of love. Even if one is not liberated, he gains the eight good qualities that are love natures (*maitrī-dharma*):
>
> 1. There is love of gods and men; 2. those in turn protect; 3. there is satisfaction, 4. and many joys, 5–6. no harm from poison and weapons, 7. the attainment of one's aim without effort, and 8. birth in the Brahman world.

Thus, if there is love, there is love of gods and men. These naturally assemble. The conquerors also overcome the Māra troop by the power of love, so it is the best protection, and so on.[16]

Now, as it is difficult to produce, one should endeavour. The *Śikṣāsamuccaya* states:

> And the following verses from the *Suvarṇabhāsa*, filled with love and compassion, should all be paid heed to with thoughtfulness and rehearsed even with the voice: "By the drum of the *Suvarṇabhāsottamasūtra* let sorrows be assuaged in the three thousand worlds, sorrows of misfortune, sorrows of Yama's world, and the sorrows of poverty here in the three worlds!"

The steps of cultivating love are first its cultivation toward kinsfolk, then its cultivation toward enemies; after that, its cultivation toward all the sentient beings. The method of cultivation is as follows: Contemplating again and again the manner of suffering by which the sentient beings suffer, as in the case of compassion's arising, one should contemplate again and again that the sentient beings have property of happiness, being unhappy whether with flux (*sāsrava*) or without flux (*anāsrava*).[17] Having by repetition made that part of one's nature, there naturally occurs the desire that they meet with happiness. Then, orienting one's mind to various sorts of happiness, one is to dispense those to the sentient beings.

b–2) the cultivation of compassion (*karuṇā*). The meditative object (*ālambana*) is the sentient beings suffering in various ways with the three miseries.[18] The mental aspect (*ākāra*) is thinking, "It would be nice if they were free from those miseries"; thinking, "May they be free (from them)!" and thinking, "I must make them free (from those miseries)." The sequence of cultivation is the contemplation first of kinsfolk, next the neutrals, and then the enemies; and at the time of equipoise (*samāpatti*) of the mind toward enemies in the manner of kinsfolk, one gradually contemplates also all the sentient beings of the ten quarters.

Kamalaśīla, following the *Abhidharmasūtra*, takes as a very important essential point the cultivation in that way, distinguishing the objects for impartiality, love, and compassion. When one begins by not distinguishing them and exercises on a generality (*spyi*) as meditative object, there is (only) a semblance of arising (of love, etc.) and there is no arising in the sense of when one contemplates each one of them; and having omitted the experience of mental change through each one, as they were previously explained, one casts away much more; because in the end when one guards by having a generality as meditative object, either the group or the isolated ones taken as meditative object is a mere arising.

The method of its cultivation is as follows: One gives thought to the experiences of general and diverse suffering of the sentient beings who have become as mothers, as they fall into the cyclical flow—those sufferings have already been explained. Besides, if this (giving of thought) has already happened in the course of training of the 'middling person' one reviews it in one's mind; and it arises easily by this cultivation. When one contemplates those (sufferings) in terms of oneself it amounts to a cause of arousing the resolve of escape (from phenomenal life); while contemplating the same (sufferings) in terms of others, it amounts to a cause of arousing compassion. However, if there is no preliminary of giving thought in terms of oneself, one does not get to the essential. Those (previously mentioned sufferings) are only illustrations; the *Bodhisattvabhūmi* states them extensively as the 110 sufferings that are the meditative objects of compassion, and they should be contemplated by those with (the requisite) mental power. Furthermore, it is said in many places that the Śrāvaka sees suffering by way of realizing the Truth of Suffering and by way of the sorrowing mind at the final end (of his path); while in contrast the Bodhisattva gives more thought to suffering by cultivating compassion. There are many periods of love and of compassion when one contemplates the manner of suffering and of unhappiness by the numerous approaches; and if one contemplates (these) for a long time, one gains an energetic steadfastness. (On the other hand,) when one is satisfied with a few precepts and neglects the cultivation explained in the great texts, one has meager force (of compassion).

Besides, as was previously explained, when one has well distinguished the meditative objects, to wit, generation of the Thought (of Enlightenment) as the entrance gate of the Mahāyāna, the way of becoming with compassion as seed, and so forth, finally one must experience the occurrence of pondering and guarding by discriminative insight. However, one goes nowhere with the sporadic experience of endeavor like a stabbing while not well distinguishing the meditative object with cognitive dawning; and one may understand likewise in other phases of the stipulated procedure.

The standard for the arising of compassion is told in the *Bhāvanākrama One*:

> When one applies compassion the same as if were the beloved son in pain [that were the object], applies it to all sentient beings, carried on as a passive reflex [of one's habituation], with the mental aspect [*ākāra*] desiring to relieve them of their sufferings—then it is perfect and gets the name "great compassion."

This sets forth that when compassion arises by a passive reflex toward all sentient beings with just that standard of mind as the extent of compassion of a mother toward her small son, very dear to her heart, who is in pain, there are the complete characteristics of Great Compassion. One may also know by this the standard for the arising of Great Love (*mahāmaitrī*).

Also, the continuation of that text (i.e. *Bhāvanākrama One*) says:

> Thus, by dint of having made compassion part of his nature, with a vow to lead all the sentient beings (out of suffering), without exerting he generates the mind of enlightenment with its mental aspect of aspiring to the incomparable right complete enlightenment.

This states that one requires the great compassion, treated above, as the basis for generating the aspiring mind. One may also know by this the standard for generating the thought of enlightenment. Now, this need not be the generation of the Thought which proceeds to the exalted path, for it is said that the beginner's generation of the Thought is that way. Besides, the *Mahāyānasaṃgraha* (Chap. 5, final *gāthā*) states:[19]

> When he possesses 1. good power, 2. aspired power, and 3. steadfast mind and distinguished going, the Bodhisattva enterprises the three incalculable eons.

Consequently, even the Bodhisattva who begins the first of the three incalculable (eons) must generate such a Thought. Therefore, one commits a grievous error if one allows himself to think, "There being no (Buddha) in their direction and country, I must achieve Buddhahood for the sake of all the sentient beings; for this purpose I shall do this virtuous deed," and is confirmed in the manifest pride of thinking he has obtained what is not obtained. This is because when one does not practice by taking deeply to heart the precept of the Thought of Enlightenment, but seeks through something else, one evidences only the desire to direct the multifarious through endeavor; and when one knowing the essential point (i.e. the Thought of Enlightenment) of the

Great Vehicle looks at their (endeavor) it appears as a joke. And because, since many texts mention that the illustrious children of the Victor practice through taking it deeply to heart in many *kalpas,* how much less (is it practiced) by those who have nothing else than intellectual dawning! Furthermore, we do not claim that it is improper to cultivate other paths; but we do claim in regard to the matter of exercising the Thought of Enlightenment, that one must protect it by taking to heart the precept.

In general, even when such an experience as has been previously explained does not arise, if one has steadfast faith in the Great Vehicle, knowing what is to be practiced in the Great Vehicle, first one generates the Thought and takes the vow ritually. Thereupon, there is also the exercise of the Thought of Enlightenment, as in the *Caryāvatāra,* which sets forth at the outset the taking of vow and Thought (of Enlightenment), and then, in regard to what is to be practiced for that, presents extensively the ways of exercising the Thought of Enlightenment in the section of *Dhyāna* among the six Perfections.

However, for making one a fit vessel (*snod du rung*) there is the need of much previous mental exercise. That is, one should practice in purifying the mental continuum by the resolve of benefit, the seven members (*yan lag bdun*),[20] and the taking of refuge; and should generate the desire to protect them.

Thus, the requirement to walk the path and proceed ever further, by exercising the understanding of voidness, appears as a "name-only." Yet the requirement to be like that, and well guarding the Thought of Enlightenment, and to walk the path that proceeds by engaging the distinction ever higher, does not appear as a "name-only." This, the sole path of all the Victors, the *Prajñāpāramitopadeśa-śāstra*[21] refers to as the twenty-two generations of the Thought[22]; and one may know it from the great waylayers of the Victor by their explanations of the method of walking the path.

b–3) *cultivation of aspiration (adhyāśaya)*. At the conclusion of cultivating love and compassion in that way, one should think, "How these sentient beings are pleasing, gratifying to me! And as they are in this way poor in happiness and tormented with suffering, in what way can they be freed from suffering and brought to happiness?" Thus one exercises his mind, even with just words, to carry the burden of rescuing them. This is a little way of showing gratitude for kindness, but it is taught here that it does not suffice to think with love and compassion, "Might they meet with happiness and be free from suffering," because we teach that one needs to generate the love and compassion that are capable of drawing forth the resolve, "I must perform the benefit and happiness of all the sentient beings."

Now, those (cultivations) are not just a matter of a session (i.e. a meditative interval in day or night); for afterwards it is a great thing if one protects continuously by being mindful in all (four) postures of later sessions, and so forth. The *Bhāvanākrama Two* says this:

> It is not only proper for compassion to be present in a *samādhi* of compassion, but also proper in all postures [i.e. standing, etc.], that is, it should be cultivated toward all sentient beings at all times.

"Compassion" is just the illustration; the same applies to any meditative object with mental aspect to be guarded.

Also, the great *ācārya* Candragomin has written:[23]

> The tree of mind, infected since beginningless time with the drippings from the open [sore] of defilement, is unable to actualize a pleasant aroma. What help would be a drop of good water?

Here one understands that just as it is not possible to sweeten a huge trunk of the bitter Tigta dripping with a most offensive odor, by applying a single drop of molasses fluid, so also when the mind continuum has been cultivated from beginningless time with the bitter taste of defilement, what help is the good qualities of love or compassion cultivated in a single brief period! Since that is the case, one must guard continuously.

Secondly, as to the exercise in exerting oneself toward the Thought of Enlightenment, having driven (in a textual sense) by the previously explained stages, and having seen enlightenment as needed for the sake of others, even if one should arouse the desire to obtain that, still this alone does not suffice. As explained previously in the section of taking refuge, it is said that one must greatly increase faith at the outset by means of pondering the good qualities of the Body, Speech, and Mind (of the Buddha), and thereupon, by means of faith make a basis of longing. Hence, one generates the desire to attain those good qualities by tying the heart to those. And one draws upon certainty that it is necessary to have one's own aim — the attainment of omniscience. There are many causes for arousing the generation of the Thought; and the *Bhāvanākrama One* reports from the (*Ārya-Tathāgata-*)*Jñānamudrāsamādhi* a very special one to be the generation by oneself, compelled by compassion.

c) *determining the generation of the Thought as the fruit of the training*. The generalizing character is like the meaning (found) in the scripture *Abhisamayālaṃkāra*, as was previously cited. Its difference (*bheda*) is stated by the *Caryāvatāra* (I, 16), following the *Gaṇḍavyūhasūtra*:

> Precisely the difference that dawns [in the mind] between "he who desires to go" and "he who is on his way," just that difference is to be understood by the learned respectively among the two [kinds of mind, *citta*).

This is said concerning the two, the aspiration (*praṇidhi-citta*) and the entrance (*prasthāna-citta*) (kinds of mind, *citta*). Although there are many inconsistent (views) about this, there is the aspiration mind when there is the aspiration of thinking, "May I become a Buddha for the sake of the sentient beings," or, "I shall become a Buddha . . . "; and there are the practices 'giving' (*dāna*), and so forth, be it in the stage of training (*śaikṣa*) or in the stage beyond training (*aśaikṣa*); and for so long as one does not hold the vow (*saṃvāra*). There is the entrance mind when one holds the vow. This is because *Bhāvanākrama One* states:

> The aspiration mind is the goal-directed volition, thinking first of all, "May I become a Buddha for the benefit of all the world." The entrance mind is the subsequent taking of the vow and the applications to the collections [of merit and knowledge].

This matter being controversial, we shall not enlarge upon it (here).

The Stages of Exercising the Thought of Enlightenment, Part II

There are three parts to the practice by taking recourse to the texts of Śāntideva (being the resolve, the steps, and basic method of changing places).

1) *resolve on the benefit of changing places with another and the disadvantage of not changing places;* cf. *Caryāvatāra*, VIII, 120:

> Whoever desires to speedily rescue oneself and others too, he should practice the highest secret, which is changing places between himself and another.

And (VIII, 129–131):

> All those who are unhappy here are unhappy because they have sought their own happiness. All those who are happy here are happy because they have sought the happiness of others.
>
> To what avail need words be multiplied? Observe the gulf separating the fool who aims for his own aim and the Muni who works for the aim of others!
>
> Buddhahood is not accomplished, and nohow is there happiness in cyclical flow for the one whose own happiness is not exchanged with the suffering of another.

According to that (passage), one resolves on the situation by way of all the trouble in holding oneself as dear and on all the perfection in holding others as dear. If one makes part of one's own nature the resolve to interchange oneself with another, the ability to (so) generate is as follows: While formerly the one who was taken as one's enemy aroused fear if this one's name was heard; later, having become agreeable, as a kin, if absent, great sadness is aroused. In that way, by imitative repetition of the mentality, there is the generation by repetition of the view of oneself like another and another like oneself. The same work states (VIII, 119):

> One should not retreat from a difficulty. So by the [magical] power of making it part of one's nature, even that person who [formerly] terrorized through hearing [this one's name] cannot be absent without sadness.

And (VIII, 112c–d):

> That depositing of one's own body in another is not difficult.

Suppose it be asked: "Since the body of another is not the body of oneself, how can it be proper to conceive in it anything like our own mentality?" Not only is this body produced from the semen and blood of the father and mother, likewise it is produced from portions of other bodies; but by dint of former habit one takes them as his self. So also, if one makes it a habit to hold the other's body as dear as one's own, it (the interchange mentality) arises. The same work says this (VIII, 158):

> Therefore, just as you constructed your self in the *bindus* of menstrual blood and semen, belonging to others, so also imagine it in others!

Having in that way well resolved about the benefit and the disadvantage, if one ties his heart and repeatedly applies enthusiasm to its cultivation, one will witness an ability to generate it.

2) *the steps of cultivating the method of changing places between oneself and another*. Now, the expression "I shall change places with another," and the expression "I shall put myself into another; the other into myself," is not the exercise of mind that thinks, "I am the other," or thinks, "That one's eyes and so forth are mine." Rather, it is exchanging the two attitudes, 1. holding oneself as dear, and 2. neglecting the other; by generating the attitude of holding the other as dear as oneself; and by neglecting oneself as though one were the other. On that account, it is also expressed as interchanging one's own happiness with another's suffering, thus regarding as the enemy the holding of oneself as dear. Or, having quit putting uppermost one's own happiness, one sees the merit of holding another dear. Or, having avoided the neglect of another's suffering, one puts uppermost its dispelling. In short, not looking toward one's own happiness, one engages the purpose of dispelling the suffering of others.

When one exercises that attitude, there are two obstacles—a) and b).

a) One decides that the basis of happiness and suffering of oneself and others is a respective matter as though oneself and the other are like the colors blue and yellow; and positing that as though proved, one treats in the same manner the happiness and suffering that are based on (oneself and others), thinking, "This is mine, to be kept or dispelled," and "This is the other's," thus neglecting it. The way to counteract that is as follows: Without deciding oneself and the other to be a respective matter, one regards oneself and the other to be a mutual notion, because regarding the other as oneself, like the other side and this side of a mountain. For example, from this mountain side one has the notion of the other side of the mountain; and going to the other side, one takes it as this side of the mountain. In contrast, when one looks at a blue color, one has the notion of blueness, but not of other colors; hence the case is not the same. The *Śikṣāsamuccaya* also says this:

> Because of the habituation in the sameness of oneself and the other, the Thought of Enlightenment would be firm. Relativity—oneself and otherness, like this side and the other side [of a river]—is false.
>
> Not because of our own, is that side the other one; for, relative to what is there a "this side?" Egoity is not proved by our own. Relative to what, would there be the other [where the "other" is ourself]?

This sets forth that the establishment is merely related to a related place, but that there is no proof in terms of (each one's) natural existence.

b) There is the obstacle of thinking, "Now, another's suffering does no harm to me; so I shall not try to dispel it." To get rid of it, one thinks, "In such a case, one would never store up resources in the time of youth through apprehension of being a suffering person in the time of age, because the suffering of the aged does not harm the youth. Likewise, a pain to the foot would not be removed by a hand, because it is 'another.' While the old man and the youth exemplify the former and later life, they correspond as well to "earlier and later" and to "morning and evening." Suppose one thinks, "The old man and the youth have a single (mental) series (*saṃtāna*), and the foot and hand are in a single group, so it is not the same case of oneself and the other." The (mental) series and the (corporeal) group are subject to many moments and to many groupings, and do not have a self-nature that is self-capable; and one ought to place one's own self and another's self in a continuous group, but (granted) it is not a self-existence, since one cannot establish oneself and another through relation. However, by dint of repetition in holding (oneself) as dear from beginningless time, there is no tolerance when one's own suffering occurs. Similarly, if one repeatedly holds another as dear, there is also non-tolerance when his suffering occurs.

In that way, one gets rid of the obstacles to changing places between oneself and another. Then:

3) *the basic method of cultivation*. One thinks, "By the force of clinging to a self, this holding my self as dear has generated in beginningless cyclical flow up to the present, the multiform undesired objects. Although desiring to create self-perfection, holding chiefly one's own aim, one winds up without the means. So even after the passage of eons, neither one's own nor the other's aim is accomplished. And not just not accomplished, for also one reaps unceasing suffering. If I had engaged myself in shifting to another that resolve of own-aim, no doubt, how much earlier would I have become a Buddha with the perfection of all the aims of myself and others. But because I did not act like that, time has passed by with fruitless difficulties. Having now recognized this, I shall hold as my greatest enemy the thought of self-cherishing; and take recourse with mindfulness and awareness (to this holding). Then, by (my) numerous endeavors that (enemy) not (already) arisen, will not arise; and if arisen, I shall avoid its prolongation." Having (by such thinking) gained steadfast certainty, he avoids many times (the self-cherishing); cf. *Caryāvatāra*, VIII, 154c–d, 155:

> Because of this [self], we have in all [eons] by the myriads been afflicted in cyclical flow.
>
> You have sought your own aim while uncountable eons passed by. And by this great effort you have gained only suffering.

And (VIII, 157):

> If previously you had done this [virtuous] deed, there would not be this [miserable] state. It is out of the question that there would be the blissful perfection of the Buddhas!

Thus, one should exercise again and again the mind of giving away to the sentient beings in a way that does not hold to one's own side and does not uphold one's own direction, and in a way that disregards one's own body, possessions, and roots of merit; and one should perform the aim of those to whom one gives. Since it is wrong to go astray in this matter, one should turn off the mentality that dwells in body, and so forth, as one's own aim; cf. *Caryāvatāra*, VIII, 137–138:

> O my mind, know with certainty, thinking, "I belong to the other," and henceforth you must not give thought except for the aim of all the sentient beings.
>
> These eyes, which are theirs, must not longer see my aim. These hands, which belong to another, must not work my aim. So also all the other senses and organs of action.

One should think, "If the body and so forth escape being consciousness-supports for the aims of others, and are consciousness-supports for one's own aim; or if body, speech, and mind provide a condition of harm to another, these have added to the harm previously without limit, and now mistake the counterfeit for a benefit. When one passes into its control, one has no tolerance at all for (one's own) suffering." One should turn off (that mind); cf. *Caryāvatāra*, VIII, 169–172:

> Those were by-gone times, when I came to grief through you! I have seen you. Now, where can you go? I will destroy all your conceit.
>
> Now renounce the hope, "But today it is my own aim!" Not caring for the many vexations, I have sold you to others. [Now serve!]
>
> If through heedlessness I would not deliver you to the sentient beings, surely it is you that would hand me over to the hell wardens.

> Thus did you often give me away for long torment! Recalling your hostilities, I destroy you, O slave of own-aim!

Having in that way considered again and again the benefit of holding another as dear, one should generate a joy from the depth of one's heart, so that the (former) thought of neglecting either has not arisen and one should not let it arise, or should it have arisen, one does not let it continue. One should arouse the attitude of holding another as dear as one formerly held oneself as dear, by way of taking the other person as the favorite, the dear one, and gratifying; thinking, "I should hold others as I did myself."

As to the cause thus giving rise to the holding of a sentient being as dear, one needs to remember that person's kindness or to notice how one was useful to oneself. Furthermore, just as when from the sowing of viable seed one observes a bountiful, fortunate harvest, and gets to regard the fertile field as dear; so also from sowing the seed of giving, and so forth, on the field of sentient beings, one derives the certainty of accomplishing the happiness and goodness in (temporary) states and the final goal, and gets to regard (that field) as dear. One should give thought to those (matters); cf. *Caryāvatāra*, VI, 113:

> From [love and compassion to] the sentient beings, and from [faith and offerings to] the Victors, there is like deriving of the Buddha natures. Then, what is the rule for veneration to the Victors and not to the sentient beings?

Furthermore, one should give thought that killing of sentient beings leads to the three bad destinies; while desisting from any killing leads to good destiny, to prosperity as well as to long life; that taking what is not given and evincing hatred lead to evil destiny, while giving away possessions and cultivating love and compassion lead to good destiny; that in particular having paid attention to those beings one generates the Thought (of Enlightenment), engaging in the practices for their aims; that even a Buddha is dependent on them, i.e. one fulfills the perfections of giving and so on by recourse to the sentient beings—as is stated in *Verses that Delight Sentient Beings*.[24] That is also stated in the *Bodhicittavivarana* (of Nāgārjuna):[25]

> That worldling's fruit, desirable and undesirable, of good destiny and bad destiny, derives from benefit and harm to the sentient beings.
>
> It is by recourse (with benefit) to sentient beings that one gains the incomparable rank of the Buddha.
>
> No wonder that in the three worlds there is none of the enjoyments of gods and men, which Brahmā, Indra, Rudra, or the (four) World Protectors, take recourse to—for one who does not benefit the sentient beings!
>
> Whatever the experiences by the sentient beings of the numerous sufferings among hell-beings, animals, and hungry ghosts, they arise from harm to the sentient beings. The misery of hunger and thirst, mutual beatings, and tortures, that can hardly be averted and are inexhaustible, is the fruit of harm to sentient beings.

The inferior fruit of the Śrāvakas is from not having acted chiefly for the sake of sentient beings; while the gain of the ultimate fruit of the Buddhas is from having acted chiefly for the sake of sentient beings. Having given thought to this rule, one should not be atttached to one's own aim, even for a moment. This is said in the same work:[26]

> Dispassion toward the sentient beings, one should avoid as though it were like poison.
>
> Hence, the Śrāvakas, not enamored [of sentient beings], can only achieve the inferior enlightenment. By not abandoning a sentient being, one achieves the enlightenment of the complete Buddha. Having in that way differentiated the sources of the beneficial and the non-beneficial fruit, how can those [Bodhisattvas] remain even for a moment attached to their own aim?

Then one should recognize that the single-minded application to other's aim and the fruitional enlightenment arise from the shoot which is the Thought of Enlightenment. Having seen its root to be compassion, the Sons of the Victor assiduously cultivate it. They, having become steadfast through greatly cultivating it, are drawn spontaneously into magnanimous practices of the exceeding difficulties. This is said in the same work:[27]

> Arising from the shoot which is the Thought of Enlightenment whose root is steadfast compassion, the single aim of others and the fruitional enlightenment are cultivated by the children of the Victor.
>
> Whoever, steadfast with the cultivation, having empathy with the suffering of others, would even abandon the bliss of meditation (*dhyāna*) and enter the hell Avīci—this is a marvel; this is worthy of fame; this is the highest kind of rule of the illustrious ones.

Now one should generate certainty in these rules by the manner of exposition used by the illustrious ones. It was heard from Jo-bo (i.e. Atīśa):

> Some Tibetans recognize a person as a Bodhisattva even when he does not know the exercise in love and compassion. Well, then! How does one go about it? At the outset, one must proceed by practicing in sequence.

It was heard from Glang-ri-thang-pa:

> Both Sva-bo-pa and myself have the eighteen human methods[28] and one total of nineteen horse methods. What does the human method do after generating the thought of highest enlightenment? It practices for the sake of the sentient beings. The horse method, when the Thought of Enlightenment has not arisen, does not arouse it; when arisen, does not dwell in it or allow it to expand; holds oneself as dear.[29]

One should exercise to see self-serving thoughts as harmful; and always exercise to benefit the sentient beings.[30]

Mahāyogin said to Kalyāṇamitra Ston-pa: "You may even have performed this and that *samādhi*, 'equipoise of the winds,' and so on. And if someone beats a large drum at the root of your ear, your contemplation might not break up. But if you are without love and compassion or the Thought of Enlightenment, you will be reborn in a place requiring confession for the day and night." This appears to imply that ordinary persons who have attained the formless realms are in a condition causal for being born in an unfavorable place.

It was heard from Kham-lung-pa, "We work for sentient beings like a neglectful workman. And sentient beings treat us the same way."

Whether there is installation or non-installation of the root of the Mahāyāna (Thought of Enlightenment), and whether one enters or does not enter the (spontaneous) sincerity in the Mahāyāna, all those depend on this. Therefore, one should observe how to put his mind on this in all times. If it happens it is good. If it does not happen, without remaining that way, one should always resort to a spiritual friend who teaches it. One should always associate with scriptures and authoritative commentaries which teach that way. On that basis, one amasses the collection (of merit and knowledge). One purges the hindrances that are an obstacle to it. And if oneself has exercised the mind that way, surely the seed will issue forth completely. Hence, the significance of the action is not trivial. It is right to be joyful. It is as said by the great master (i.e. Atīśa):

> The one desiring to enter the gate of the Great Vehicle Dharma, ought to generate by exertions for an eon the Thought of Enlightenment which like the sun and moon dispels the darkness and alleviates distress.

Standard for Generation of that Thought

It is to be known just as already explained.

Taking it Ritually

It is just as the great master (i.e. Atīśa) states it:

> The one desiring to arouse it and exercise it should cultivate energetically for a long time the four sublime abodes of love, and so forth. So he must dispel clinging and envy, and arouse it by rightly performing the ritual.

Having thus exercised the mind, when there is firm certainty as to generating the Thought, one must make a ritual of taking it. This has three parts: 1) attaining what is not attained; 2) protecting what is attained against breakage; 3) if broken, the way of mending.

1) *attaining what is not attained*. This has three sections: a) the object (*viṣaya*) by which it is taken; b) the basis (*ādhāra*) on which it is taken; c) how it is ritually taken.

a) *the object by which it is taken*. When the *Gurukriyākrama* states "a preceptor (*ācārya*) possessing the characteristics," Jo-bo (i.e. Atīśa) has not made it clear. The former teachers maintained that it did not suffice to have the aspiration thought and to abide in what is to be practised in this, but that one must have the entrance vow. This appears consistent with what Jetāri says: "One goes straight to a spiritual friend having the Bodhisattva vow." In regard to generating the Thought, according to the *Daśadharmaka*,[31] through being drawn into holding it by means of another person, the *'śrāvaka'* explanation states that one is drawn into holding it through being urged by that person and made disgusted (with one's current inferior conduct); so a ritual is not done.

b) *the basis on which it is taken*. In general, it is as Jetāri cites: "Son in the lineage, or daughter in the lineage! Since one has the perfection of basis and of resolve . . ." Thus, it is proper to arouse the aspiration thought by means of the body and resolve of a god, serpent, and so forth; all are proper as the basis of this. But, in this regard, the *Bodhimārgapradīpapañjikā* mentions mindfulness of death, insight, and great compassion for the emergence of the (Bodhisattva's) mind from cyclical flow. According to that, the exercise of the mind in steps of the path as previously explained [for the lesser and middle persons] would scarcely gain the experience of mental change into the Thought of Enlightenment.

c) *how it is ritually taken*. There are three parts to this (being the preparation, main part, and conclusion).

c–1) *preparation*. This has three parts: special observances for taking refuge; accumulating the collection; exercising the resolve.

1) *special observances for taking refuge*. This has three parts: (a) decorating the place, preparing the icons, arranging the offerings; (b) making entreaties and taking refuge; (c) what is to be learned by the person gone for refuge.

a) *decorating, preparing, arranging*. The sinful person, having well prepared a spot in a secluded place; polishes and anoints that clean place with the five cow products;[32] makes it fragrant with excellent perfumed water of sandalwood, etc.; and scatters pieces of sweet-smelling flowers. On a throne, miniature throne, or good stand, one installs cast images of the Three Jewels, and the like (religious) books, and replicas of the bodies of Bodhisattvas. One should make arrangements with offering implements such as canopies, etc. and flowers, etc. to the extent they are available; and with music, food, and ornaments. One decorates with flowers the throne for seating the spiritual friend (*kalyāṇamitra*).

According to the former teachers, first one collects and offers the set of things by way of reverencing the Saṃgha and sacrificing food cakes to the spirits; and in their absence, as is said in the *Bhadrakalpika*, one manages with offering of cotton fringes, etc.; but if those things are available, one must seek them with much unperturbed zeal, and arrange them in a way incomprehensible to one's friend. At the time the Tibetan teachers received (precepts) from Jo-bo in Mang-yul and Bsam-yas, he said, "concerning the generation of the Thought, it would not arise with a bad offering." He also said that the method is lacking for the basis when there is no placement of a statue of the Lord of the Teaching[33]; and that one should place (religious) books (i.e.), the *Prajñāpāramitā*, at least starting with the *Sañcaya* (*-gāthā*).[34] After that, according to the explanation in the *Gurukriyākrama*, one invites the Ārya-Sāṃgha, and is to praise it, three times muttering the *Pūjameghadhāraṇī*.

Thereupon, the disciple bathes, dons one's good clothes, joins the palms of one's hands; and one's *guru* gets this one to show faith, tying one's heart to the good qualities of the fields of the host (of Buddhas and Bodhisattvas). One imagines that oneself dwells in the presence of each one of the Buddhas and Bodhisattvas. One is led to leisurely perform the 'seven members'[35] (of the recitation). In that regard, it was formerly customary to perform the 'seven members' in the way descended from Nāgārjuna and Śāntideva; and to perform only the bowing and offering (of the seven) in the way descended from Maitreya and Asaṅga. Besides, that when one makes the confession of sins, one should have regret; but that when one has dissatisfaction, one should generate the Thought of Enlightenment with enthusiastic satisfaction is not the case. Because the great Jo-bo has included such things as the bowing and offering rites in his *Cittotpāda saṃvaravidhi*; and has clearly stated in his *Gurukriyākrama* that the 'seven members' are the preliminary acts for generating the Thought. And for that reason, even though it does not occur in the tradition of Nāgārjuna and Śāntideva, the vow is mandatory.

b) *making entreaties and taking refuge*. Then one must plant the idea that one's *guru* is the Teacher. According to this instruction, one bows to the person convinced that this one is the Buddha. One offers to this one gifts and the *maṇḍala*. And having kneeled down on the earth with the right knee cap, one joins the palms, entreating for the aim of the Thought of Enlightenment. Then one recites thrice:

> Just as formerly the Tathāgata-Arhat-Samyaksaṃbuddhas and the great Bodhisattvas, when dwelling on the great earth, at the outset generated their Mind into the Incomparable Rightly Perfected Enlightenment; in the same way, also I named so-and-so, implore that through the *guru* I may generate my mind into the Incomparable Rightly Perfected Enlightenment.

Then one should take refuge in the special manner, as follows: The Buddha Bhagavat is the object (*viṣaya*). The Dharma is the truth of path that chiefly produces the cessation of (i.e. appropriate to) the Great Vehicle. The Saṃgha is the irreversible Bodhisattava-Āryas. Thus holding from this time onward as long as the 'terrace of enlightenment' (*bodhimaṇḍa*) is not attained, for the sake of protecting all the sentient beings to be served, one imagines petitioning the Buddha as the refuge-teacher, the Dharma as the refuge-substance, and the Saṃgha as the refuge that is the companions for accomplishment — this is the general resolve. There is the resolve in particular according as stated in the *Bodhipathapradīpa* 8b – 9): "With a mind that cannot be turned back . . ."; and one puts strong longing in the thought, "In all times I shall not turn back." Thus one should take refuge with a posture as previously explained, reciting thrice:

> Preceptor, pray listen to me! I, named so-and-so, take refuge in the best of the bipeds, the Buddha Bhagavats, from this time until I shall arrive at the terrace of enlightenment.

> Preceptor, pray listen to me! I, named so-and-so, take refuge in the Dharmas, the Dharmas that are tranquil, free from passion, from this time until I shall arrive at the terrace of enlightenment [*bodhimaṇḍa*].

> Preceptor, pray listen to me! I, named so-and-so, take refuge in the best of hosts, the irreversible Saṃgha of Ārya Bodhisattvas, from this time until I shall arrive at the terrace of enlightenment.

These respective prayings for cognizance in the taking refuge in each of the (three) Jewels as well as the alternate and different words for the refuge in the Dharma are in accordance with the rite composed by Jo-bo.

c) *precepts for the person gone for refuge*. As was previously explained in the section on the lesser person, the precepts are here also to be explained by the preceptor.

2) *accumulating the collection*. This is a phase in the *Cittotpādavidhi* (of Jo-bo). Here it is in addition explained as performing the bowing, offering, and the like. One should do it as explained in the commentary, i.e. performing the 'seven members' and reviewing in mind the Buddhas, Bodhisattvas, the former and present spiritual friends. Here, 'offerings to the *gurus*' is also to be understood as the offering in former times; and the 'seven members' are to be performed with the text either of *Bhadracaryā* or of *Caryāvatāra*.

3) *exercising the resolve*. The *Bodhipathapradīpa* states it as generating the Thought while one observes the suffering of sentient beings, having previously cast the mind of love. As was previously explained, this clearly sets forth love (*maitrī*) and compassion (*karuṇā*) as the aspects constituting consciousness-supports.

c – 2) *the main part*. In the presence of the preceptor, one kneels down on the ground with one's right knee cap, or squats, as appropriate; and remaining in that position, unites the palms of one's hands, and is to generate the Thought (of Enlightenment). Moreover, the *Bodhipathapradīpa* states (k. 11):

> . . . one should generate the Thought of Enlightenment, pledged not to turn back.

And the *Vidhi* states: ". . . until the terrace of enlightenment." Therefore, one does not generate the Thought by just thinking,

"I shall attain Buddhahood for the sake of others"; but taking one's consciousness-support in generating that Thought one pledges, thinking, "I shall not give up as long as enlightenment is not attained." So one should generate it by recourse to the rite with resolve of it.

Accordingly, if one is unable to practice what needs to be practiced concerning the aspiration thought, one should not do it. And if one generates with a rite that amounts just to thinking, "I shall become a Buddha for the sake of all the sentient beings," whether one is able or unable to practice what needs to be practiced of generating the Thought, one is satisfied that one has done everything. While in that way there are two proper things for the aspiration thought (i.e. thinking "... for the sake of others," and "... as long as enlightenment is not attained"), indeed this is not practicing what needs to be practiced in regard to adopting the entrance thought with a rite, and it is not valid that one has (thereby) done all the aspects! Hence, the claim to distinguish what is valid and not valid in the many rites of vow in descent from Nāgārjuna and Asaṅga, is a great misunderstanding. Moreover, some persons having explained the beginner's practice of Dharma as the repeated holding with a rite that holds the entrance vow, do not know at all the fundamental transgression in the general and particular of what needs to be practiced. Hence, their non-teaching of the distinction in how to do it, is an exercise in futility. Also, the *Ārya-Rājāvavādaka-sūtra* mentions that when one is unable to practice what needs to be practiced of giving and the other perfections, even so one gains many merits in generating only the Thought of Enlightenment. Appealing to this as textual source, the *Bhāvanākrama One* states:

> Even when someone is incapable of practicing the perfections [*pāramitā*], all, completely, in every respect, that one, with control of the means, should also generate the Thought of Enlightenment since it has a great fruit.

Thus, it is very clear that it is proper to perform the generation of the Thought in one who does not practice what needs to be practiced of giving and the other perfections, and while it is not feasible for him to hold the vow (of entrance).

The rite of holding the Thought is to recite the following three times:

> All the Buddhas and Bodhisattvas dwelling in the ten directions, pray listen to me! Preceptor, pray listen to me! I, named so-and-so, have the root of virtue [*kuśala-mūla*] of this and other lives, consisting in the nature of giving to others, the nature of morality, and the nature of contemplation; and by means of that root of virtue consisting in what has been done by me, what has been granted to do, and in sympathetic joy with what is done [by others], just as the former Tathāgata-Arhat-Samyaksaṃbuddhas and the great Bodhisattvas dwelling on the great earth were made to generate their mind into the incomparable rightly perfected enlightenment; in the same way, I, named so-and-so, also holding from this time on, up to reaching the terrace of enlightenment, shall generate my Thought to the incomparable rightly perfected great enlightenment; shall rescue the unrescued sentient beings; shall save the unsaved; shall encourage the discouraged; shall bring to Nirvāṇa those who have not attained complete Nirvāṇa.

In the case of these two and the rite of taking refuge it is mandatory for the candidate to repeat after the precepts, even if it is not very clear.

There are in the situation where there is a preceptor. How it should be done if a preceptor is not available, is just as told in the *Cittotpādavidhi* which Jo-bo has composed:

> When there is no preceptor like that, the rite of generating the Thought of Enlightenment by oneself is as follows: One reviews in his mind the Tathāgata Śākyamuni and all the Tathāgatas of the ten directions, and performs the rites of bowing, offerings, and so on. Then, omitting the entreaties and the word "preceptor," one is to perform, in the sequence as above, the taking of refuge and the like.

c–3) *concluding rite*. The preceptor is to tell the disciple what needs to be practiced concerning the aspiration thought.

2) *protecting what is attained against breakage*. For this, it is necessary that what needs to be practiced should be known. Hence, this will be explained, in two parts: a) teaching the cause for no

breakage of the Thought generation of this life; b) teaching the cause of not being separate from it in the other lives.

a) *teaching the cause for no breakage of the Thought generation of this life*. This has four parts: teaching the mindfulness of benefit for expanding the enthusiasm in generating the Thought; teaching the six-time generation of expanding the basis of generating the Thought; teaching the non-rejection by the mind of the sentient beings for whom there is the generation of the Thought; teaching the amassing of the collection of merit and knowledge.

a – 1) *teaching the mindfulness of benefit for expanding the enthusiasm in generating the Thought*. One gives thought to the benefits of the Thought of Enlightenment by reading the scriptures or listening to the *guru*. Since they are set forth extensively in the *Gaṇḍavyūha,* one should peruse them there. Also, this work, as it was previously cited, states it to be "the seed, so to say, of all the Buddha natures." And when it states, "In short, for comprising all the practice and fervent aspiration of the Bodhisattva" — there would be an infinity in expounding the members extensively—it is "in short" because it comprises all in short. As to its compactness, it is said to be compact as it comprises the essentials of all the Bodhisattva path.[36]

As the *Bodhisattvabhūmi* states the benefit, it pertains to the aspiration thought; and it states two benefits for the beginning generation of the Thought to be a firm generation: (1) one becomes an illustrious field; (2) one has the assistance of unassailable merits.

(1) As to the first (benefit), it states that one is saluted by the world together with its gods and men. According to this, no sooner does one generate the Thought than that one becomes an honorable object (*dakṣiṇīyabhūta*) of all the sentient beings. And no sooner is the Thought generated than one overcomes through one's family even high-souled Arhats. Accordingly, one becomes a *guru* or an abbot. It states that one is a field of merit (*puṇyakṣetra*), since when one does a merit, even if done in a small way it yields an infinite fruit; and that one is like the earth, since one is a support for the whole world. Accordingly, one is like a father of the creatures.

(2) As to the second (benefit), one is always protected by the doubling of guardians who guard and the king who is the wheel-turner.[37] Thus, if one is asleep, or intoxicated, or heedless, one cannot be harmed by *yakṣas* or *kinnāras*[38] that are in one's district. With syllables of incantations and charms[39] one appeases epidemics, agents of illness, and plagues. What is lacking to the hand of sentient beings, one brings to their hand; and how much more does one accomplish (for them)! If one has a firm generation of the Thought, even the set of ritual acts of appeasing (the deities),[40] and so forth, are taught as easy to fulfill, so that, given it (the firm . . .) even the 'shared' occult powers (*siddhi*)[41] are speedily accomplished. Furthermore, wherever one may be dwelling, whatever the harm from dangers, possible dangers, famines, and *kinnāra* spirits as have not arisen, do not arise; while those that have arisen are suppressed. Upon dying and shifting one's abode, there is little harm in the lower regions and one is free from natural illness; and if harm should occur, it does not last for a long time or in severe form. If one is engaged in teaching the Dharma for the sake of the sentient beings, one's body does not weary; there is no forgetfulness or loss of thought. The one stationed in the Bodhisattva family[42] has meager natural contamination (*dauṣṭhulya*)[43]; and if one has generated the Thought (of Enlightenment) there is very little contamination of body and mind.[44] Because one has forbearance and certainty, tolerates whatever harm comes in his/her direction, and does not create harm in another direction. When seeing another person harming another, one is much saddened. Hatred, envy, deceit, and hypocrisy can hardly arise in that person, and if arisen, are of weak intensity, not long lasting, and quickly depart. It is difficult to be born in evil destinies;[45] and if born therein, one is quickly liberated; besides, in those places one has minor suffering. When one takes that (Thought of Enlightenment) as a condition, that person gets very weary of cyclical flow[46] as well as compassionate toward the sentient beings (in it).

If the merit of the Thought of Enlightenment took on a form, it would not find room even in space; and the measure of offerings of material goods to the Buddha would not equal it, as is said in the *Vīradatta-paripṛcchā:*

If the merit from the Thought of Enlightenment had a form, it would fill up the realm of space and extend still beyond.

Suppose a man would donate to the lords of the world and fill with excellent jewels Buddha fields numbering the sand grains of the Ganges.

And suppose someone unites the palms and offers one's Thought of Enlightenment. This offering is superior. Its end cannot be found.

When the great master (i.e. Atīśa) was circumambulating he diamond seat (*vajrāsana*) he reflected on how to do it so as to peedily gain the perfect enlightenment; and he decided there vould be a speedy Buddhahood for the great ones who have contructed small images of the body (of the Buddha). Then, when e was asked, to whom this should be taught (he responded), "It s to be taught to the one with the Thought of Enlightenment." It s reported that a certain youth asked it of an old woman who was n the space above a *gandhola*, who gave the same reply as above – hearing which his mind became very sure about the Thought f Enlightenment. In that way, the concise essential of all the preepts of the Great Vehicle, which is the great treasury of all the ccult powers (*siddhi*); the special Dharma that separates the Great Vehicle from the lower one; the sublime basis exhorting the hildren of the Jina to magnanimous conduct—was informed as he Thought of Enlightenment. To ever expand the enthusiasm in s contemplation, one should do it like a thirsty man who hears report of water, because for many eons the Victor together with is children have pondered the paths, finely analyzed by their vondrous wisdom; and have seen this very (special Dharma) as he illustrious means of becoming a Buddha. The *Caryāvatāra* , 7a–b) also says this:

The powerful *munis*, with superior pondering for many eons, have seen just this as beneficial.

a–2) *teaching the six-time generation of expanding the basis of genrating the Thought*. This has two parts: (1) not abandoning the eneration of aspiration thought; (2) practicing its expansion.

(1) *not abandoning the generation of aspiration thought*. Given that someone in that way has put himself under the power of the Buddha, the Bodhisattvas, and the spiritual guides (*kalyāṇamitra*); and has with their witness taken the vow to rescue the unrescued, and so forth. If, because of seeing the multitudes of beings doing evil, or the long time required for endeavor in many eons, or the necessity to practice the difficulties to perform in regard to the two immeasurable collections (of merit and knowledge)—that one would get timid and lay down the burden of the Thought's generation, it is even a greater sin than violating the Prātimokṣa (of the monks); cf. the *Saṃcaya* (XXXI, 5):

> Even when one has practiced the ten-fold virtuous path for a 100 millions eons, if he arouses the desire to be a Pratyeka-Arhat, at that time faulty morality occurs; also broken morality; and the generation of the Thought is more weighted down than [by] the 'defeat' [of the Prātimokṣa].

This sets forth a morality violation of that Bodhisattva, for the reason that the Bodhisattva morality is superior to the vow in the mental orientation of the Śrāvaka or Pratyekabuddha, and if it is lost, morality is rent; and because if it is not abandoned, the unshared avowed mind of the Bodhisattva is not rent, even when he practices without shrinking in the sense objects ("distinct powers of desire," *kāmaguṇa*); cf. the same scripture (XXXI, 4):

> If the Bodhisattva enjoys the five sense objects [*pañcakāmaguṇa*], he [still] takes his refuge in the Buddha, the Dharma, and the Noble Sāṁgha. If, orienting his mind to omniscience he thinks, "I shall become a Buddha," a wise person should know the [Bodhisattva's] place—the perfection of morality.

If one abandons the Thought pledged that way, he must wander for a long time in evil destinies; cf. *Caryāvatāra* (IV, 5–6):

> There is a saying: "Even if it be a mere slight thing one had thought over in his mind [to give], and the man does not give it, he becomes a hungry ghost." How much more of you sir, when loudly inviting the whole world to the incomparable joy and deceiving it! What will be your destiny?

Now, that same work (III, 27) states:

> Just as a blind man finds a jewel in a heap of rubbish, in the same way, by some coincidence, this Thought of Enlightenment has arisen in me.

As that passage indicates, one should think, "How marvellous that such a thing as this is found by me!" and should not abandon it in any circumstances. Moreover, dwelling on that in diverse ways, one should always incline one's heart to not abandon it even for a moment.

(2) *practicing its expansion*. It does not suffice to merely refrain from abandoning it in that manner, but one should expand it by great endeavors in the three times of day and in the three times of night.[47] Furthermore, if one has fulfilled extensively the rite previously explained, one should perform like that. If one has not fulfilled, having clearly visualized the field of the host (of Buddhas and Bodhisattvas) one extends offerings (to it). Then exercising love and compassion, one should hold (the Thought) during the six times.

The (condensed) rite for that is as follows:

> Until the enlightenment, I take my refuge in the Buddha, the Dharma, and the Best of Hosts [i.e. Sāṃgha]. May I, by these deeds of giving and so forth, accomplish Buddhahood so as to benefit the world.

This is said three times for each of the three (i.e. three times using the word "Buddha"; three times each, using the words "Dharma" and "Best of Hosts").

a – 3) *teaching the non-rejection by the mind of the sentient beings for whom there is the generation of the Thought*. This is not treated in the *Bodhipathapradīpa* and the *Cittotpādavidhi* in their sections on what needs to be learned; but the *Bodhipathapradīpa Commentary* in the section on 'Protection' explains that one should assist the sentient beings and not abandon them, because (the protection) is of the Thought of Enlightenment as the consciousness-support, its benefit, the rite of generating it, the common expansion, and the non-forgetting. Since this is not in contradiction with the basic purport, one should also learn this.

The measure for the abandonment by the mind is as follows: One takes recourse to just a condition that renders something not valid; and thinks, "One would never perform his aim at this time!"

a–4) *teaching the amassing of the two collections*. Having taken the aspiration thought ritually, as the cause of expanding the Thought of Enlightenment in each day one should endeavor at amassing the collections while honoring the (three) Jewels, and so on. Although one does not see textual sources for this, except in the sayings of the former (Tibetan teachers), it appears to be of great benefit.

b) *teaching the cause of not being separate from it in other lives*. This has two parts: practicing the rejection of the four evil natures that cause loss; practicing the acceptance of the four good natures that cause non-loss.

b–1) *practicing the rejection of the four evil natures that cause loss*. The *Kaśyapa-parivarta* of the *Ratnakūṭa* states that there are four natures (*dharma*) regarding forgetting or the non-manifestation in other lives of the generation of the Thought; and that there are four natures regarding the not forgetting of the Thought of Enlightenment in the intermediate period as long as one has not attained enlightenment. This information needs to be learned about the aspiration thought.

Among them, the four evil natures include two that deceive regarding the 'abbot' (*upādhyāya*), the 'master' (*ācārya*), the *guru*, or the 'sponsor.' The 'abbot' and the 'master' are easily understood to be the 'object' (*viṣaya*). The '*guru*' is claimed to be the benefit. The 'sponsor,' although not included, does possess good qualities. This is the explanation in the *Kaśyapa-parivarta Commentary*.

Should it be asked, "What sort of action toward that object constitutes going with an evil nature?" (the response is:) if one deceives knowingly either of those objects, it is an evil nature. The way of deception is explained by the commentary as talking compassionately about transgressions with those 'objects' and confusing with false words. The *gurus*, being cheated by deceptive thought, do everything that creates the means. While there is a craft and deception devoid of falsehood, as will be taught below, they must constitute a cheating by causing falsehood.

The *Śikṣāsamuccaya* states that the good natures eliminate the evil natures, which is the reason that the adversary of this (first) one is the first of the four good natures.

Furthermore, a disciple might ask his *guru* for one advice, asserting that he secretly got another advice when he went to hear it from the spiritual guide. Thus with bad intent he speaks, deluding the *guru*.

In regard to not discouraging another and to effecting discouragement, for the two the 'object' is the other person doing virtue and not discouraged. Here, how one does it (i.e. the bad nature) is as follows: with resolve to install in discouragement, one generates discouragement in a person who is presently undiscouraged. The commentary explains it as confusing those who are presently engaged in pure conduct, in words that teach with craft and deception. Our thesis that in the two there is a capacity and no capacity of deception, and that these are the arousal or non-arousal of discouragement, appears consistent with the commentary. However, the commentary sets forth that it (the bad nature) incites a later confusion.

In regard to uttering dispraise, etc. of the sentient beings rightly installed in the Great Vehicle, the 'object' is maintained by some persons as anyone who has generation of the Thought, and it through a rite. Some others claim that since the Thought was generated formerly, now it is not possessed; this is in contradiction to the scriptures, and so is not valid. Apart from the mere mention of 'Bodhisattva' the commentary does not clarify the matter. In another section (i.e. in the *Śikṣāsamuccaya*) the one possessing the Bodhisattva's vow practices the instruction, and there are many explanations about rightly entering the Great Vehicle. But it seems the requirement is to generate the Thought and to hold onto it. As to how it (the bad nature) is done: it is the speech of dispraise, etc. The claim that it entails a speech made vehement with hatred, is consistent with the commentary.

To whatever 'object' it speaks, it speaks to those aiming at the Dharma which is the Thought of Enlightenment, so as to turn away their faith in the Great Vehicle or their desire to accomplish (in it); and the commentary's explanation suffices for understanding the meaning.

The speech with dispraise is like this: "He has an evil disposition," which one says without weighing the disadvantage (of so talking). The unpleasant speech is like this: "He has impure conduct," which one says upon weighing with this object in mind. The not-to-be-said is like this: "He has impure conduct this way and by means of this," which one says upon weighing. The commentary explains that one may add at the end of each of those foregoing three the expression "non-*śloka*" (bad sound).

It is also a great disadvantage arising close to ourselves, as has already been explained in brief.[48] Furthermore, when one who has generated the Thought reviles another Bodhisattva, then, as is pointed out in the *Praśāntaviniścayaprātihārya-sūtra*, that former one, though that one be with the Thought of Enlightenment, as many times as that one has reviled is the number of eons that one must dwell in hell; and the *sūtra* mentions that there is no possibility for a Bodhisattva to fall into evil destinies other than through defaming a Bodhisattva. Besides, the *Saṃcaya* (XXIV, 5) declares:

> If any Bodhisattva who has not received a prophecy should instigate a quarrel with one who has received a prophecy,[49] for so many seconds as his mind possesses the fault of antagonism, exactly that many eons from his starting point he must be attired in armor.

This states that to the extent one arouses an angry resolve of such sort, for eons to the same extent that one must walk a path from this starting point, taking that one far away from Enlightenment. For this reason, it is mandatory to suppress all forms of anger; and if they arise, to promptly confess them and to endeavor in the vow. The same work (XXIV, 6b, c, d = 6a, c, d of Sanskrit) declares:

> If one arouses the idea, "that person's mind is not good," one should individually confess, and then practice one's vows, as one unhappily studies here the Buddha's Dharma.

When one ponders the anger phase (it is advised), that given love and compassion already present but in meager force, one should practice them for a long time; and if not already present, one should take up the task of generating them for the first time — thereby one bears the root of the Thought of Enlightenment. And if one exercises, as previously explained, by suppressing anger, which is the opposing condition, however more he does, so much more they (love and compassion) expand, becoming boundless; cf. *Pramāṇavārttika*, Siddhi Chap., 129c–d:

> (When compassion) is not supplanted by the adversaries, it reaches its true self in consciousness.

And (Siddhi Chap., 126):

> And since, when they are repeatedly exercised, the mental factors (*buddhi*) compassion and so on, are matured from the concordant prior seed, how can there be their standstill?

When approaching another with deceit and guile, and not with aspiration, the 'object' is another sentient being, whoever it may be. The way it is done is the practice with guile and deceit. 'Aspiration' has resolve as its bare nature—so the commentary's explanation. It is said that 'deceit and guile' are such things as cheating on the weight of a sold article; and such things as when Rgyal-ba-ye-'byung formerly gave a thanksgiving offering in the Stod-lung district, and later used the thanksgiving (offering) for himself.[50] The (*Abhidharma-*)*Samuccaya* says that both arise under the aegis of attraction to riches and honour and belong to the category of either lust (*rāga*) or delusion (*moha*); and that while 'guile' professes presence of good qualities where there are none, 'deceit' is the cover-up of one's own faults. Here, 'cover-up' is the tactic of keeping one's faults away from disclosure.

b–2) *teaching the acceptance of the four good natures that cause non-loss*. The 'object' of the first good nature is all the sentient beings there are. The practice of it is to refrain from knowingly speaking an untruth, even for one's life (depending on it) or in jest. If one acts that way, the 'object' in particular of one's abbot (*upādhyāya*) and preceptor (*ācārya*), etc. is not confused with lies.

The 'object' of the second good nature is all the sentient beings. The practice of it is the abiding with aspiration free from deceit and guile, and the abiding with upright resolve. This is the adversary for the fourth bad nature.

The 'object' of the third good nature is all the Bodhisattvas. The practice of it is arousing the idea that they are like the Teacher, and speaking in the four directions praises of their abiding in their aims. When we ever more scratch in the way virtue does, in the end there are no scars. But hatred and defamation make many scars on the Thought of Enlightenment and associates. When we end by removing wounds, being capable of two eliminations, i.e. removal of wounds in this (person) and the Thought of Enlightenment, according to the *Śikṣāsamuccaya* there is reliance on a person, and what was stated as the supplanting (by anger, etc.) does not happen at all. Because, as mentioned in the *Kaśyapa-paripṛcchā*, since one does not know in whom resides the Thought of Enlightenment, one arouses the idea, "He is a teacher," toward all sentient beings, and is controlled by exercising the "pure shining" (*samādhi*). Expressing the good qualities is also taken up in the section of the hearer; and there is no fault if one does not express them by going into the four directions. This (third good nature) is the adversary of the third bad nature.

The 'object' of the fourth good nature is the sentient being who is brought to maturity by oneself. The practice of it is to engage toward holding the perfect Enlightenment without desiring the inferior vehicle. Furthermore, from one's own side it is required to assist the candidate (*vineya*); but if the resolve does not arise in the candidate no fault occurs, because he is unable to accomplish it. This (fourth good nature) eliminates the second bad nature; because if there is the desire, tied to the heart, to place another person in all the ultimate bliss, one would not work to arouse in that other person the discouragement of dissatisfaction, i.e. to assist that person to arouse dissatisfaction, cf. the *Siṃha-paripṛcchā*:

> Therefore in all one's lives one does not lose the Thought of Enlightenment. Even in dreams there is this Thought; even more in the wakeful state.

And he declared:

> Whether in pleasure groves, towns, or cities, one assumes the duty, thereby one does not lose the Thought toward Enlightenment.

Besides, the *Mañjuśrībuddhakṣetraguṇavyūha* states that one does not abandon his fervent aspiration, if one has these four: defeat of pride, elimination of envy and of avarice, and satisfaction when one observes another's success. The matter is clearly taught by the following and other remarks in the *Ratnamegha*:

> One exercises the Thought of Enlightenment in all one's postures [standing, etc.]. If one has let in the Thought of Enlightenment prior to whatever virtue one practices, that one should not be separate from the jewel of the Thought also in whatever other lives. For that many times one should review it.

3) *if broken, the way of mending*. Now, there is the basis of breakage (or, loss of the Thought) when there are (any of) the four bad natures; or as fifth, the mind's abandonment of the sentient beings; or as sixth, giving up the generation of the Thought by thinking, "I am not able to accomplish Buddhahood"; or, after the measure of session is passed, to disregard the aspiration thought; or, within the measure of session, to give way to discouragement. Or, if one breaks off the acceptance of six times or the practicing in the two collections, there is the basis of the breakage alone. If it be the case of the basis of abandonment (i.e. the four bad natures, etc.), it is required to repeat the rite of taking the aspiration thought. And if it be the case of the basis of breakage alone, it is not required to repeat the rite; it suffices to confess. So many (authorities) state.

Among them, when one thinks, "I am not able to accomplish Buddhahood," if one had planted the generation of the Thought, it is immediately abandoned in that case (of so thinking). But it is not required to fix the relation in terms of session measure: this is invalid in every way.

As to the four bad natures, while they are not the basis for abandoning the generation of the Thought in the present life, they are the cause for the non-manifestation of the Thought in another life. Consequently, one should suppress them in this life.

The *Bodhipathapradīpa* explains (k. 18c–d):

> So as to remember those even in other lives, one guards the instruction as it was taught.

Here, the words "as it was taught" mean the way it was taught in the *Kaśyapa-paripṛcchā*. And it is the meaning of the scripture itself.

> Kaśyapa, there are four natures which, if the Bodhisattva has them, direct him to the Thought of Enlightenment in all his births as soon as he is born; and he does not get confused [about them] in the interval, up to being seated at the terrace of enlightenment.

This has been clearly set forth in the section on the four good natures. Hence, even though in the section on the four bad natures, this life does not elucidate the next one, one knows a control of the next one. However, if in the present life, one comes under the influence of the bad natures, the generation of the Thought gets weak in strength. If one does not (exert control); and the Bodhisattva possessed of the vow speaks a little lie for raising a laugh, performs a small deceit and guile toward a sentient being, expresses in a small way language vile with hatred toward a Bodhisattva, and generates in a small way discouragement of another's producing a root of virtue; then, having passed the session measure during which he was not discouraged, he abandons the vow of *bodhi*-thought. This is because when in those ways he abandons the aspiration thought, he casts away the vow thought —as is said in both the *Bodhisattvabhūmi* and the *Śikṣāsamuccaya*. Since it is so held (by these authoritative works), those (acts) must also be appraised as fundamental transgressions; such as those were never recommended, and they are invalid.

Furthermore, as to calculating the session, while (some persons) appear to base it on the *Upāli-paripṛcchā*, one should not construe it by the meaning of that scripture. In the *Śīlapaṭala Com-*

mentary I have established the matter extensively, so it will not be expounded here.[51]

As to rejecting sentient beings with the mind, the rejection by the mind by considering sentient beings in general and thinking, "I am not capable of the aim of this much of sentient beings," is clearly (mentioned as) the casting off of the aspiration thought. And generating the Thought by considering sentient beings in particular and thinking, "At no time will I perform the aim of this person," is like destroying the collection (e.g. chariot) in favor of a part (e.g. axle), thus destroys the Thought generation which is on behalf of all those sentient beings that exist. If it were not so, one could reject the second sentient being, the third, the fourth, and so on up to many of them, and generate the Thought for the sake of the remainder; so it is mandatory to generate the Thought of Enlightenment in a complete way.

As to what needs to be practiced for generating the Thought that way (i.e. in a complete way), according to the *Bodhipathapradīpa Commentary* there arose a diversity of interpretations—those of King Indrabodhi, Nāgārjuna, Asaṅga, (Ārya)Śūra, Śāntideva, Candragomin, Śāntarakṣita, and so on. Some maintained there are as many things to be practiced as there are for first generating the Thought, and second, entering into its career (*caryā*). Certain ones maintained, "All that is said in the scriptures should protect." Certain ones maintained, "as much as is to be practised of the path of accumulation (i.e. of merit and knowledge)." Others denied that it is this training and like this. According to others, "One should practice the taking of refuge and on top of that should watch out for the eight natures of forgetting and of not forgetting the Thought." When making these formulations, the traditions of these preceptors were derived from the scriptures (*sūtra*). But my guru (Tib. *bla ma*) said that one should follow the tradition received from one's own guru. And all maintained (what they said) was the meaning of the scriptures.

The great *kalyāṇamitras* descended in the lineage from the *kalyāṇamitra* Ston-pa maintained that this commentary, generally speaking, is not written as a commentary by Jo-bo (i.e. Atīśa); while those in the lineage from Nag-tsho maintained it is written by Jo-bo, asserting that it was a secret doctrine of Nag-tsho's.

However, it was of common acceptance among the former teachers that he made a brief commentary when in Pu-rangs; thereafter, they assert, when he proceeded to Bsam-yas, the Translator asked him for an addition, and he did it extensively. Thus, Jo-bo composed a brief commentary; and in consultation his explanation grasping the essentials was rightly extended in many points. Hence, while there have been on the side some mistaken showings, there have also appeared numerous fine explanations for the meaning of the text. So also I explain by drawing upon the errorless ones in the steps of the path as well as in other types (of Buddhist literature).

It is hard to believe the previous explanations of what needs to be practiced about this. Taking the generation of the Thought to be what needs to be practiced of the 'entrance thought' is not valid, since on top of the precepts of taking of refuge, there would be no possibility of allowing the engagement and disengagement (respectively) for the eight good and bad natures. And if one performs the aspiration thought alone, all that was stated in the scriptures regarding what needs to be practiced about this, and the practice of those practicing with engagement in the career and its sequel, would be not required; because otherwise there is no distinction from what is to be practiced of the vow.

What needs to be practiced, except for the two things to be practiced as previously explained,[52] is in accordance with the *Bodhipathapradīpa* and the *Cittotpādavidhi*. And what the *Sūtra of the Seven Dharmas*[53] says of the instruction, to wit, "It should be done by one desiring speedy supernormal power (*abhijñā*)," does not appear for the practice, but is peculiar to the generating of the Thought, so it is not written up.

Accordingly, our school (of interpretation) is as follows: If one violates one's practice—excepting the non-abandonment of aspiration thought, and the non-abandonment mentally of the sentient beings — one violates what is to be practiced of the pledge of virtue in the interval starting with not having the vow of enlightenment thought and going up to the time of not falling from the dominion of enlightenment thought. Since there would be evil practice, one should confess by means of the four powers.[54] And when one has gained the vow of enlightenment thought, it would be a fall that violates the practice of the vow; so it suffices to perform as was stated for mending the fall. Since this is included in the practice of the entrance thought, there is no alternative. However, the generation of the Thought in the six times is not in common with the practice of the aspiration.

The Method of Practicing the Career after Having Generated the Thought

This has three divisions: the reason for requiring the practice of the instruction after having generated the Thought; the teaching that Buddhahood is not accomplished by practicing the means or insight in isolation; exposition of the steps of practicing the instruction.

The Reason for Requiring the Practice of the Instruction after Having Generated the Thought

When one has in that way generated the aspiration thought, if one then does not practice giving (*dāna*) and the other perfections, there is still a great benefit as was already cited from the scripture *Maitreya-vimokṣa*. However, if one does not do the main thing of accomplishing the instruction of the Bodhisattva, there is no possibility of becoming a Buddha. Hence, one should practice the career (*caryā*); cf. the *Gayāśīrṣa*:

> Enlightenment belongs to the Bodhisattvas who have the main thing of performance, not to those who lack the main thing of performance.

And the *Samādhirāja* puts it this way:

> Hence, you should think, "I shall do the main thing of performance." Why so? O youth, because the incomparable, rightly accomplished enlightenment is easy to gain for the one having the main thing of performance.

Here, the term 'performance' is the means of accomplishing Buddhahood, because it is the practice of the instruction going with the Thought of Enlightenment. And the *Bhāvanākrama One* states:

> The Bodhisattva who generated the Thought of Enlightenment in that way, should realize that the one who is untamed cannot tame others, and apply himself to the performance of giving, and so on, for enlightenment is not gained in the absence of performance.

This is also alluded to in the *Pramāṇavārttika* (Siddhi chap., k. 132):

> Being compassionate he applies himself to the means for destroying [his own and others'] suffering. When the goal and its cause are out of sight, to explain them is a difficult matter.

Thus, if there is great compassion toward another, one must dispel that one's suffering; and it does not suffice to have the good resolve, "May that (cause) be dispelled and one be free of suffering!" but it is required to apply oneself to the means for it. Furthermore, when one has not previously applied oneself to the means, one is unable to rescue another; so the one desiring to perform the aim of another should first tame oneself. For that, it is said one must do the main thing of performance; and it is said that one should learn the instruction for that performance when one takes the vow. Hence, it is very important that one not mistake the doing that constitutes the doing of the main thing, i.e. the performance.

The Teaching that Buddhahood Is Not Accomplished by Practicing the Means or Insight in Isolation

Given that it does not suffice for one to desire to gain Buddhahood, but that one should engage the performance-means for Buddhahood. Besides, the means must be errorless. Thus, no matter how much one may endeavor on a faulty path, the (desired) result does not occur, like pulling a goat when one desires to draw some milk. Again, even when one has concluded that it is faultless, if one endeavors with parts incomplete, the (desired) result does not occur; just as when any one of the essential conditions of seed, water, soil, etc. are missing, the shoot does not arise. Now, the *Bhāvanākrama Two* says it this way:

> If one creates assiduously a faulty cause, no matter for how long a session [''watch''] one does not obtain the desired result. For example, it is like getting milk from a [he-]goat. When one does not practice all the causes, no result ensues; because when any one among seed, and so on, as the case may be, is missing, the result, i.e. shoot, and so on, does not arise. Therefore, the one desiring that result should take recourse to faultless causes and conditions, and all of them.

However, there is the question of what is the 'faultless' complete causes and conditions. (As though answering the question,) the *Vairocanābhisaṃbodhi* declares:

> O Master of the Secret Folk! The omniscient knowledge has compassion for a root, has the Thought of Enlightenment for a motive, and has the means for a finality.

Among them, compassion has already been expounded. Thought of Enlightenment means the two Thoughts of Enlightenment, conventional (*saṃvṛti-tas*) and absolute (*paramārtha-tas*);[55] and means is the fulfillment of giving and the other perfections—as the great waylayer Kamalaśīla explains.

In regard to that path, certain persons such as the Chinese Hva Shang have reflected perversely that if there is a discursive thought (*vikalpa*) followed by a good reflection, how much more if it be a bad reflection, one is bound to the cyclical flow (*saṃsāra*); so the result of that (discursive thought) does not transcend the cyclical flow. It is just as when one is bound with a gold strap as compared with a cotton thong; or just as when the sky is obscured by both white or black clouds; or as when it is either white or black hounds that bring pain to the cave (of an anchorite). So by all means, making a place (in the mind) without discursive thought is the path for becoming a Buddha; and the giving, guarding of morality, and so on, are unnecessary for cultivation in the final meaning (*nītārtha*), but are stated on behalf of foolish persons. Therefore, when one has gained the final meaning, the application to those practices is like a king descending to the level of the mob; or like one who has acquired an elephant to be searching for an elephant. So they say. Hva Shang has (tried to) prove that position by quoting eighty sources of scriptures that praise "by all means no discursive thought."

Asserting, "(Your) 'all parts of the path' are not the basic path of the Buddha," this position casts severe aspersion on 'convention' (*saṃvṛti*). Opposing the heart of the Buddha's teaching, which is the pondering by way of discriminative insight of the reality of non-self, it largely rejects the rule of the 'absolute' (*paramārtha*). This vileness of wayward views which they posit as a lustre of the path and occupying the mind as a substitute for the category of calming (the mind) which is how one applies excellently — the great Bodhisattva Kamalaśīla well refuted with an immaculate multitude of scripture and principle, and then he indeed wrote up extensively the auspicious path that delights the Jina.

However, there came a decline of the teaching. There was a depletion of the illustrious ones who have fulfilled the essentials of the path and are certain as to the alternatives by scriptures of final meaning and by immaculate principles. The merit of sentient beings was at a low ebb; they had scarce faith in the Dharma; were mostly of meager power of insight. Still more, some persons actively opposed the categories of the career, i.e. protective vows and so on; and at the time of contemplating the path acted just like Hva Shang by abandoning those (protective vows, etc.). Some persons refrained from condemning the part of means, but well accepted, for understanding the viewpoint, the Hva Shang position. Others abandoned the discriminative insight and well espoused the Hva Shang contemplation — the no thinking at all.

The path of those persons does not show in terms of category and object a contemplation of voidness. However, if they are drawn into a contemplation of voidness, even though gaining an errorless meaning of voidness; and their manner of contemplation have an understanding of errorless contemplation, those persons will contemplate voidness alone; they say that they do not contemplate the side of practices that have the domain of convention (*saṃvṛti*); or they say there is no requirement to hold those (practices) deeply and to endeavor in them by many gateways. They are in contradiction with all scripture, and transgress the path of principles.

What is to be accomplished by the Mahāyānists is the Nirvāṇa of no-fixed abode (*apratiṣṭhita-nirvāṇa*). For this, they must accomplish the no-fixed abode in cyclical flow (*saṃsāra*) by means of the insight that understands reality, the steps of the path based on the absolute (*paramārtha*), the "profound path," the collection of knowledge (*jñāna-saṃbhāra*), and the part of insight (*prajñā*). And they must accomplish the no-fixed abode in the quiescent *nirvāṇa* by means of the insight realizing a phenomenon, the steps of the path based on conventional truth, the "broad path," the collection of merit, and the part of means (*upāya*). Consistently, the *Acintyaguhya-sūtra* declares:

> The collection of knowledge eliminates all defilement [*kleśa*]. The collection of merit sustains all the sentient beings. Bhagavat, that being so, the great Bodhisattvas are to strive in the collections of merit and knowledge.

Besides, the *Ārya-Ākāśagarbha* says this:

> By the insight-cognition, all defilement is cast out. By the means-cognition, all the sentient beings are taken inside.

The *Ārya-Saṃdhinirmocana* says it this way:

> I deny that those who are completely outside the aim of sentient beings, or completely outside all the motivations to be instigated, are in the incomparable, rightly completed, enlightenment.

The *Vimalakīrtinirdeśa* states the point extensively:

> "What is the bondage [*bandha*] of the Bodhisattvas; what their liberation [*mokṣa*]?" "The fencing-round of the wandering in phenomenal life without the means, is the bondage of the Bodhisattvas. The wandering while wandering in phenomenal life with the means, is their liberation. The fencing-round of the wandering in phenomenal life without insight, is the bondage of the Bodhisattvas. The wandering while wandering in phenomenal life with insight, is their liberation. The insight not held by the means, is bondage. The insight held by the means, is liberation. The means not held by insight, is bondage. The means held by insight, is liberation."

Now, at the time of the path subsequent to the desire for Buddhahood, it is mandatory to be based on both parts, means and insight, while (the goal) is not accomplished if either is missing; cf. the *Gayāśīrṣa*:

> The path of the Bodhisattvas, in short, is twofold. What are the two? They are the means and insight.

Furthermore, the *Śrī-Paramādya* declares:

> Perfection of Insight is one's mother. Skill in the Means is one's father.

In the words of the *Kāśyapa-parivarta* (#42):

> O Kāśyapa, for example, just as the king who is governed by ministers performs all the duties of a king, so also the insight of the Bodhisattva which is governed by the means performs all the acts of the Buddha.

For that reason, one should contemplate the voidness possessing the best of all aspects, being complete with all parts of the means, i.e. giving, and so on; while the path of the Mahāyāna does not lead anywhere with only voidness; cf. the *Ratnacūḍaparipṛcchā*:

> Thus, attired in the apparel of love [*maitrī*], based on the foundation of great compassion [*mahākaruṇā*], he meditates the meditation possessing the best of all aspects, bringing out the aspects [images] of voidness. What is the voidness possessing the best of all aspects? That which is not without giving, not without morality, not without forbearance, not without striving, not without meditation, not without insight, not without the means.

That is the promulgation *in extenso*; the meaning is provided by the *Uttaratantra* (I, 92):

> The painters, i.e. giving, morality, forbearance, and the rest, are its aspects [images]; and the voidness possessing the best of all aspects—is the picture.

According to this, one likens the situation to the case where many artists have assembled to draw the picture of a king. One knows how to draw a head, but nothing else; another knows the hand, but nothing else; and so on. As a single artist is incomplete, there would not ensue by that person a completion (of the picture). Here the picture of the king is the voidness, and the artists are likened to giving, and so forth. Thus, if the means consisting in giving, and the rest is not complete, it is like a picture with mutilated head, mutilated hand, and so on.

Furthermore, as to the attitude, "We take the contemplation of the void alone as basic, and do not require contemplation of the others," this is refuted by the Bhagavat himself when he accepted in former lives those directions. If it were that way (as in your attitude), (the Bhagavat) in many eons when he was a Bodhisattva would have had poor insight that does not understand the 'final meaning' (*nītārtha*) when he dispensed gifts, guarded his morality, and so on. So states the *Sarvadharmavaipulyasaṃgraha-sūtra*:

> "Maitreya, as regards the performance of the six perfections on the part of the Bodhisattvas for the complete enlightenment, these men of delusion will say: 'A Bodhisattva need only train in the perfection of insight. What is the need of the other perfections?' They think any other perfection should be disparaged. What do you think, O Ajita: Was the King of Kāśi foolish when he gave parts of his flesh to the hawk for the sake of the dove?" Maitreya answered, "Not so, O Lord." The Bhagavat [then] said: "Maitreya, when I was practicing the Bodhisattva career and collected roots of merit associated with the six perfections, did I do wrong as regards those roots of virtue?" Maitreya replied, "Not so, Lord." The Bhagavat declared: "You, Ajita, in the meantime [of your rebirths] performed the perfections of giving, morality, forbearance, striving, meditation, and insight, sixty eons for each perfection. These men of delusion will speak thus: 'Only by one rule is there enlightenment, to wit, by the rule of voidness.' Now, will they be pure in conduct? [Of course not!]"

So, the one who says, "If there is comprehension of voidness, there is no need to cultivate with great endeavor the part of the means," casts aspersion on the auspicious former lives (*jātaka*) of our Teacher, as though to say: "Those were times when the final meaning (*nītārtha*) was not understood."

If one thinks, "There is a performance in diverse ways of the practices, giving, and so on, as long as there is no firm comprehension of voidness; but, if there is (the firm . . .), it suffices," this is also a tremendously perverse view. If such as this were right, then the sons of the Jina who have entered the great stage where they gain the non-reflecting knowledge (*avikalpika-jñāna*) that comprehends in immediacy absolute truth (*paramārtha-satya*), and in particular the Bodhisattvas of the Eighth Stage where they gain power over the non-reflecting knowledge, would not be required to practice. But that is not right, because the *Daśabhūmika-sūtra* states that giving (*dāna*) and the other (perfections) are respectively predominant on each of the ten stages, and still there is no lack of practice of the remaining ones, thus saying that on each stage there are six (perfection fractions) of the six perfections or practice of ten (perfection fractions); and (because) their meaning has been commented upon that way by the Venerable Maitreya, Nāgārjuna, and Asaṅga, so one cannot draw out a different interpretation.

In particular, in the phase of the Eighth Stage there is the end of all defilement, so one is stationed in the absolute where all elaboration (*prapañca*) abates. At that time the Buddhas could not have become Buddhas with merely this comprehension of voidness in that (state), because this non-reflection (*nirvikalpa*) is also attained by the Śrāvakas and Pratyekabuddhas. The *sūtra* urges (the Bodhisattva in that Stage) with such imperatives as these: Look at these immeasurables of our body, knowledge, and field! Since you do not have our powers, and so on, begin to strive for these! Consider that the untamed sentient being is troubled by diverse defilements! Do not abandon this forbearance! When it expounds the requirement to practice the career going with the Thought of Enlightenment, when others convey their contentment over a single subtle *samādhi*, what they set forth should raise laughter among the wise. That is the message of the *Daśabhūmika-sūtra*:

> O Prince, you should know concerning the Bodhisattva who has entered this Motionless Bodhisattva Stage, who abides, drawing upon the force of his former aspiration, in that stream which is the

> entrance to the Doctrine [*dharma*], that for him the Buddha Lords make a providing by way of Tathāgata-knowledge, and they speak thus to him: "Very well, very well, son in the lineage! This absolute forbearance is for approaching the Buddha-natures. However, you should know, son in the lineage, that our attainment of Buddha natures consisting of the ten powers, the four confidences, and so on, this is not in you. Begin your striving! Apply yourself to searching for that attainment of Buddha natures! Do not turn away from forbearance's gateway!
>
> "Moreover, you should know, son in the lineage, that when you have obtained in that way the peaceful liberation, again observe the foolish ordinary folk, who are without peace, are generating diverse defilements, and whose minds are struck with manifold reflections!
>
> "Furthermore, son in the lineage, remember your former aspiration for bringing about the aim of sentient beings, and [remember] the inconceivable knowledge gateway!
>
> "Also, you should know, son in the lineage, that this is the underlying nature of all the *dharmas*. Whether Tathāgatas arise or do not arise, there remains this underlying nature, the staying of the Dharmadhātu, which is this voidness of all the *dharmas*, the non-apprehension of any *dharma*. But not by this alone are the Tathāgatas differentiated, for also all the Śrāvakas and Pratyekabuddhas attain this non-reflecting underlying nature.
>
> "Furthermore, son in the lineage, now observe our immeasurable body, immeasurable knowledge, immeasurable Buddha Field, immeasurable realization of knowledge, immeasurable light disk, immeasurable purity of speech members; and may you generate a like realization!"

For example, a great vessel is caused to embark upon the ocean, is moved by a conformable wind, and its time of journey is a single day. But however much one may figure the requirement of movement (by the wind), not having caused (the ship) to embark, and endeavoring ahead of time on that behalf, one does not figure it out in the time of a hundred years. In the same way, while the path of omniscience takes a single moment and is not concerned with the great effort of one who has entered upon the Eighth

Stage; as much as one may figure when one has not attained that (Buddha) Stage, one cannot do it even with prior endeavor in a thousand eons. Because it is (thus) stated in the *Daśabhūmika*, when one claims there is a "quick path" (*myur lam*) while one has not learned the Bodhisattva practice, one deceives oneself.

Suppose one thinks, "Even though one does not desire giving and so on, there being no requirement for them in the person with no thinking at all, those are complete; because when one is not attached to the receiver, the giving, or the gift, one has complete giving of the non-apprehension kind, and in the same way the others are complete, as the *sūtra* mentioned that each (stage) includes each of the six (perfections)." If one were complete with just that, the heretics (i.e. non-Buddhists) would also have all the perfections complete at the time when they are equipoised in the one-pointed calm of the mind because in that way they would be unattached (to the triad). In particular, as previously cited, the Śrāvakas and Pratyekabuddhas at the time of their non-reflection toward underlying nature (*dharmatā*) would be in the Great Vehicle (*mahāyāna*) since they would have all the Bodhisattva practice complete (in themselves). Again, if you claim it suffices with just that, since it was said that in each one (of stages) is included each of the six, well, then, in the case of offering a *maṇḍala*, when one provides cow dung together with water, and so on, it would be right to do only this, since it is said there is (a fraction of) the (remaining) six perfections (when there is one of them, as here: giving).

Now, as to the practice held by view and the insight held by means, there is the example of the mother depressed with grief at the death of her beloved son. The force of grief does not leave her at the time she engages in such things as speaking with others; and whatever notion arises, it is unnecessary that all those notions be notions of grief. So also, when there is the fierce energy of insight that understands voidness, at the time the person engages in dispensing of gifts, bowing, circumambulation, and reciting; given that the notions having these (activities) as consciousness-supports are not the comprehension of voidness, the engagement does not contradict the possession of the coloring or energy of that (insight). Also, if at the outset of a session, a person first puts fierce energy in the Thought of Enlightenment, at the time he settles in a *samādhi* of voidness; given that this is not actually the Thought of Enlightenment, the holding is not contradicted by the coloring of that (Thought of Enlightenment). Now, what is called "giving without apprehension (of an object)" is like that; but the thinking of dispensing is without duration, and the giving is not convenient; and one may understand also the remaining (perfections) the same way. One may also understand that way the rule of the means not lacking insight.

Furthermore, one should not be mistaken in regard to what is said about body, possessions, and long life in cyclical flow (*saṃsāra*) as the fruit of merit collections. If there is skill in the means that lacks (perfection of) insight, even so, if one is held by those (merit collections), that is very properly the cause of liberation and omniscience, just as said in the *Ratnāvalī* (III, 12a–b):

> The Form Body [of the Buddha], in brief, O King, is born from the merit collection.

And there is no end of scriptures that teach this.

Furthermore, you say, sometimes the bad deeds and all the defilement that become the cause of evil destiny (*durgati*) can be converted into the cause of Buddhahood. And you assert, sometimes the giving, morality, and other virtues that are the cause of a high state, are the cause of (staying in) cyclical flow and are not the cause of enlightenment. (Sir,) put your mind in a tranquil state, and (then) speak!

Well, a *sūtra* states that the (mental) attachment to the six, beginning with giving, is the work of Māra.

The *Triskandhaka* explains that the one who transgresses in terms of consciousness-supports, by unworthy clinging to gift giving and morality, should individually confess all those guardings of morality, and so on.[56]

And the *Brahmaparipṛcchā* declares: "However much one practice, all that is discursive thought. Non-discursive-thought is enlightenment."

One should not make a mistake regarding what those passages state.

The meaning of the first (passage) [unnamed *sūtra*] is that by wayward clinging to the 'selves' (i.e. of person and of *dharma*), the aroused giving, and so on, is impure and so explained as "work of Māra," but that does not teach that giving, etc. are (in themselves) the work of Māra. Moreover, since it is stated for the six, claim that meditation and insight are also the work of Māra (if that is what you think the passage means)!

As to the meaning of the second scriptural passage [*Triskandhaka*] when it (giving, etc.) is aroused by wayward clinging, it is impure, and accordingly explained; but it does not teach that one should not resort to giving, and the others. Otherwise, when it says, "who transgresses in terms of consciousness-supports, . . . gift giving," the words 'who transgresses in terms of consciousness-supports' would be unnecessary; because when it mentions that gift dispensing is confessed, it does not speak that way from speech as the principle. According to *Bhāvanākrama Three*, the manner of answering done like this is very important, because when one understands this waywardly, all sides of practice are construed as holding a personal-self or a *dharma*-self as sign-source, and are claimed to be possessed of sign-sources.

If it is adherence to the self of *dharmas* to adhere to the three spheres,[57] to wit, the abandonment thought that thinks, "I dispense this substance"; the vowed thought that thinks, "I withhold this bad act"; and all virtuous constructive thought of that sort—then those who gain the view of *dharma*-non-self would be right to suppress all aspects (images) like hatred, pride, etc., but it would not be valid for them to take recourse for the sake of that (suppression) [as it would be adherence to *dharma*-self].

If all constructive thought which thinks, "this," or "that," i.e. constructive thought in the three spheres, is construed as holding *dharma*-self, then [so is] giving thought to the good qualities of the spiritual friend; giving thought to the favorable states, to death, and to the suffering of evil destiny; and all the applications to what needs to be practiced of taking refuge; [so is, thinking] "from this act that fruit occurs"; [so is] love, compassion, exercise of the Thought of Enligtenment, and the entrance thought. They amount to thinking, "This," "From this, that arises," "This is the good quality," and "This is the disadvantage." And when one so thinks [according to you, sir] they are only a requirement to gain certainty; so to the extent there is merely the great certainty about those, one would proceed ever more in holding the *dharma*-self. And [according to you, sir] the more one would guard the certainty in non-self of *dharmas*, to that extent one would derive ever less certainty in those paths. So [you, sir] are mistaken, as one would be about temperature, regarding the two sides of practice and view; and nowhere generates with strong energy and for a long time a certainty cognition in those two.

For that reason, [we conclude as follows:] in the phase of the fruit there is no conflict between positing the Dharmakāya as the obtainable, and taking the Form Body as the obtainable. In the same way, also in the time of the path there must be no conflict between 1. guiding the certainty cognition about the two selves (i.e. of person and of *dharma*) while free from elaboration (*prapañca*) without remainder, even an atom, when fixing as consciousness-supports the holding of sign-sources (in those two); 2. guiding the certainty cognition in [thinking,] "From this arises that," and "This is a fault and that is a merit."

Moreover, with dependence on establishing the basic view, the two truths, by way of scripture and principles, there is 1. the authority which supports the *paramārtha*, by establishing that there does not exist even an atom of self-existence in their own layout or manner-of-being of all the *dharmas* whether of *saṃsāra* or *nirvāṇa*; 2. the authority of convention which supports cause and effect with respective certainty, while not confusing in the slightest the *dharmas* of cause and of effect. What is the use of taking those two mutually as the assailant and the assailable? When one gains certainty that they each associate with the other, then one counts "understanding the meaning of the two truths" and "gaining the purport of the Jina." This rule will be explained in the section devoted to Discerning the Real.[58]

As to the meaning of the third scriptural passage [*Brahmaparipṛcchā*], that part of the scripture is a context of considering arising, etc. So it teaches that there is no arising in reality of giving, and so forth; and it teaches with the expression "discursive thought" (*kalpanā*) only what was imagined by discursive thought; but it does not teach that one should not take recourse to those (i.e. giving and the rest) and abandon them.[59] Consequently, there is no phase as long as one is not yet a Buddha where learning those practices is not mandatory. So it is required to study the practices of the six perfections and so on.

Moreover, if one performs with endeavor upon tying the heart at this time, the accomplishments are accomplished by the endeavor. In the meantime those who are unable to perform (the perfections) should act in the domain of aspiration, i.e. should act in many fervent aspirations to purify obscurations and to amass the collection as the basis of the capacity to take (those perfections) to heart; and there will occur, not long delayed, a wealth in the heart. If, not doing it that way, one says, "I, taking the position that there is no knowing and no doing of it by myself, do not need to practice those," one creates a calamity for oneself and a calamity for others; besides, one serves as a condition for decline of the Teaching, so one should not act (that way); cf. the *Sūtrasamuccaya*:

> The weariness for discriminating the unconstructed [i.e. voidness] or for constructed virtue [i.e. the collection of merit] is a work of Māra. If one well knows the path to enlightenment, and does not seek the path of the perfections, it is a work of Māra.[60]

And:

> The Bodhisattva who lacks skill in the means should not exert himself in the profound underlying nature.[61]

The *Acintyaguhya* declares:

> Son in the lineage, for example, fire blazes from a cause; without a cause, it becomes inert. In the same way, a thought blazes from a meditative object; without a meditative object, the thought becomes inert. The Bodhisattva skilled in the means, since his Perfection of Insight is pure, also experiences the close pacification of the meditative object. But he does not perform the close pacification of the meditative object when it is the root of virtue, and does not perform it when the meditative object happens to be a defilement. But he stops on a meditative object when it is a perfection

> [*pāramita*], discriminates the meditative object when it is voidness, and beholds the meditative object with great compassion for the sentient beings.

One should differentiate what that passage states variously as the manner when it is not a (proper) meditative object and the manner when it is a (proper) meditative object.

Accordingly, the requirement is to loosen the bondage of defilement and of holding sign-sources; the requirement is to tie tightly with the cord of instruction. The requirement is to shatter the two sins,[62] and the requirement is to not shatter the virtuous deeds. Hence, the tie by the instruction and the bondage by holding sign-sources are not identical. The loosening of the protective vow, and the loosening of the bondage of self-positing, are not identical. Omniscience is accomplished through many causes. Each one by itself does not suffice, as in the saying, "To chase a hundred birds with one sling-shot." What suffices is to obtain the auspicious basis of favorable conditions and to take the main thing through diverse doorways. But practicing only some sections of the path obstructs the doorway to the two collections (i.e. of merit and knowledge), and should be recognized as unvirtuous guidance. Also at the time of the procedures of the great and small vehicles one respectively trains and does not train in the unbounded collection. Restricted vehicle (*prādeśika-yāna*) and lesser vehicle (*hīnayāna*) are alternate names, because the meaning of 'restricted' is a single direction.

Now, the present-day lower fruit, the food and drink, etc. obviously requires an accomplishment by many causes and conditions. Neither is it right to be satisfied with a single direction for the accomplishment of Buddhahood, which is the supreme aim of a person, because the result, patterned after the cause, is the underlying nature of dependent origination. Consistently, the *Karuṇāpuṇḍarīka* declares that the restricted accomplishes the restricted, and the all accomplishes the all. The *Tathāgatotpattisaṃbhava-sūtra* also says this:[63]

> The origination of the Tathāgatas is not by a single cause. Why so? O son in the lineage, the Tathāgatas are rightly accomplished by

> the ten-myriad immeasurable causes of right accomplishment. What are the ten? As follows: 1. the unsatiated right cause by way of the immeasurable collection of merit and knowledge; . . .

And so on, extensively. The *Vimalakīrtinirdeśa* explains it broadly:[64]

> O friends! The body of the Tathāgata is surely born from the "hundred" merits. It is surely born from all the virtuous natures. It is surely born from the immeasurable path of virtue.

Moreover, *nātha* Nāgārjuna writes (in the *Ratnāvalī*, III, 10):

> At the time the cause of the Form Body of the Buddha is immeasurable like the world, at that time the cause of the Dharmakāya is accordingly measurable [i.e. realizable].

Such means (*upāya*) and insight (*prajñā*) are encompassed by the six perfections (*pāramitā*); and their practice, as previously set forth, is shared by the Mantra(-Vehicle) and the Perfections(-Vehicle), because when the great texts of Mantra (i.e. the Diamond Vehicle) explain that as many as are the palaces and the arrays of gods they are all the good qualities of inner consciousness, they again and again mention the complete Pāramitā path with its six perfections, thirty-seven natures bordering on enlightenment, sixteen voidnesses, and so on. Hence, one should know them as shared except for the practice on the path of the sense objects (the five *kāmaguṇa*) going with certain special persons, and the taking and rejecting in certain explanations of the Prajñāpāramitā literature.

Taking the above explanation as a seed, and thinking it over well, if one does not gain certainty in the complete parts of the path—not a single direction—it is clear that he does not hold the pith of the general path of Mahāyāna. So wise persons should arouse firm certainty therein, and should let in ever greater capacity in the lineage of the highest vehicle through many doors.

Part II

Precepts for the Great Person

Exposition of the Steps of Practicing the Instruction

There are two parts: rules of practicing the general Mahāyāna; rules of practicing the Diamond Vehicle, in particular.[65]

Rules of Practicing the General Mahāyāna

This has three sections: 1) exercising the desire to practice the instruction of the enlightenment mind; 2) having exercised (that way), to take the vow of the Jinaputra; 3) having taken (that vow), what be the rule of instruction.

1) *exercising the desire to practice the instruction of the enlightenment mind*. As long as one has not taken at the outset the individual vows of the Vinaya (i.e. *Prātimokṣa*) and of the Mantra (i.e. Vajrayāna), it is not proper to listen to what needs to be practiced; and those (Vinaya and Mantra) are dissimilar — because when one well knows ahead of time what needs to be practiced, has (so) exercised one's stream of consciousness, if one then is enthused to hold (the vow), the vow is loose. That is the message of the *Bodhisattvabhūmi*:

> For the Bodhisattva who wishes to take the vow of morality, the points of instruction of the Bodhisattva that derive from the exegesis of the Bodhisattvasūtrapiṭaka are declared points of transgression when taught ahead of time. If, upon considering from his heart and upon analyzing with insight he should then get enthused [for the vow], he should know that neither on account of another's inducing him to rightly hold it, nor on account of contending with another, would the Bodhisattva be firm [in the vow]. He should [first] take hold of it. The vow of morality rightly taken should be imparted to him with the rite.

Hence, when one is informed of things to practice, one should make them objects of that one's mind. Then exercising a desire to practice by tying the heart to those, if one takes the vow it becomes very firm; so this is the good means. Furthermore, if it were explained both in this section and in the one below, there would be a great burden of words; so it will be explained below.

2) *having exercised (that way), to take the vow of the Jinaputra.* In the *Śīlapaṭala Commentary* I have set forth extensively and established how it is first taken, promptly thereafter how to guard against the basic transgressions and against transgressions of bad deeds, and if broken the way to mend (the vow). Prior to taking the vow, one must observe it in certainty; so one may know it there (in that Commentary).[66]

3) *having taken (that vow), what be the rule of instruction.* This has three parts: wherein is the basis of instruction, the method of gathering the instructions there, how the steps of instruction are in that place.

a) *wherein is the basis of instruction.* Although there is no end to the clear distinctions, if one assembles into principles, one assembles what the Bodhisattva needs to learn into six perfections; hence the six perfections are the 'great vow' that comprises all the essential points of the Bodhisattva path. Also the four persuasions (*catvāri saṃgrahavastūni*) are assembled therein for the reasons shown. 1. *the persuasion of giving.* This is obvious. 2. *the persuasion of pleasant speech.* Taking its point of departure in the six perfections, it instructs the candidates (*vineya*). 3. *the persuasion of aim inducement.* This is the installation of others in the aim of the precepts. 4. *the persuasion of common pursuits.* This is an accomplishment like the candidate (aims at), but by oneself. Furthermore, although the two collections, the three instructions,[67] and so on, encompass all the Bodhisattva path; an assembling that generates understanding as the six perfections do, is not equalled in capacity by any other. So it is best to take the six perfections as the basis for categories.[68]

b) *the method of gathering the instruction therein.* Here are two topics: teaching certainty of number as the main topic, teaching certainty of sequence as the subordinate topic.

b–1) *teaching certainty of number as the main topic*. The Bhagavat only made the contents of the six perfections; and the illustrious heir-apparent (i.e. Maitreya) explained, according to the purport, the essentials that are the reason for making them that way.[69] Thus, generating the cognition of certainty amounts to these rules for certainty of number. If one gains the certainty where these (rules) are captivating to the mind, one will emphasize the precept regarding the procedure of the six perfections. So one should gain the certainty. For this, there are six points.

1. *certainty of number relating to commencement*. There is required an immeasurable lineage of past lives for the completion of the magnanimous acts of the Bodhisattva. In those (lives) there may occur breaks in the stages of the path; and without each characteristic of the basis being completed, a present-day basis like this amounts only to single parts, so that, even though one performs, practically no profit ensues. Therefore, it is mandatory that all parts of the basis be complete. Besides, one must have four endowments: a. the possession where one practices; b. the body by which one practices; c. the retinue together with which one practices; d. the occupation which begins it. Moreover, with merely those endowments there are many movements into conditions of defilement. So in addition it is required that one not move into the dominion of defilement, and one should not be content with that, but also well distinguish the consciousness-supports with errorless engagement and disengagement toward the situations of taking and rejecting; because otherwise one is infatuated by those endowments, like the infatuation of craving the fruit of reeds and of the plantain tree, or by the pregnancy of a mule.

If there is insight, one should acknowledge it as the fruit of former good acts, and again move to ever increase the endeavor in those causes. And if insight is lacking, it was exhausted by enjoying the formerly collected fruits. If it is not newly expanded, one falls headlong into suffering in a later life.

Now, in another life those six (perfections) may arise, but do not arise without a cause or from a discordant cause. There is certainty as to the six perfections when the cause is concordant; so in this life one should many times repeat the thorough reliance on the six perfections; because in whatever amount one especially engages the cause, in that amount the fruit arises with its particulars.

Those constitute the commencement of states; and the commencement of the ultimate endowment of body, etc. happens in the Buddha Stage. Consistently, the *Sūtrālaṃkāra* (XVI, 2) says:

> Endowment of possessions [giving] and of embodiment [morality]; endowment of retinue [forbearance] and of enterprise [striving] are the commencement; also, not going under the influence of defilement [meditation] and always being without waywardness in duties [insight].

2. *certainty of number relating to the two aims*. If one practices the Bodhisattva career with that sort of basis and in that way, the duties of the Bodhisattva amount to two, namely, performance of one's own aim and of another's aim. For that reason, there is the certainty of number relating to the performance of the two aims. a. In this connection, for performing the aim of another, one should first benefit him with material things; moreover, there should not be any gift attended with harm to sentient beings. Since warding off in good fashion an action attended with a thing of harm to another, is a great aim for others — morality is required. It would put an end to that, if one does not forbear harm directed to oneself once or twice: there would not be pure morality; so one must have a forbearance with no thought of how harm is directed toward oneself. If one does not respond by this (nonforbearance), he is not sullied by the sin which another has collected. And so that the (other person, harm-doer) might supplicate and be one applied to virtue by that (astonishing forbearance), would be a great aim of others. b. As to one's own aim: There should be the bliss of liberation through the (magical) power of Insight. Besides, there should be no straying of the mind (to outer objects), so the mind must be equipoised by meditation (*dhyāna*) and just as desired in regard to the meditative object (in the mind). Hence, one must gain the adeptness to fix as desired (on that meditative object), which does not happen in the

lazy person, so one must enterprise with untiring striving through day and night. Hence, that (striving) is the substratum of those (other perfections).

Thus, for performance of those two aims, there is certainty in the six perfections (cf. *Sutrālaṃkāra*, XVI, 3):

> Well applied to the aim of sentient beings, one performs by means of renunciation [giving], non-injury [morality], and patience [forbearance]. One practices in every way one's his own aim by means of fixation [meditation] and liberation [insight], together with their substratum [striving].

In that passage, the words "in every way" mean (in this case) no aspect of other's aim. "Fixation and liberation" mean, respectively, the signature of meditation (*dhyāna*) when the mind is fixed on the meditative object (*ālambana*), and the signature of insight (*prajñā*) when there is liberation from cyclical flow (*saṃsāra*). If one differentiates these two, one makes no mistake in terms of Calming (the Mind) and Discerning (the Real). Accordingly, even those who desire a deep holding of the mind must gain certainty in the complete body of the six perfections, since they occur fractionally in the meditation of those persons.

As to the certainty of number relating to complete performance of all aspects of other's aim: First one gives away material possessions, thereby dispelling poverty. Besides, one does not do harm to another, no matter to what sentient being. Even more, one prâctices forbearance toward the harm directed to oneself. And does not tire of making (those harm-doers) one's friends by using one's striving. Resorting to meditation, by means of magical acts one creates what their minds long for. When there happens to be a fit vessel (i.e. candidate), resorting to insight one explains well, thus removing that person's doubts. Hence, for liberating one should be certain regarding the six perfections (cf. *Sūtrālaṃkāra*, XVI, 4):

> No pettiness; no injury; bearing with injury; never tiring of performance; bringing joy; speaking good words — on account of those the aim of others is one's own aim.[70]

This shows that it is not right to not rely on the six perfections, since they serve in two ways, i.e. the aim of oneself and of the other; and if one gains certainty in the manner of accomplishing, through those (perfections), the aims of oneself and others, there arises a devotion to perform those (aims).

3. *certainty of number relating to comprising all the Great Vehicle.* It is like this: One is not attached to possessions that are obtained, and does not pursue those that are not obtained; so one does not look for possessions. That (giving) being present, one is able to protect the instruction; so one adopts morality and is devoted to it. One forbears the suffering that occurs when one is involved with sentient beings and non-sentient entities; so one does not get weary. Besides, one is not wearied of enthusiasm for attending to whatever type of virtuous deed. One cultivates non-discursive thought in the *yoga* of Calming (the Mind) as well as non-discursive thought in the *yoga* of Discerning (the Real). By means of those six, one comprises all the Great Vehicle that moves thereby; and by means of the six perfections one performs in sequence—and because apart from them, little is required (cf. XVI, 5):

> Not delighting in possessions; intense devotion; in two, no weariness; and in two, the *yoga* without discursive thought. This in short is the Supreme Vehicle.[71]

Accordingly, it is a contradiction to desire to enter the Great Vehicle and to reject the six perfections by not having their procedure.

4. *certainty of number subject to all the aspects of the path or means.* The path or means that is unattached to possessions belonging to the domain holding acquisition, is *giving*; because by making renunciation part of one's nature by repetition, one is free from attachment to those (possessions). The means which stops the straying (of the mind) that issues for the purpose of acquiring the unacquired domain, is *morality*; because when one stays in the vow of the monk (*bhikṣu*), one does not allow any straying (of mind) to (worldly) occupations. The means which

does not abandon sentient beings, is *forbearance;* because when they do harm (to oneself), one's mind is not changed by all the pains. The means which enhances virtue, is *striving;* because that (virtue) is enhanced through engaging the striving. The means which purifies obscurations, is the last two perfections; because *meditation* purifies the obscuration of defilement, and *insight* purifies that of the knowable. For that reason, there is certainty in the six perfections (cf. XVI, 6):

> One path is non-attachment to sense objects. Having attained it, another is in [the vows] which restrain the wandering [of mind]. Still others in non-desertion of sentient beings and in the enhancement [of virtue]. And others in the purification of [two] obscurations.

The teaching in terms of their (perfection) requirement confers a great certainty in the six perfections, to wit: *Giving* stays away from the influence of (mental) straying to sense objects; and is unattached (to them). *Morality* prevents the straying that has not already occurred, and restrains the straying that is aimless and meaningless. *Forbearance,* when sentient beings commit many evil deeds nearby, takes a stand in opposition to turn them back from their (evil) purposes. *Striving,* with the power of repetition, and by way of performing for a long time innumerable virtues, enhances (virtue); and by way of thinking about the benefits of those (virtues), exerts for long with keen enthusiasm. *Meditation* suppresses the tops (i.e. the manifest part) of defilement. *Insight* destroys the seed of that (defilement) as well as the obscuration of the knowable.

5. *certainty of number relating to the three instructions*. The bare nature of the *instruction of morality* is morality. It is also the giving that disregards possessions; and by right adoption this is the set of morality. Also, rightly taken, it is protected by the forbearance which, upon one's being reviled does not revile in turn. So those (three perfections) are the retinue of that (instruction). The *instruction of mental training* is meditation. The *instruction of insight* is insight. Striving belongs to all three instructions. Hence, this is a certainty regarding the six perfections (cf. XVI, 7):

> Pertaining to the three instructions, the Victors have promulgated six perfections. Three [perfections] go with the first [instruction]. Two [perfections] go [respectively] with the last two [instructions]. One [perfection] goes in [all] three [instructions].

Accordingly, by whatever endowment of basis one completes the aim of oneself and others; being located in what sort of vehicle one would have whatever aspects of means; namely, the basis for performing whatever instruction, the aim, the Great Vehicle, the means, what completes and condenses the instructions —one has recognized as the six perfections themselves. They contain all the essentials of the procedures going with the Thought of Enlightenment. They should be contemplated as long as one has not gained the great certainty (regarding them).

Furthermore, from the outset there are two causes for not transcending cyclical flow or ignobility; they are: attachment to possessions, and attachment to home. Their adversaries are giving and morality.

There are two causes for backsliding when someone has been noble once and not arrived at the goal: being unhappy because of the evil deeds of sentient beings; being weary by application for a long time to the side of virtue. Their adversaries are forbearance and striving. If one exercises through many approaches while recognizing the rule for protection of eagerness—how one gives no thought to the suffering and harm, and regards time without measure as a single day; this arouses the forbearance and striving capable of counteracting the causes of backsliding—so it is great among essential points.

That much of Bodhisattva practice is not all there is. In regard to the present-day application to virtue, there is little taking on of difficulties, small endurance of forbearance, many starts on whatever path is cultivated by reason of feeble thrust of eagerness; and while in the meantime there is no great reversal, there is no going forward; and a response by not acting upon the precepts of forbearance and striving.

Even when one does not in the meantime backslide, there are two causes for lack of success: straying of the mind that is not fixed on a virtuous meditative object; deficient insight. Their adversaries are meditation and insight; because it is said that when the mind strays elsewhere, such practices as muttering (of incantations) are useless; and if the insight that well analyzes the scriptures of inner science (i.e. Buddhism) does not grow, one errs even in gross (i.e. non-subtle) situations of engagement and disengagement and practices in a wayward manner.

That is certainty of number subject to the adversaries that eliminate the discordant sides.

6. *certainty of number for the basic situation of accomplishing all the Buddha natures*. The first four perfections amount to the set of *samādhi*, because those four accomplish the meditation perfection of not straying (to external objects), and based thereon, by cultivating discerning, there occurs the comprehension of reality.

As to the certainty of number subject to what is concordant with maturation of the sentient beings, this has the same meaning as the third one explained above.

The foregoing is explained in accordance with Ārya-Asaṅga's position and *ācārya* Haribhadra's formulation; and show the main essentials for arousing certainty in the six perfections.

b–2) *teaching certainty of sequence as the subordinate topic*. There are three types (sequence of arising, as lower and higher, as crude and subtle). (1) *sequence of arising*. When one disregards possessions, there is the giving without attachment. Given it, when one adopts morality and well restrains sinful acts, he possesses morality. Given it, there is the forbearance toward harm. When there is the forbearance that does not weary of difficult acts, there is scarce condition for backsliding, so one can start striving. When one exerts striving in day and night, there arises the *samādhi* adept in helping the mind (to stay) on a virtuous meditative object. When the mind is equipoised, there occurs the understanding of the genuine as it really is.

(2) *Sequence of lower and higher*. The earlier ones are lower; the later ones are higher.

(3) *Sequence of crude and subtle*. The earlier ones are cruder, because it is easier to enter and perform in them than in the later ones. Each later one is more subtle than the preceding one, because they are successively harder to enter and perform; cf. *Sūtrālaṃkāra* (XVI, 14):

By that sequence is taught the arising not only by the later on the former, but also by stages of lower and higher, as well as by the crude and the subtle.

c) *how the steps of instruction are in that place*. This has two parts: the rules for learning the general practice; the rules for practicing the last two perfections in particular.

c–1) *the rules for learning the general practice*. This has two sections: practice of the perfections which mature the Buddha natures for oneself; practice of the four persuasions which mature the mental series of others.

(1) *practice of the perfections which mature the Buddha natures for oneself. There are six: giving (dāna)*, morality (śīla), forbearance (*kṣānti*), striving (*vīrya*), meditation (*dhyāna*), and insight (*prajñā*).

Perfection of Giving

There are four parts to the Perfection of Giving. 1) the actuality of giving; 2) the means of entering its cultivation; 3) varieties of giving; 4) summarizing their goal.

1) *the actuality of giving*. It is as stated in the *Bodhisattvabhūmi*:

> What is the actuality of giving? A volition arisen together with non-attachment belonging to the Bodhisattva who disregards all his furnishings and his own body; and, aroused by it the body and speech action [*karma*] of giving away the thing to be given.

Thus, the virtuous volition is the nature of giving, and the body and speech *karma* are aroused by it. Now, the fulfillment of the Perfection of Giving does not concern removing the poverty of living beings by handing over to another the material to be given. Otherwise, there being poor persons, the former Jinas would not have taken giving to its fulfillment. Thus, body and speech do not govern, but mind governs. Accordingly, one should cut off the covetous grasping toward body, possessions, and roots of merit as all belonging to one's own wealth; and should tie one's resolve to others and give those (possessions, etc.) away. And that is not all: Also the fruits are renounced, because the Perfection of Giving arises from the complete making part of one's nature the mentality of consignment to sentient beings. So also *Caryāvatāra* V, 9–10:

> If the Perfection of Giving is in making the world wealthy—and the world is today impoverished—how could former saviors have had that perfection? The Perfection of Giving has been explained as the mind of abandoning to all people everything, together with the fruits. Hence, that [Perfection] is precisely the mind [of that abandoning].

Hence, the path-procedure of the Perfection of Giving is not the giving of materials to others in a concrete sense: It is the volition of giving, with the giving generated in many directions and in ever increasing measure.

2) *the means of entering its cultivation*. The Perfection of Giving does not arise merely through completely eradicating covetousness toward body and possessions, because covetousness belongs to the category of desire (*kāma*) and even the two *arhats* of the lower vehicle completely eliminate it along with its seed. For that reason, it does not suffice to merely dispel all the adherence to the covetousness kind of hindrance of giving; but one must generate the resolve to give away to others all possessions, and (generate it) by tying the heart (to it). For this, one must contemplate the disadvantage of holding on (to things) and the benefit of giving (them) up; so this should be discussed (confer) *Candrapradīpa-sūtra:*

> The fools that cling to this foul body, to life that sways uncontrollably, [properly] like dreams and illusions, come into power of delusion, committing outrageous acts; and not knowing that they have fallen into death's vehicle, travel to the hells.

Thus, having viewed the body as impure and life as shifting as is a stream of a steep mountain; and the *karma* of both body and life as controlled externally, so without self of self-control, and false like a dream and an illusion—one must stop the clinging to those. While if one does not turn off that (clinging), one comes into the power of clinging, amasses highly sinful conduct, and proceeds to evil destinies. The *Anantamukhanirhāradhāraṇī* puts it this way:

> Wherever sentient beings get in fights, clinging is the basic cause there. Therefore, one should abandon any place where craving arises. For the incantation belongs to him who has abandoned craving.

Moreover, the *Śikṣāsamuccaya* states:

> For my body and mind are in each second passing away. If by means of a body that is impermanent and carrying defilement, I could obtain the Enlightenment that is permanent and immaculate, should it not be obtained by me [without payment]!

It is also as the *Jātakamālā* mentions ("The Story of the Tigress," k. 22):

> This body being non-self, breaking up, pithless, pained, ungrateful, always impure — one is not wise who wouldn't rejoice at its being beneficial to another.

That is, however one may guard (the body) with numerous exertions, one must certainly (i.e. inevitably) give it up; but by giving away the pithless body with a resolve to another, one may accomplish many aims of oneself and the other person. One should think, "I being stupid do not purify my mind that way." Thus, as much as is possible, one should generate the mind that gives body, and so forth, away to others. Also, the *Caryāvatāra* (III, 11) says:

> Nirvāṇa is the abandonment of everything, and my mind has the aim of Nirvāṇa. If I must abandon everything, best it be turned over to the sentient beings.

Besides, the *Pāramitāsamāsa* (I, 49–54) has this:

> Observing possessions as impermanent and then compassion become one's 'second-nature,' one comprehends with certainty: "What is given away, that is mine; not what is in my home." There is no fear [of robbers] through what is given; it is what is in the home that occasions fear. A community entity has to be protected and does not satisfy; when it is given away, those petty concerns do not arise.

> The given creates happiness even in the other world; the not-given yields suffering in this very life. For the wealth of men is like the self-presence of a firebrand: not tossed away, it confers ruin. What is not given away, passes away. What is given, yields a treasure. Wealth, pithless and weak, has a [strong] pith when given away by one looking to the benefit of the world. The wise praise that which is given away. A foolish person likes its hoarding. Generally, loss is due to [belief in] ownership. Through giving arise good fortune and fame. What is given away does not have defilement as owner. Greed, the doctrine of the ignoble, is on behalf of defilement. What is given is [itself] the illustrious path. Therefore, any other the noble ones declare "bad path."

Besides, whatever the roots of merit, great or small, one has created, one should consign all of them to sentient beings after having tied one's resolve to the aim of accomplishing extensively the benefit and happiness (of those sentient beings) in temporary conditions and finality. Then, when renouncing as a gift, one would obtain as many merits as are based on each one of those sentient beings, so one easily completes the collection (of merit). The *Ratnāvalī* states (V, 86–87):

> If whatever merit has been alluded to were to take a shape, it would not be contained in world realms numbered as the myriad sands of the Ganges.
>
> That is said by the Bhagavat, and there is reason herein. Like that is the one wishing the benefit of sentient beings in realms immeasurable.

Furthermore, one should act so as not to give rise to an interruption in the increase of giving, to an increase in miserliness or to the non-occurrence of the relinquishing thought; and if arisen, so as to squelch them. Thus whatever was one's former retinue and goods, one does not hold onto them; and even when given by another, is not to take them. So the *Pāramitāsamāsa* (I, 3–4):

> Whatever serves to increase the fault of miserliness or to not promote the relinquishing thought, that the Bodhisattva should abandon. This hindrance is the deception of ownership.

> Therefore how could a Bodhisattva accept jewels, wealth, or even precious sovereignty, since each contrives opposition to the relinquishing thought and obstructs the path to complete enlightenment.

If, at the time of so acting, one is still attached to goods on account of miserliness, one should recall that the Muni (i.e. the Buddha) succeeded in enlightenment after giving up every last thing, and that oneself had taken a vow to understudy his example. One should think, "I formerly bestowed upon the sentient beings my body, possessions, and virtues—all of them; and if I now act attached to possessions, my practice would be like that of an elephant which, oppressed by the sun enters the water and bathes; returns to the shore, and to restore (his previous condition) rolls over on the ground; then, seeing his body dirty with soil, re-enters the water, and repeats the performance." So thinking, one would not act with attachment; the same work tells it (I, 5–6):

> Bearing in mind the superb practice of the *munis,* and also one's own vow directed to that, one should review in one's mind these sublime thoughts so as to dispel the clinging to possessions.
>
> "When I hand over this body to the world, and even the relinquishing nature [itself]—at that time a thought of attachment to an external given thing, is as unsuitable for me as the bathing of an elephant."

If one can get eager by way of thinking of the many benefits of relinquishing in that manner, and of thinking of the disadvantages of merriment and possessions, one would arouse the relinquishing mind as a 'second nature.' Likewise, also at the conclusion of exercising love and compassion, and of contemplating the lives of the Buddha and his spiritual children, one should generate the relinquishing thought. The way of generating it, is as told in the *Caryāvatāra* (III, 10):

> My embodiments, likewise my possessions, even my merits of past, present, and future, I renounce without regard [for reward], to make succeed the aim of all sentient beings.

That is, having taken as meditative object the three — one's embodiment, possessions, and roots of virtue — one gives them away by a resolve to all sentient beings. Having in that way turned off the craving to hold anything at all as one's own, and exercising again and again the volition to donate it to others, one is called 'Bodhisattva' (enlightenment being) (confer) *Pāramitāsamāsa* (I, 11cd; 12):

> "Why is this 'mine' which is only yours? There is no pride of 'self' in me with respect to it." To whom such marvellous reflections — following the nature of the complete Buddha — arise again and again, that one, outstanding among enlightenment beings [*bodhisattva*] the Buddhas, who are the inconceivable beings [*acintyasattva*], call "great being" [*mahāsattva*].

At present, conviction is not mature, and one's force is meager, so that while one has given one's body by resolve (i.e. imaginatively) to the sentient beings, one has not concretely given away one's flesh, etc. Nevertheless, if one does not purify one's resolve to give away body and life force, one does not make (this resolve) part of one's nature, so as the *Śikṣāsamuccaya* mentions, in the future one is (predictably) incapable of giving away one's body and life force. Hence, from the present time onward one must purify the resolve. When one ties one's resolve whereby one engages oneself in the food, clothing, dwelling places, and so forth, that should be given to the sentient beings, forgetting to think, "I shall use these for the sake of others," engaging in those with a craving for one's own sake, it is the defiled fall (*kliṣṭāpatti*); or, in the absence of craving, if one forgets to assign one's ideation to take all sentient beings as object, or craves for the sake of (only) some other sentient being, it is the undefiled fall (*akliṣṭāpatti*).

When one has consigned to others those (i.e. the three, embodiment, etc.) with the idea "They are substances belonging to others," and then uses them for one's own sake, it is the (transgression) "taking what was not given"; and, as the *Śikṣāsamuccaya* mentions, if it is valuable, it is a 'defeat' (mandating expulsion) of the *Prātimokṣa*. In this regard, some persons maintain that since one has consigned to all sentient beings, there is no possibility of a full value to a single sentient being, so there is no 'defeat' (requiring expulsion from the *saṃgha*). Some other persons deny the validity of that thesis, on the grounds that one has (contemplatively) consigned the entire stock of goods to each and every sentient being; but also, since it was consigned to those others, but no one owns it, there is no 'defeat.' As to the purport, one consigns it by tying the resolve to the world of men; hence, realizing this, and having the idea that it belongs to others while keeping it to oneself; indulging in it for one's own sake, at the full value, it is the 'defeat' (of the *Prātimokṣa*), so that is the purport. On that account, what is said in those other sectarian positions is not valid.

(On the other hand), the person who thinks, "I am making use of what belongs to that sentient being, and thus perform his aim," incurs no fault in so practicing; confer *Śikṣāsamuccaya:*

> But if one thinks that one's embodiment is the servant of sentient beings and that it is protected by usages as a servant of sentient beings, there is no fault. For a servant always busy with the master's work [*karma*] does not own what he/she busies oneself with.

Suppose it be thought, "Having already consigned this property to the sentient beings, if I use it without their permission I will incur a fault." In fact, there is no fault; confer the same work:

> When a servant is fully devoted to master's purposes, but one's mind is troubled with disease and so forth, there is no fault if one uses (the property) even without asking permission.

One should not act without faith, thinking, "If I do not donate it all to the sentient beings concretely, just giving it away mentally seems a prevarication; so there is no substance to such (a giving)." The same work states:

> Nor is it right for a Bodhisattva so acting to be without faith when someone in his presence is unaware of the [giving] event [concretely], because he knows that the relinquishing thought is marvellous. Nor is it right to have any doubt for this rule.

3) *varieties of giving*. This has three parts: how one acts by means of every basis; the varieties dependent on respective bases; the varieties of giving's bare nature.

a) *how one acts by means of every basis*. Here the action by having six lustres is as follows:

1. *the lustre of basis*. It is the reliance on the Mind of Enlightenment; thereby one's acts (of giving) are precipitated.

2. *the lustre of substance*. In general it is the use of all substances for giving; and when involved in particular ones, it is the non-casting away of the resolve (to give).

3. *the lustre of the high goal*. It is the giving away so that all sentient beings may be happy temporarily and be benefitted ultimately.

4. *the lustre of skill in the means*. It is said to be associated with non-reflecting wisdom. With the beginner, it means to be associated with the insight which comprehends the non-self-existence of *dharmas*.

5. *the lustre of consignment*. This is the consignment of virtues given away, for complete enlightenment.

6. *the lustre of purity*. This is the removal of the obscurations of defilement and of the knowable.

These have been explained according to the *Mahāyāna-saṃgraha*.

When there is, for example, a giving of the Dharma, the deed involves the six perfections (the others, as follows):

The vowed morality which is the mental orientation of the Śrāvakas and the Pratyekabuddhas.

The faithful tolerance of the Omniscient Dharma, and the forbearance of mistreatment by another.

The striving that generates the longing to develop ever higher that very (giving).

The meditation which, by a single-area thought having nothing in common with the lower vehicle, consigns the virtues, for complete enlightenment.

The insight which knows as illusion the gift, the giver, and the recipient.

When one acts with the complete six, one exhibits great power. These are set forth in the Great Commentary (by Haribhadra) on the *Aṣṭasāhasrikā (Prajñāpāramitā)*.

b) *the varieties dependent on respective bases.* Speaking generally, the giving of material things is done by the home-based Bodhisattva; and the gift of the Dharma by the Bodhisattva who has become a monk. This is said in the *Bodhisattva-pratimokṣa:*

> Śāriputra, suppose a home-based Bodhisattva fills the Buddha fields numbered like the Ganges sands with the seven jewels as gifts to the Arhat-Tathāgata-Right-Complete-Buddhas. If a Bodhisattva who has enterėd monkhood teaches one four-lined stanza, from this greater merit flows. The Tathāgata, Śāriputra, does not permit the gift of material things by one in monkhood.

Even so, the *Śikṣāsamuccaya* mentions this in connection with an interruption of hearing (the Dharma), and so on. This text adds that when the one gone forth (to monkhood) works for material things and practices donating, this is prohibited (by the Buddha) so as not to harm one's virtuous acts. But, if one obtains much by the power of former merits, one must give away the material things. Also, it was heard from Śa-ra-ba: "I am not talking to you about the benefit of giving; I am talking about the disadvantage of keeping." Thus, the one gone forth, who wearies his flesh in seeking and collecting treasure inflicts many wounds in his morality; in terms of gift-giving, this course made him (Śa-ra-ba) unhappy.

c) *the varieties of giving's bare nature.* Of the three, c–1) the giving of the Doctrine (*dharma*) is teaching the Illustrious Doctrine without error; or teaching it with study principles of worldly occupations such as the mechanical arts, so long as they are free from sin; and enrolling people into holding the points of instruction (*śikṣāpada;* or 'moral commandments'). c–2) the giving of security (*abhaya*) is the protection of the sentient beings from the fear (or danger) of men, such as kings and robbers; from the fear (or danger) of non-human beings, such as lions, tigers, and sea serpents; and from the fear (or danger) of the elements, such as water and fire. c–3) the giving of material things is of two kinds: the giving that gives away material things concretely; and the giving of them only by resolve (or, imaginatively).

(1) *the giving that gives away material things concretely.* This has three topics: (1)–1. the rule for giving material things; (1)–2. how

one acts when one cannot give; (1)–3. recourse to the adversary of the hindrances to giving.

(1)–1. *the rule for giving material things.* This has four parts: the object person to whom one gives; the resolve with which one gives; what manner to give; the thing which is given.

(a) *the object person to whom one gives* is of ten kinds: 1. the friend who benefits oneself; 2. the harm-doing enemy; 3. the neutral who neither benefits nor harms; 4. the person with the good qualities of morality, etc.; 5. the person with the faults of immorality, etc.; 6. the inferior; 7. the equal; 8. the superior; 9. the happy, prosperous man; 10. the unhappy, poor man.

(b) *the resolve with which one gives.* Of the three (kinds), 1. of what sort is the resolve one is required to have: one takes as aim the requirement, and thinks, "Based on this, I shall complete the Perfection of Giving, the collection (of merit) for the incomparable enlightenment." 2. One takes as aim the entity, and thinks, "At the outset the Bodhisattva should give away every last thing to the sentient beings, so he should dispense in the manner of a sacred trust: my materials belong to others." 3. One takes as aim the object person, and thinks, "These object persons among those who ask for or do not ask for (something) fulfill my Perfection of Giving, so they are my spiritual guides (*kalyāṇamitra*)." One should have (all) the three resolves.

The *Pāramitāsamāsa* (I, 55) tells this:

> And when the petitioner approaches him, he [the Bodhisattva] so as to increase the collection for Enlightenment, will plant in himself the idea of being the servant of that person [the petitioner] and in him[self] a love for the spiritual guide.

The resolve to take as meditative object the requirement, thinking, "It is required to give away each entity; and so I shall give it away," is to be known extensively in the works *Subāhuparipṛcchā* and *Pāramitāsamāsa*.

The resolve of taking as aim the previously mentioned objects must be done in every case, so it is the generalized resolve. Varieties of the resolve are the resolve of having a loving thought for the harm-doer and of having compassion for those who suffer; the resolve of sympathetic joy when someone has good qualities; and the resolve of equanimity toward beneficial persons. And having planted these, one is to give. One must also equipoise the mind on those objects. The fruit of the virtue consisting in the gift-giving should also be turned over to the sentient beings such as the petitioner; and, in particular, one should be compassionate toward a suffering object. Candrakīrti states:

> Whatever gift is free from stinginess and is given with equipoised mind evenly to the illustrious vessel and to the degraded vessel, that gift is purer than the giver. Whatever gift is given with compassion, and without stinginess, namely, the gift and fruit of giving simultaneously to the supplicant—that is extolled by the illustrious ones.

Furthermore, the *Guṇāparyantastotra* puts it this way:

> Whoever, upon seeing a depressed, poverty-stricken person, who has hopeful thought; and still, cold-hearted, looking for the reward, would seek another goodly vessel [as object person for giving], this man, his resolve forsaken, may practice his charity and still is "equal to the askers." Hence, You, compassionate, stayed wishing to give.

As to what sort of resolve one should abandon (may there be) the lack of resolve that values bad views, e.g. thinking, "Giving is fruitless"; "Since it is a gift of sacrifice (with violence), it is within the Dharma"; "Giving (symbolically) the name 'virtue' and wishing good-luck,[72] there is giving and completion of giving; with just this, I shall be free from mundane and supramundane attachment." One should not give, thinking like that.

(May there be) the lack of arrogant resolve, e.g. despising the asker; vieing with another; and also, having given, to think, "I am generous; while that other person is not." One should not act with such conceited thoughts. Also, the *Karmāvaraṇaviśuddhisūtra* mentions the obscured giving:

> The [foolish] worldlings [Mañjuśrī], when they are giving a gift, despise the stingy; and by this [despising], [both] feel hostility; . . . and so are reborn in the hells. Thus, giving is stated as an obstacle [in this case]."

> "They, when guarding their morality, . . . speak in dispraise of those with bad morality . . . and cause many persons to lose faith. By reason of [inducing] that lack of faith, they fall into bad destinies.

The Sūtra explains (the obscured perfections) for those dwelling in forbearance, and so on, in that they blame those who dwell in the opposing practice.

Hence, this amounts to what occurs in the *Guṇāparyantastotra:*

> At the time you had great learning and awareness you did not praise yourself. Instead, you highly honoured even those other beings whose good qualities were meager. When you dwelled in the collection of good qualities, you pointed out even your tiny sins.

(May there be) lack of (badly) based resolve, e.g. no giving with the hope of getting goodly fame.

(May there be) lack of resolve that shrinks (from action), e.g. agreeably disposed prior to the donation, at the time when giving acts with faith, and after having given is without regret; then, hearing about the vast extent of giving on the part of Bodhisattvas, one's mind becomes timid and one does not act, despising oneself. But one should rather increase one's enthusiasm, not castigate oneself or not act.

(May there be) lack of turned-away resolve, e.g. though giving with compassion to enemies, friends, and neutrals, being partial to one of them, i.e. one should be without partiality.

(May there be) lack of resolve that imagines retribution, e.g. with the hope of benefitting others, there is no giving, because one looks upon persons as poor in joy, burning with the fire of desire, without power to dispel suffering, and suffering naturally.

(May there be) lack of resolve that imagines maturation, e.g. there is no hope for a subsequent maturation consisting in the fulfillment of possessions and body, because one looks at all constructed things as pithless and at the benefit as the incomparable enlightenment. One should not stop hope for those fruits in the temporal condition, but stop the positing of an attainable in only the body and possessions of phenomenal life.

Besides, there is the lack of resolve called "wayward living," when dispensing gifts, thinking, "The king and others will know that I am generous, and give me respect for it." There is the not-giving through fear of becoming indigent, and the resolve that deceives the petitioner. The resolve should be to communicate with another, free from dissatisfaction, anger, or straying of mind; not being put off by various wayward pursuits of the petitioner; and even when seeing the faults of the petitioner of self-deception, not reporting this to others, and so on. There is the giving with a trust that from respective gifts there arise respective fruits which cannot be misled by another.

(c) *what manner to give*. This has two parts.

1. *By what manner one should not give*, as follows: One bestows with postponement, so no quick bestowal. One bestows just after causing hardship. Bestows upon having engaged in conduct opposed to the code of Dharma or of the world. Bestows poorly or meagerly, contradicting his former pledge to give a set amount. Bestows, after mentioning the 'kindness.' While it is proper to give in one time, gives in small installments. Bestows, if one has become a king, involving the robbing of the wife and son of another. Bestows upon another, by urged taking of the chattel of one's father, mother, servant, etc., and then giving it to others. Bestows a gift in a way that brings harm to another. Becoming lazy, one asks someone (else) to do the giving. Bestows after scoffingly disparaging the request, after rebuking with insinuated detraction, and after bragging with harsh words. Gives in contradiction with the training prescribed by the Buddha. Not giving presently what he received, but gives after collecting for a long time. Those are the manners to be abandoned. One should cast them aside.

Moreover, one should observe that it is sinful for a Bodhisattva to collect a lot and then give; and that the giving of possessions as they arise lacks sin, because (in the first case) there is no more merit when he donates on one occasion after collecting that way, and during the lengthy collection refuses many a request for the goods. This torments (the askers') minds. And having been asked (formerly), now gives just to a few (who did not ask for it). This important point is stated that way in the *Bodhisattvabhūmi*, because for that length of time he had generated many defilements of stinginess, etc., had interrupted many virtuous acts by the trouble of guarding, etc. (the possessions), and since in time they can be lost, he cannot complete a gift. Such things we have seen.

2. *By what manner one should give*, is as follows: One bestows, with a bright expression on the face, and previously making a smile, showing sincerity of expression, and with respect rendered to whatever field (of giving), with one's own hand, at the right time, with no harm to another, and after having endured the pain of austerity. Their fruits are just as told in the *Satyakaparivarta*:[73]

> By transmitting with honor, there arises the honor [to the donor] by kinsfolk and so forth. Giving with one's own hands at the proper time, one's purposes are accomplished in proper time. By transmitting with no harm to another, one gets steady enjoyments. By transmitting with forbearance of (any) unpleasantness, one's retinue will be like-minded.

The *Thesaurus* (*Kośa*, by Vasubandhu) states that by giving fittingly with one's hand, one obtains vast enjoyment. According to the *Thesaurus Commentary* (by Vasubandhu), the expression "steady enjoyments" means the enjoyment is not interrupted by others and is not destroyed by fire, etc.[74]

Furthermore, the preparation which cooperates with another's gift, is as follows: If one has property, one should go into the house of stingy people with no experience of giving and make them happy. One should put oneself into a contented and relaxed frame of mind, speaking thus: "I have a great extent of property. So that I may complete the Perfection of Giving, I need petitioners. If you see some petitioners, don't send them away. Take my wealth and give it to them; or, bring them to me, and rejoice in my gift!" So one asks (others). Then, with no loss in one's wealth and with pleasure one will do it like that. In that way one casts the seed for dispelling the blemish of stinginess. As a result of gradually making it part of one's nature, by oneself one denotes a little wealth; on the basis of that small non-attachment (donates) a middling amount; and on the basis of that, attains the great (stage of giving). Accordingly, when one's own master, disciples, and friends, cannot give while clinging to their wants; or if that is not the case, lack property; having supplied them with the property, get them to donate to the Three Jewels, while oneself refrains. Thereby, one's own merits expand greatly. The defilements of some other persons are overcome. Others fulfill their desire for the Dharma. And the sentient beings are brought (into the fold) and matured. Likewise, if oneself lacks property, by the possibility of work and action one might gather wealth and donate. Or tell a *Dharma*-story to others such that even poor and stingy persons want to give.

Besides, there is the cooperation of giving a gift insofar as possible when requests have arisen, by its being given in a home where the people have faith and possess wealth, and where oneself has gone (for the urging).

Moreover, having selected the materials to be given, one gives them away in the order of starting with the better ones. One should give those things in the arrangement (for giving, i.e. in the order best, middling, inferior).

(d) *the thing which is given*. This has two parts: teaching in brief the entity which is given away and the one not given away and teaching that extensively.

1. *teaching in brief the entity which is given away and the one not given away.* The Bodhisattva should give to another whatever entity that promptly upon its being given one generates a joyful feeling of being free from going to an evil destiny, and (in which case) one is placed eventually in benefit, elimination of sin, or placed in virtue; or that promptly (upon its being given) joy does not occur, but eventually there is benefit. And one should not give to another whatever thing that promptly upon its being given one gets depressed, and (in which case) eventually there will be harm; or that promptly (upon its being given) (depression does not occur), however eventually there is harm.

2. *teaching extensively the entity which is given away or not given away.* Here, there is the corporeal entity which is given or not given; and there is the external entity which is given or not given

A. *the corporeal entity which is given or not given.* If one understands the rule for not giving away one's own corporeal entity, one will understand the reverse, namely those to be given; hence, at the outset the rule for not giving away will be explained. There are three topics here.

the impropriety of giving in regard to the time. The Bodhisattva at the outset ties his resolve that he may give his body, etc. to the sentient beings. However, there should not occur despondency by the mortification of donating the flesh of his body, etc., that is to say, as long as the resolve of great compassion has not expanded (sufficiently) he should not give that gift. This is stated in the *Śikṣāsamuccaya:*

> And what is this kind of striving, whereby there is depression? What there would be if a man of weak strength should undertake heavy work; or if out of due time; or if a man whose conviction is immature should undertake a difficult task like giving away his flesh. [Certainly,] he has given his embodiment to the sentient beings, but he must prevent an untimely usage. Otherwise, by the destruction of the seed, i.e. the Mind of Enlightenment, by reason of the Bodhisattva's depression, there would be destruction of the large pile of fruit for those sentient beings. That is why the *Gaganagañja-sūtra* mentions that untimely expectation is the work of Māra.

Also, the *Caryāvatāra* (V, 87) states:

> Hence, one should not abandon one's life when one's resolve of compassion is impure. It should be abandoned in this and other lives so as to accomplish the great aim [of enlightenment].

the impropriety of giving in regard to the purpose. One should not give away the body for the sake of a trifling purpose. The same work states (V, 86):

> Not for a trifling purpose should one ruin the body which serves the Illustrious Doctrine. For only so [conducting oneself], may one quickly fulfill the hopes of the sentient beings.

When it is a matter of oneself, one should be free from greed, etc. that hinder the giving; and when it is a matter of the other, there is the great purpose of accomplishing the aim of many sentient beings by not giving away the body (to one); at that time, even if requested one does not give the members and so on (of the body). And if the request for the cutting off of life, etc. is to bring about the sinful conduct of harm to another and oneself, one should not put oneself at another's disposal at the asking, even briefly.

the impropriety of giving in regard to the petitioner. If asked for the limbs, etc. with expectation of doing injury, by a deity belonging to the Māras or by a sentient being bedeviled by it, one does not give, because it would harm those (petitioners) themselves. If asked by madmen and by those with delirious minds, again one does not give, because they do not ask sincerely but only with false words. There is no transgression if one does not give to those beings; and that is not all!—if one does give, there is a transgression.

One should give one's body at request in a situation excepting those (three) cases; and furthermore, there are two (such) giving: the giving of limbs and so forth, arranged in their order; and the giving in the sense of becoming a servant pursuant to the purpose of gaining the Dharma of another.

B. *the external entity which is given or not given.* This has two sections: the rule for not giving the external entity; the rule for giving the external entity.

B–1. *the rule for not giving the external entity.* This has five topics.

the impropriety of giving in regard to the time. For example, giving evening food to Buddhist monks and to those who are fasting.

the impropriety of giving in regard to the object of the giving. For example, these: Giving excess food and drink to someone striving to hold a vow. Giving food and drink polluted with excrement and urine, spittle, vomit, pus and blood. Giving garlic and onions as well as prohibited flesh or alcoholic drinks to someone holding a vow whereby it is improper for him to desire to eat and drink those or to partake of those; giving such things as garlic and what is defiled by them. Being enchanted by well-turned phrases about charity, to give away a son, servants, and so forth, at the request of an unfriendly person, a harmful spirit (*yakṣa*), demons (*rākṣasa*), one in the grip of a terrible spell, or someone who is ungrateful and forgetful of what is done (for the person). Giving to a sick person unwholesome food and drink; or, although wholesome, in undue proportion. Giving to those begging their food with too much clinging and measuring. Giving (religious) books to the unbeliever, the fault-finder, the one who does not wish to understand the meaning of the book, but regards the book as wealth. That is stated in accordance with the *Bodhisattvabhūmi;* and one may know it extensively from a passage in the *Viniścayasaṃgrahaṇī* of the *Bodhisattvabhūmi;* it states:

> If one gives a written book of the Dharma to beggars whose insight is infantile, that (deed) is attended with sin. If one requests others to give it to them, that is also attended with sin. There is no sin if, upon giving it, the recipient is made to think, "I have been enrolled into holding the profundities of the Dharma, and am capable of the devotion which it deserves."
>
> If one allows beings who have faith in books of heretical teachings, or in books that are counterfeit as contrasted with the Illustrious Doctrine, to copy the latter, or hands over a finished copy to them, or asks others to give it to them, that is attended with sin. If [a heretic] has in hand a book written by a Bodhisattva and defaces it, why get that person to copy the words of the Buddha's scripture? One should know by oneself that it would be just meaningless. One should recite to others only what is good [in the circumstances]. If someone requests a book that is blank, the Bodhisattva should thoroughly question that person, saying, "What will it do for you?" and if that one answers, "I will enjoy bartering it"; or if the Bodhisattva puts a Dharma [such as the 8000 scripture] into book form, he should not give it to that person, but if it has a [paper] value, that person should be given this value. If it has no [paper] value, that one should be given neither [the book or its price], and there is no sin. If it was not put [into book form] as the meaning of Dharma, so that one may enjoy it happily, the book should be given to that person.

> Likewise, when the request is due to a desire to ask for a vile book; and it is not given, again there is no sin. Just as is the case of desire to ask for a vile book, so is the case of desire to ask for a middling text. But when the request is due to desire to ask for a superior book, to not grant the request is attended with sin.

the impropriety of giving in regard to the situation. In illustration, when oneself has not finished the purpose of the book and would not be soiled by stinginess were it absent, and desires to know (the book), he should not give the book to one who requests it, and would not incur sin (thereby). The reason it is improper to give this, is that it is the giving of Dharma and such a giving is subject to one or other of three requirements; thus, the requirement that it not be given and there be two remaining (requirements), since if it were given away there would be no remainder, and since the first requirement cannot operate (by itself). It is this way: given that oneself is not soiled by stinginess, there is no requirement to dispel the defilement of stinginess. If one does not give (the book) one may foresee much promotion of his knowledge; while if it were given, the considerable promotion would not occur. If it were not given, one may complete the collection of knowledge for the benefit and happiness of all sentient beings. Hence, when there is a giving capable of gladdening this sentient being and all other sentient beings, this is the sole gladness (needed). It is for those reasons; and the *Bodhisattvabhūmi* states in that manner the greater and lesser requirements. The *Caryāvatāra* (V, 83c) puts it this way: "One should not renounce a great thing for a small one." Hence, if one does not give it, there is no fault; just not only this.

The manner of not giving is as follows: One should avoid the harsh words of saying, "I shall not give it to you"; but send that person away, using the skillful means of good language. The skillful means is this: At the beginning the Bodhisattva consigns with a pure resolve all his property to the Buddhas and Bodhisattvas of the ten directions. Just as, for example, a monk having considered the religious garments, and so on, consigns them to the teacher and his disciple, who wear them. Because of consigning that way, the property accumulates, and the 'Bodhisattva living in the Noble Family' increases his merit unfathomably. Thereby, those property items are held as though in trust by the Buddhas and Bodhisattvas. If a soliciting person comes, one should give the property item to that person, if it is lawful to do so, thinking, "There is no property not given to the sentient beings by the Buddhas and Bodhisattvas," and give it. And if it is not lawful to do so, using one's consideration one should consign it ritually to those (Buddhas and Bodhisattvas); and based thereon, one should inform (that petitioner) with mild words, "O dear one, this belongs to others, so it cannot be given to you."

Again, when one gives double or a triple the value of the book, it follows that the Bodhisattva has not failed to give (something). But this (petitioner) may think, "That (Bodhisattva) is so attached to it, he has no power to give it."

Acting that way is how a wise person gives.

the impropriety of giving in regard to the entity. Such things as giving away one's own father and mother, food and drink that involve animated beings, when not informing. Or, even informing, (giving away) the son, wife, servant, etc., who do not want to be given. Or a man of pleasant family surroundings — his son and wife.[75] This states (also) that one does not give away the servant-entity; as this appears to be a chief entity, it is counted among the entities (not to be given away). The *Viniścayasaṃgrahaṇī* of the *Bodhisattvabhūmi* states that when there is no stingy expectation toward the three religious garments and the remaining implements other than those, as were permitted by the Buddha, and if they are necessary for the virtuous side, there is no fault in not giving them away at a request; and this text says:

> The Bodhisattva who is in the religious life incurs no sin in dispensing excess implements exclusive of the three religious garments, bodily enjoyments and things consistent with a pleasant abode, as permitted by the Buddha, when he individually considers the desired things that were begged.

> The only case where he incurs no sin by not giving away at request is when (the requested entities) are needed for the virtuous side and are not included among wants.

The *Bodhisattvaprātimokṣa* has this:

> Śāriputra, if a Bodhisattva gives away his three robes, there would be a serving of the asker, but this one's lesser wants would not thereby be supported.

Thus, when the Bodhisattva who is in the religious life gives away the three religious robes, he has a transgression.

the impropriety of giving in regard to the purpose. Such as these: Giving for the harm of oneself or others; the dispensing of poison, weapons, fire, and liquor. Meeting the request for prohibited pleasures that pile up causes for evil destiny, and for things used for playing games. In the case of study and request for mouse and game traps, etc. for the purpose of harming sentient life, to instruct and give those. This also shows the impropriety of teaching precepts to persons in the purpose of inflicting harm on the life and enjoyments of living bodies. Furthermore, it is such as these: Meeting requests for soil-parts and water meant to inflict harm on the sentient life based in dryness or in moisture. Meeting request for a governed district meant to inflict harm on the men of that district or of another one. When the request is by unfriendly persons, to give to their enemy.

B–2. *the rule for giving the external entity.* One should give when for that situation it is a time not interdicted by the Teacher; it being not unlawful to give the thing to be given to a person, and it being suitable for him. And if it be the reverse of the previously mentioned situation, and one possesses stinginess for a book, then even if one has not finished what needs to be done with the book, he must give it to the asker who makes known his desire for it. Furthermore, if there is a second copy of the book, one should give that; and if there is not (a second copy), one should give the price of making a copy. Furthermore, if there is not (a second copy), one should think, "If I do not give this, it is better that I should become mute in this life; I will not submit to greed," and so thinking will certainly give.

Also, except for the previously mentioned entities, when one is installed as king, it is not lawful for him to separate from their master the wife, son, and so forth, of another, and give them away; still, upon request, he may give towns and their accessories. Likewise, one should give, upon request, things used for happy games that are not causes for going to bad destiny, as well as traps and so on that do not harm others, provide the drying or wetting of a place of sentient life if it does not harm the sentient life, also food and drink that are free from living beings. And at a request that is meant to benefit oneself and others, one also gives poison, blades, fire, and liquor.

At the time of giving material things, how is one to do it if both a poor and a wealthy asker appear? If one is able at the outset to satisfy the wants of both the two askers, one should fulfill the wants of both. But if one is not able to do so, one should think, "First I will satisfy the wants of the poor one." Then, at the time of no giving, should one be unable to fulfill the wants of the second person, one should make him cognizant with gentle words, "Dear one, do not think you are being turned away, because these goods are first transmitted to this poor man," and thereupon should satisfy the wants of the unwealthy man.

These rules to learn the giving of such sorts are of highest importance for the beginner who has taken the vow of the Bodhisattva. Hence, they are (here) written, and these non-exceptional cases are explained according to the purport of the *Bodhisattvabhūmi*.

(1) – 2. *how one acts when one cannot give*. If one is pressured by stinginess at the time the petitioner asks (the former) should think this: "This entity and I will surely part (some day). Either it will abandon me, or I will abandon it. Thus, this abandoning will be done at the time of dying and I should (then) be glad and satisfied. If this were given away (now), at the time of dying I would be unattached to wealth, would have no regret, and would be glad and contented." If, thinking that way, one is still unable to give away, the *Ugraparipṛcchā* mentions one's communication to the asker with three communications: "I at present have little power (of former merit); my virtuous roots not matured, as a beginner in the mahāyāna; am dominated by non-giving mentality; my view is indulgence; I adhere to 'I' and 'mine.' " "Illustrious person, I pray that you be patient with me; do not be tormented!" "I shall conduct myself to fulfill the hopes of you and of all sen-

tient beings." These (communications) are for eliminating other faults of lacking faith in each other, but are not free from the fault of stinginess. The *Śikṣāsamuccaya* states that the Bodhisattva's stinginess is blameworthy. Yet, if one does it this way, because of the stinginess, it avoids the 'defeat' of not giving the treasure of the Dharma. The *Pāramitāsamāsa* (I, 57–58) puts it this way:

> When due to feeble power [of former merit] one cannot give when meeting a supplicant, may this person be not disappointed, and rather be conciliated with gentle words. One's duty is to renounce stinginess, one's task is to eliminate craving [Skt. means "delusion"], so that a supplicant does not leave that one looking downcast.

(1)–3. *recourse to the adversary of the hindrances to giving*. The hindrances are four according to the *Saṃgrahaṇī*:[76] lack of habituation, poverty, attachment, not seeing the result.

(a) *lack of habituation* is the lack of desire to donate materials to the asker according as they are present to be given. For its adversary, one should think, "This fault is due to not in the previous life making myself habituated in giving; hence there was certainty of retribution." Having thus quickly made oneself cognizant, one should think, "And if I do not give the gift, in my next life also I will not like to give." Thus considering in each case, one is made to give. But there is no giving when one is dominated by the fault of non-habituation.

(b) *poverty* is the not thinking of giving on the grounds that one's possessions are very small. For its adversary, one should think, "As long as I am revolving in cyclical flow and have not rendered benefit to other beings, on account of the former *karma* or lack of independence, I shall experience many sufferings difficult to bear, of hunger, thirst, etc.; but if I do render benefit to others, while there is the suffering of the present life arising dependently, when I die the giving will indeed be a good thing for me (to have done), while turning away a supplicant is not that way (a good thing for me). So even if I have no possessions (left), I shall live even by just eating vegetables." And having so thought, one submits to the suffering of poverty, and gives (as possible).

(c) *attachment* is the not thinking of giving the requested object by attachment to the giveable entity that is very appealing and excellent. For its adversary one should think, "I have quickly understood the fault of attachment: I am happy in suffering"; that is, one should think, "This (present) adherence to a wayward idea will generate suffering at a later time (or, next life)." And having understood and eliminated (that wayward idea), one makes oneself give the entity.

(d) *not seeing the result* is the not seeing the benefit of becoming fully enlightened by recourse to renouncing the thing to give away, i.e. thinking that giving concerns the benefit of great possessions. For its adversary, one should quickly recognize the fault; and view, in general, all constructions (*saṃskāra*) being destroyed at each instant, and, in particular, possessions as breaking up and becoming separated (from oneself); and any gifts that are given, all of them one should consign to the great enlightenment. When one sees just the maturation of possessions, etc., for a price one gives everything without losing. As to that one, one can achieve profit but not merit. Similarly, when one gives for enjoyment, one achieves enjoyment, but not liberation. The *Catuḥśataka* says (V, no. 95):

> When one thinks, "The giving of the gift here gives rise to a great fruit," then give and take is degrading, like the profit of commerce.

(2) *the giving of things only by resolve.* Going into solitude, gathering one's mind within, one ties the heart with a pure resolve and imagines the far-spread, unfathomable diversity of things to be given whole-heartedly. One is convinced that this materializes as gifts to the sentient beings. It states in the *Bodhisattvabhūmi* that this expands to unfathomable merit in a time of little trouble, and that it is the giving on the part of a wise Bodhisattva. Although the *Subāhuparipṛcchā* mentions that this is to be done by one lacking possessions, it is not improper to be done also by the one who has possessions. As to how is the wise giving when the giving leaves no possessions, this is in the stage of pure conviction and as long as one has not attained the first stage (of

the Bodhisattva). But having attained that stage, there is no possibility of poverty by way of possessions, since the *Bodhisattvabhūmi* states:

> Accordingly, as long as the Bodhisattva has not attained the pure resolve he gives wise gifts until no possessions remain. The Bodhisattva with pure aspiration, in how he has attained transcendence over bad destiny, so in all his lives he obtains inexhaustible possessions.

4) *Summarizing their goal*. After taking the Bodhisattva vow, one practices by making as object of aspiration the rules for learning the giving of the high level. One gives gifts as previously explained, from now on learning through becoming cognizant of the importance of the engagements. In particular, one resorts to the adversaries of stinginess regarding body, possessions, and virtuous roots; with relinquishing mentality one exerts to give away in ever increasing measure; and cultivates a joy in the path-procedures. And one should be sad when one has not trained one's mind that way. If one does it that way, as told in the *Subāhuparipṛcchā*, in other lives one is able to complete the Perfection of Giving in time of little trouble. But if one abandons all those (rules) with his stance, even in the present life one is continually tainted with weighty sins; and in other lives one dislikes the entrance heart, so it becomes very difficult for that one to enter the Bodhisattva practice. Moreover, the *Pāramitāsamāsa* (I, 61) explains:

> The root of that giving is the Mind of Enlightenment. The one desiring to give such a gift, that one the Buddhas call "best of givers." And the one who wishes to receive the donation, that one they call "best among worldlings."

According to that passage, one should remember and cultivate the Mind of Enlightenment which is the basis of the practice. And the casting of fervent aspiration, aspiring to enlightenment, is the root of all giving and is the best of all gifts. So one should exert oneself in it. This is the sublime essential of the *Subāhuparipṛcchā*.

Perfection of Morality

There are five parts to the Perfection of Morality. 1) the actuality of morality; 2) the means of entering its cultivations; 3) varieties of morality; 4) how one acts at the time of their practice; 5) summarizing their goal.

1) *the actuality of morality*. Morality is the abstinent consciousness that turns the mind away from anything attended with harm to another. Thus, by accomplishing ever higher the making of that consciousness part of oneself, there is the Perfection of Morality. But in an external sense the Perfection of Morality does not occur by an arrangement entirely free of harm to sentient beings. If that is not the way it is, even so in our day the sentient beings are not free from harm. So the victors (Buddhas) of yore, when accomplishing the Perfection of Morality, were unable to lead the sentient beings to a place free from harm. Hence, whether any sentient being in an external sense is free or not free of harm, when one makes part of one's stream of consciousness that abstinent consciousness that turns away from harm to those (sentient beings) — this is the superior path-procedure of morality; confer *Caryāvatāra*, V, 11:

> How am I to chase away all the beings, fishes and the rest, so as not to kill any? To obtain the abstinent consciousness, this is the Perfection of Morality.

Although there are three types of morality, here the abstinent consciousness is explained as chiefly in the control of vowed morality. Moreover, when it is a matter of a precipitating cause, it is the ten abstinences that eliminate the ten non-virtues; and when it is a matter of its bare nature, it is the abstinence from seven non-virtues, i.e. the seven eliminations of the nature of body and speech *karma*. So the *Avatāra-Commentary* (on II, 1a):

> Now, morality, whether because it does not tolerate defilement, because it does not produce sin, or because it "cools" [i.e. liberates] by putting out the fire of mental flare-ups in consciousness, is the cause of happiness, on which account illustrious persons

take their stand on it. Besides, morality has for character the seven eliminations. The three natures [*dharma*] [of mind-*karma*], absence of lust, absence of hatred, and right views, are precipitating causes. For that reason, when morality is in the matter of these precipitating causes, it is explained as the tenfold path of *karma*.

2) *the means of entering its cultivation*. Accordingly, the pledge to train in the (Bodhisattva) practice after having generated the Mind (of Enlightenment), is the pledge to get all sentient beings to have the Complete Buddha's ornament of morality. Thus is it required to accomplish their aim. Furthermore, it is required to first generate the power of one's own purified morality, because if one's own morality is impure or damaged one will fall into evil destiny, and then does not fulfill even one's own aim, let alone the aim of others! Consequently, the one who endeavors for the aim of others must tighten up one's protective vow so as not to relax in acting with esteem for morality; so *Pāramitāsamāsa* (II, 1):

> The one who has aroused the aim to make people adorned with the Complete Buddha's ornament of morality, should first purify one's own morality, for morality draws to itself the strength of [magical] power.

And (II, 48):

> The one who falls from morality is impotent even in one's own aim. How is one competent in the method of another's aim? Therefore, a relaxed devotion to this, is especially not right for one who works for another's aim.

Thus, the purification of morality is dependent upon path-procedures according as are the rules for possibilities of engagement and avoidance. Moreover, the one who duplicates the mentality keen and firm with desire to protect (one's vow) should generate the desire to protect it by way of contemplating for a long time the disadvantage of not protecting and the benefit of protecting. In regard to the former (case), it is just as the same work states (II, 49a–b):

> Therefore, observing the overwhelming danger, reject what should be rejected, no matter how minute!

So, having feared by reason of the disadvantages, one should industriously eliminate even minute sins, and should imagine, as was previously explained, the disadvantages of the ten kinds of non-virtue which are the coarsest of the opponents to morality. The benefits, as were previously explained, are stated by *śrīmat* Śūra in the same work (II, 47):

> If from morality would arise among men a perfection with heavenly pleasure, and among gods [a perfection] with the single taste of supernal joy, how wonderful is this morality, from which, even more, the Buddha natures arise!

Furthermore, by recourse to this (morality), one has a distinguished attainment ever higher in the stream of consciousness, becomes equal in training to the great Bodhisattvas who are imbued with compassion, and obtains the pure wisdom that rejects all the seeds of bad conduct. Another ornament may be downgraded and ridiculed when termed too young or too old; while the ornament of morality, whoever has it—whether young, old, or in between—generates joy to all, so it is the best of ornaments. Another perfume is carried by certain breezes and not by some other breezes, so that it is partial; but the renowned perfume of morality pervades in all directions. The application of ointment made of sandlewood and so forth, is prohibited to the monk, even for dispelling fever; while the application of a remedy against the fever of defilement is not prohibited to the monk and is appropriate for him. A similar case is to have only the token of a monk; while the one who has the treasure of morality is distinguished over others. It says in the same work (II, 60–61):

> Morality is the path of the distinguished attainment, the affinity with persons of compassionate nature, the purity of one with superior knowledge, the species of adornment that is faultless and best.
>
> Morality is the gratifying perfume that pervades the three worlds; the ointment not prohibited to the monk. Among men it builds the superiority over ordinary persons, even when they look alike.

Moreover, there arise from morality such benefits as these: One does not speak sentences woven of falsehood. Persevering industriously, one accomplishes without difficulty and the required possessions are gathered spontaneously. One is honoured by all men without threatening them with harsh acts. There is no reproach due to the family of one's relatives and so forth. Love toward this one arises naturally, even when one did not previously benefit and even from strangers. Even the dust of his feet, being touched by the crowns of heads of men and gods, is brought into the field of offerings. The same work says (II, 62–64):

> Because it is the state of constancy of those who do not boast, and is free as well from speechlessness or fatigue—it is the lordliness whose haughtiness and pride are abandoned, that is bowed to by the whole world even though not threatened. Whether one is among those born in a non-distinguished family, or is among those who have not performed the principal services; among those stationed in the rule of morality exclusively even when not previously praised among men; men and gods bring their head crests to the dust auspicious around the feet of that one possessing morality, touching it [the dust] in respectful greeting; for that one has the most glorious of families.

The wise man who well reflects on the benefit and the disadvantage in that way, should guard (morality) as stated in the same work (II, 49c–d):

> One should not violate the morality customary to the Bodhisattva by an upsurge of personal pleasure.

And (II, 51c–d; 52a–b):

> [One rightly resorts to morality] which moves freely because self-controlled; which being the irreproachable adornment, has the praise of the wise; is complete and free from pride, because full of all the points of instruction.

Furthermore, one should avoid an aspiration in terms of just one's own fear of evil destiny, or in terms of just the perfection of gods and men, i.e. one should guard (morality) so as to install all sentient beings in morality. The same work states (II, 59, 65):

Whoever wishes to install in morality all the sentient beings in the uncountable world realms, should [himself], for the sake of benefitting the world, stand firm on morality. That [morality] is called a perfection by those who know it. Therefore, not through fear of evil destiny, not with the motive of sovereignty, and not by upsurge of longing for the affluence of heaven, should one follow morality, for not so would it be spotless. One should live on morality while keeping uppermost success of the world's aim.

3) *varieties of morality*. There are three: vowed morality, morality which gathers virtuous natures, and morality of (possible) activity for the sake of sentient beings.

a) *vowed morality*. The *Bodhisattvabhūmi* states this to be the seven divisions of the Prātimokṣa.[77] Thus, one abiding in the vow of the Bodhisattva (already) has the vow of *Prātimokṣa*. The vow of the *Prātimokṣa* is stipulated both for the 'householder' Bodhisattva and for the 'monk' Bodhisattva; and the abstinent vow common to those two is vowed morality (*saṃvara-śīla*). When one has the Bodhisattva vow, though not (holding) the proper basis of the *Prātimokṣa* vow, one is accompanied by the natural sins that are against the *Prātimokṣa* ordinances. Thus, the abstinent vow that eliminates the pointed-out sins, is vowed morality.

b) *morality which gathers virtuous natures*. Having fixed one's attention on the virtues consisting of the six Perfections and so on, one generates all those not yet arisen in his stream of consciousness; and those one has already generated one does not violate but enhances in ever higher degree.

c) *morality of (possible) activity for the sake of sentient beings*. Having fixed one's attention on the eleven kinds of help of sentient beings, one should accomplish their aims of the present life and the next life, and do it as appropriate in a manner free from sin. I have already set forth these extensively in my commentary on the *Śīlapaṭala*, so for certainty in this matter one should consult it again and again.[78]

Hence the stipulations of the *Prātimokṣa* are the single category of instruction for the one possessing the Bodhisattva vow and who has gone forth (as a monk), i.e., it is not aside from the instruction of the Bodhisattva. Besides, from among the three kinds of morality, the vowed morality is the given stipulation of the *Prātimokṣa* or is the engagement or avoidance in common with it, and is of great importance at the very outset also for the Bodhisattva, so one must train in precisely it. This is because (Asaṅga's) *Viniścayasaṃgrahaṇī* on the *Bodhisattvabhūmi* states:

> Among the three kinds of morality, there is this vowed morality, which is the comprisal [of stipulations] and what answers to it [i.e. is derivatively consistent], i.e. which is what restrains and protects, and [stipulations] other than it, that restrain and protect. Now, when one neither restrains nor protects [according to the comprisal], one does not restrain or protect [by stipulations] other than it [i.e. by what answers to it]. One should say that it is on that account that a Bodhisattva loses his vowed morality and loses all vows.

Consequently, when one comes to think, "The *Prātimokṣa* vow belongs to the auditors (*śrāvaka*)," abandons the stipulations of engagement and avoidance, and professes that the Bodhisattva instruction is a reason for studying something else, one has not grasped the essential point to learn about Bodhisattva morality. This is because it is said many times that the vowed morality is the substratum and ground for two subsequent moralities (i.e. gathering virtuous natures and for others' sake).

Also, the chief thing about the vowed morality is that it eliminates natural sins, and that it includes the essentials of the great disadvantages of the natural ones—this is stated in all the upper and lower vehicles, to wit, it is the elimination of the ten non-virtues. Consequently, one must rightly restrain the three doors (of body, speech, and mind) by way of not permitting any arousal of those (non-virtues) to go on. The *Pāramitāsamāsa* (II, 8–9) puts it this way:

> One should not stray from the *karma*-paths which are the glorious path to heaven and liberation. The distinguished resolves, aimed at the benefit of the world, of those staying therein [the karma-*paths*] become fruitful.
>
> This morality in short [the Buddhas] declare, is restraint in body, speech, and mind. Therefore, endeavor just in this [morality] totally, and you should energetically purify these [non-virtues].

Moreover, Candrakīrti, in his section on "Perfection of Morality" has explained it as the elimination of the ten non-virtues; and the same frequently occurs in scriptures such as the *Daśabhūmika*. Hence, if at the outset one purifies the restraining thought, as previously set forth, the remaining (two) moralities are accomplished easily.

4) *how one acts at the time of their practice*. One operates by having the six lustres and by having the six perfections. At the time of operating in possession of the six perfections, the installing of others in morality while oneself stays in morality, is the gift of morality; and the remaining (perfections) are as previously given.

5) *summarizing their goal*. One does not lose the Mind of Enlightenment which is the basis of the practice, and gives in increasing measure. This is the root of engaging the practice of morality and so on, and is the best turn-off of harm to any sentient beings. One purifies by making as object of aspiration the path-procedures of morality at the high level. Starting with the morality of the beginner, one studies from now on with resolve tied to the situations of engagement and disengagement. In particular, whoever recognizes the sins along with the natural ten non-virtues, should each day cast many restraint thoughts. And among these, whatever vow that was pledged should have fundamental transgressions (these) the restraint thought should again and again endeavor to cast off. If one acts like that, since the fruit corresponds to deed as cause, also in another life one is able to master the Bodhisattva training with small trouble and small pain. But if right now one abandons with scorn those (kinds of morality) he is continually defiled by severe transgressions, and in numerous lives is incapable of learning the instruction of the Bodhisattva. Hence, one should endeavor from right now.

Perfection of Forbearance

There are five parts to the Perfection of Forbearance. 1) the actuality of forbearance; 2) the means of entering its cultivation; 3) varieties of forbearance; 4) how one acts at the time of their practice; 5) summarizing their goal.

1) *the actuality of forbearance*. This is the not giving any thought to another's harmdoing; the acquiescence to suffering in

one's own stream of consciousness; certitude and well-planted faith in the doctrine (*dharma*). There are also three opponents to them: for the first, hatred; for the second, depression consequent upon hatred and dread; for the third, non-belief and denial.

Here, the fulfillment of the perfection of forbearance amounts just to the fulfillment of repeating the thought that opposes one's own anger, and so on; but it does not demand that one look toward freeing all the sentient beings from their undisciplined state, because one is unable to manage that, and because one does the needful by disciplining one's own mind. So the *Caryāvatāra* (V, 12–14):

> Bad persons are infinite in number; how many of them could I kill! Yet, when this angry thought is slain, slain are all the enemies! How is there [enough] leather to cover the whole earth? Earth is spanned by a mere boot-sole's leather! Likewise, I cannot hold back external entities. I shall hold back my own mind! What is the use of my restraining others!

2) *the means of entering its cultivation*. Although there are many gateways, for the while I shall explain how one contemplates the benefit of forbearance and the disadvantage of non-forbearance. The benefit is stated in the *Bodhisattvabhūmi*:

> At the outset the Bodhisattva observes the benefit in forbearance. He thinks, "The forbearing person in the future will have few enemies, will have few discords, will have much pleasure and satisfaction. That one will be without regret at the time of death; and with the break-up of that one's body will be born among the gods in the good destiny, the heaven world." He thus observing the benefit becomes forbearing himself and installs the other person in forbearance. He speaks praise of forbearance, and upon seeing a forbearing person is happy and delighted.

The *Pāramitāsamāsa* (III, 3–5) puts it this way:

> They say that patience is the foremost observance of those whose minds are elevated to the aims of others, for the fault of anger hems in what is better for the world as a dam, the waters.

> Ornament of the powerful; pinnacle of strength in those living austerely; heavy rain on the forest fire of hostility; forbearance dispels what has no good purpose in this world and the next.
>
> Blunted against the forbearance armor of illustrious men, the word-arrows of bad men mostly change to flowers of praise and make up garlands of their [i.e. illustrious men] fame.

And (III, 8B):

> Forbearance is the workshop for [producing] the form[79] decorated with illustrious characteristics, delightful by its virtues.

Thus, the benefit of forbearance is praised that with it there are many gateways: One is not diverted from the aim of others by the wayward conduct of sentient beings. One is protected from the anger-enemy that overcomes many roots of virtue. That even for harm-doing of meager power, there is a captivating ornament by reason of forbearance. That it is the illustrious power of ascetics to suppress defilement. That it is the heavy rain which extinguishes the bon-fire of hostility. That it is the armor which the wayward-conduct arrows of bad men cannot pierce. That it is the eye of the world of the one with golden color. That it is the artisan-skill that constructs the auspicious form which is captivating; and so on. Besides, it is as the *Caryāvatāra* states (VI, 6c–d):

> Whoever, by persisting, destroys anger, is happy in this and the next life.

Thus, if one relies on having continuous forbearance, one does not lose joy of mind, so that at all times in the present life one is happy. In the next life it eliminates a bad destiny, and yields a particularly good destiny. Eventually, it confers liberation. Therefore, it is good for this life, and for the future. One should contemplate until one gains keen enthusiasm and firmness of certainty that those and other benefits do arise from forbearance in the relation of cause and effect.

As to the disadvantage of anger, and the disadvantage of not seeing it (as such), the *Caryāvatāra* (VI, 1) informs us:

> All this good conduct — giving, offering to the Buddhas — performed through a thousand aeons, a hostility brings to nought.

This *Caryāvatāra* formulation agrees with that presented by Ārya-Śūra (author of *Pāramitā-samāsa*). The *Mañjuśrī-vikrīḍita-sūtra* mentions that it (anger) destroys the virtues accumulated for a hundred ages; and furthermore the *Avatāra* says that the virtues produced by repeating the perfections of giving and morality and accumulated for a hundred ages are destroyed by a single instant of angry resolve.

As to the sort of object the anger is (textually) stipulated, some (authorities) explain that the Bodhisattvas are stipulated, and some claim objects in general (are stipulated). Of those (possibilities), the former appears consistent with the (*Madhyamaka-*) *Avatāra* (III, 6a–c):

> Anger toward the sons [i.e. Bodhisattvas] of the Victors destroys in an instant the virtues of giving and morality accumulated for a hundred ages.

The *Avatāra Commentary* (by Candrakīrti), referring to the (person-) object where anger arises, says that if a Bodhisattva destroys his roots of virtue by anger, how much more is it the case when a non-Bodhisattva is angry at a Bodhisattva; and says that whether it is certain or uncertain that a Bodhisattva is the object, or whether it is true or untrue that one observes the (given) reason of the anger as a fault, still the destruction of virtue happens as previously explained.

In general, for destroying the roots of virtue, one should not limit it to anger against Bodhisattvas; (confer) the *Śikṣāsamuccaya*:

> And in the texts of the Ārya-Sarvāstivādins we read: "See, monks, this monk prostrating himself with all his limbs on the hair-and-nail *stūpa*, bringing his mind to sincere devotion." "Yes, sir." "Monks, given the ground covered by that monk, and the 80,000 leagues [*yojana*] down to the golden circle [*kāñcana-cakra*], as many as be the grains of sand included, so many thousands are the 'wheel-turning' kingships to be enjoyed by that monk." [and so on, down to] Then the venerable Upāli, bowing with *añjali* in the direction of the Bhagavat, addressed him: "According to what

> the Bhagavat has said, this monk has great roots of virtue. How do these roots of virtue dwindle, subside, and disappear?" "I do not see, Upāli, such a wound or damage, as when someone in the pure life [*brahmacārin*] [arouses evil thoughts] in a fellow student [*sabrahmacārin*]. Then, Upāli, these great roots of virtue dwindle, subside, and disappear. That being the case, Upāli, this is the rule: One would not rail with his mind against the *'gal ba* [the red-hot pillar for torturing criminals]; how much less should he against a body endowed with consciousness!"

As to the meaning of destroying the roots of virtue, some learned men say that (it means) destroying the capacity to speedily generate the fruit of former virtues, postponing the issuance of the fruit; that the fruit of such (faults) as hatred come forth earlier; but without denying that the respective fruits issue upon encountering the condition in the future. Their reason is: if there is no capacity by any mundane path to eliminate a seed that ought to be eliminated, there is no possibility to eliminate the seed by defilement (itself). The reason those scholars give does not appear certain (to wit:) 1. because when the ordinary person purifies non-virtue by the four adversary powers,[80] there is no elimination of a seed, even though it is purified; and when that person encounters the condition in the future there is no possibility of the maturation coming forth; 2. because there is no elimination of seed even when virtuous and non-virtuous *karma* have ceased through having issued forth their respective maturations; and when subsequently encountering the condition there is no possibility of the maturation arising; 3. because at the time of attaining "summits" and "forbearance" (consistent with truth) in the Stage of Praxis (*prayoga-mārga*)[81] one has not eliminated the non-virtuous seed which is a cause of wayward views and bad destiny; and even when encountering the condition, it is not possible to give rise to wayward views and bad destiny.

Furthermore, as was previously cited, "who by *karma* is weighted down in cyclical flow (*saṃsāra*)." That any virtuous or non-virtuous *karma* previously matured would for a while quash the opportunity for other *karma* to mature, and that just it could destroy the virtue or non-virtue—cannot be established, because it was not declared (in either scripture or principled exegesis).

Just the postponement for a while of the maturation is not valid as the meaning of destroying the roots of virtue. On the other hand, one should say that when non-virtuous *karma* becomes powerful it destroys all the roots of virtue. Hence, on this very point, the *ācārya* Bhāvaviveka states that neither the purification of non-virtue by the four powers as previously explained, nor the destruction of the roots of virtue by wayward views and hostility can bring forth the fruit upon encounter with the original condition, just as a shoot does not spring forth on meeting with the condition of a ruined seed.

Furthermore, as was previously explained, even when someone is "washed," since one's collected sin has been purified by the four powers, this does not contradict the fact that one is slow to rise in a higher path. According to some, even though one destroy the fruits (respectively), the perfections of possessions and body, of giving gifts and of protecting morality—by the natural outcome (*niṣyanda*) of repeatedly enacting in mind the giving (of gifts) and rejecting (of bad actions) one is insured against the defeat in the future of the arising of the virtuous roots of giving and morality. According to others, that one destroys the natural outcome, which arises in continuous affiliation, of performing inner morality, etc., does not defeat the occurrence of the perfections of body, property, etc. According to still others, if one does not vent anger against a Bodhisattva who has obtained a prophecy, one can proceed to fulfillment in a single eon (*kalpa*); while if someone understands the path but gets a single angry resolve (against that Bodhisattva) even though one keeps the path in his stream of consciousness, one makes little progress while proceeding on the path of a whole eon. In short, I think that when one washes a non-virtue, whatever be the act of that, it does not entail washing everything; and that in the same way, when one destroys a virtue, whatever be the act of that, it does not entail destroying everything.

However, this is of paramount importance: Having taken recourse to the scripture of only the Buddha and to the principles (of exegesis) based thereon, it appears mandatory to ponder (those). Hence, one should rightly peruse the scripture and ponder it. Accordingly, the disadvantage of the "unseen" (i.e.

dharma = the past life) is the unfathomable opposition to the issuance of one's own intensely disagreeable maturation, and (opposition to) the issuance of another person's very agreeable maturation. The disadvantage of the "seen *dharma*" (*dṛṣṭa-dharma* = the present life) is the following: the mind does not experience peace and certainty; whatever was the former pleasure and joy, they disappear and are later not recovered; sleep does not come, and the stability of the mind in a natural state is lost; with great hatred the one formerly accorded kindness and who has forgotten the kindness, is slain; even his friends weary of him and abandon him; even if he gathers them with gifts, they don't stay with him. (confer) *Caryāvatāra* (VI, 3–5):

> While the thorn of hatred pains the heart, neither does the mind experience peace or attain pleasure and joy; neither is there sleep or steadfastness.
>
> Who with gifts and respect have relied upon another, even they are wont to slay the master who has an odious share of hatred. Even his friends fear him; he gives and is not served. In short, there simply is no way by which an angry man can be happy.

Besides, the *Jātakamāla* (XXI, Story of Cuḍabodhi, k. 29–33) has this:

> A man whose beauty of complexion is lost by the fire of anger, though he be adorned with ornaments, does not look good. And lying on a goregous couch he rests painfully, the thorn of anger in his heart. Forgetting the direction of accomplishment beneficial to himself, by anger he goes off on the wrong road. So he is deprived of fame and success in aim, like the moon in its dark phase is wasted in itself [and in catching anything]. Even though dear friends try to restrain that person, by wrath one falls into the pit of wrong principle. The discrimination of the hater being slow to sort out the beneficial and the harmful, usually one ends up in a stupefaction.
>
> Having by anger made sinful acts a part of one's nature, one is tormented in evil destinies for centuries. Can enemies, provoked by severe offence, do anything worse? "This anger is the enemy within," so I know. What man may tolerate the course of its [magical] power?

One should contemplate to again and again gain firm certainty that such disadvantages as those arise from anger. That is also *Caryāvatāra*'s message (VI, 2):

> There is no sin like hatred, no austerity like forbearance. Hence, cultivate forbearance with zeal and by many sorts of methods!

Accordingly, one first applies himself to observe what are the benefits and what the disadvantages, and then endeavors to cultivate forbearance by many avenues. The reason for the first step is told in the *Avatāra-Commentary* (on III, 6):

> Thus, just as it is impossible to determine in number of *palas* the measure of the ocean water, so also here it is impossible to determine the limit of the retribution. Consequently, there is no other sin as great as non-forbearance to cast a disagreeable fruit, and to harm merit.

It says this because, while there are maturations that issue with much greater unpleasantness, for destroying the roots of virtue there is no greater sin. Besides, one may learn from the *Śikṣāsamuccaya* that there are many sins besides hatred that amass a great severity of maturation and that destroy the roots of virtue—such as the wayward view that ridicules "cause and fruit"; the rejection of the Illustrious Doctrine (*saddharma*); generation of pride; above all, the murder of Bodhisattvas and teachers; and so on.

3) *varieties of forbearance*. There are three: how one disregards harm-doing; the resignation to suffering; forbearance with certitude toward the Dharma.

a) *how one disregards harm-doing*. There are two ways: suppression of non-forbearance with harm-doing toward the one who has done harm; suppression of dissatisfaction at an enemy's wealth and of satisfaction at his downfall.

a – 1) *suppression of non-forbearance with harm-doing toward a harm-doer*. This has two parts: (1) suppressing the non-forbearance toward the one who has hindered happiness and the one who has brought suffering; (2) not encouraging anyone to hinder with respect, or anyone to commit the three, contempt, and so on.

1) *suppressing the non-forbearance toward the one who has hindered happiness and the one who has brought suffering*. This has two parts: teaching the impropriety of engaging in anger; teaching the propriety of engaging in good will.

(a) *teaching the impropriety of engaging in anger*. This has three aspects: the impropriety, upon consideration, in regard to the object, the subject, and the basis.

1. *the impropriety, upon consideration, in regard to the object*. This is (first) considering the presence or absence of independence. One should examine, thinking, "What is the valid reason to be angry at the harm-doer?" Upon examining that way, suppose one thinks, "Because first that person had a resolve of desire to do harm to me, then because that person managed to frustrate my happiness, or to generate the pain of dissatisfaction in my body and mind." "Now, given that I am independent, that one did not actually harm me; am I angry because that one sent harm in my direction? Or, given that I am not at all independent, am I angry because another did harm after that one, without independence, was enjoined (to do so)?" In the first case it is not proper to be angry, because that person doing harm was not independent toward oneself. One thinks, "It is this way: the thought that there was harm was generated when there was the set of cause and condition, to wit, the seed of defilement previously made part of one's nature, the vicinity of the object, and unmethodical mental orientation," because even if one does not so think (the thought that there was harm) is generated by those causes and conditions. And let this one think, "It is generated when those causes and conditions are not complete," because even if this one does so think, if definitely does not arise. Accordingly, those causes and conditions generate the belief of harm-doing; and while that generates the applications of harm-doing, since it generates suffering in another person, that person is also without any independence at all. That one oneself is in the power of another, i.e. defilement, because that proceeds like its servant. Suppose it is the case when oneself is definitely without independence and another has done harm after being enjoined in a manner powerless; here it is very improper to be angry. For example, suppose someone being shaken by an evil spirit passes into its power; and a specialist is willing to help this one to get

free from it; wishing to do harm to (the specialist), strikes that person and so forth; (the specialist) thinking, "This one being powerless it was (actually) done by the evil spirit; in that way this one does it," is not at all angry (with the patient) and endeavors even more to free this one from the evil spirit. Like that, even a Bodhisattva may do harm by harm-doing; and one should think, "That one being oneself powerless (or: lacking independence), its was (actually) done by the defilement-demon; in such a way that one does it"; and so thinking is not at all angry (at the Bodhisattva). Thus one should generate one's mind to think, "I shall endeavor in the Bodhisattva practice so to free (the sentient beings) from defilement." That is also the message of the *Catuḥśataka*:

> In the same way as a healer would not, by anger, provoke someone demon-possessed, so also the *muni* seeing the defilements. But there is no person free from defilements.

It is also as told by Candrakīrti:

> The wise, having considered, "This here is not the fault of sentient beings, but this is the fault of defilements," do not provoke the sentient beings.

While many participants are stated in the *Caryāvatāra*, this one easily gives rise to certainty, and it appears preeminently to be the adversary of anger. The *Bodhisattvabhūmi* also mentions a good cancellation (of anger) through cultivating the idea of Dharma alone, and this has the same significance; so one should cultivate repeatedly attainment of certainty in this (principle).

If one is independent regarding those sentient beings, one would have no suffering at all, for the reason that one does not want suffering and for the reason that one is independent regarding it. Furthermore, if a person is ruffled by their strong defilements, that one should think of how much less ought he to harm another when (that harm-doer), highly afflicted and subject to loss, opposes oneself, jumps into an abyss, does harm (to oneself) with thorns, sharp-pointed instruments; destroys (one's own) food, etc.; and so thinking, should suppress the anger (confer) *Caryāvatāra* (VI, 31):

> Thus everything is in control of another, and that control also without [self-] control. [Having understood that], how can one be angry toward the entities that are inactive like magical creations?

And (VI, 33–34):

> Hence, having seen an enemy or a friend doing an impropriety, one should think, "Such are the conditions which affect that one," and be happy.
>
> If one could obtain what one wants by desiring it, among all with bodies, none would have suffering, for no one desires suffering.

And (VI, 37):

> At a time when men are controlled by defilement, they kill themselves which are dear; at that time, how could they spare the persons of others?

In terms of examining the adventitious and the bare nature, the impropriety, i.e. the fault of doing hurt to others, either is or is not in the bare nature of sentient beings. If it is in the bare nature, it is not right to be angry, just as it is not right to be angry at the hot, burning fire. On the other hand, if it is adventitious, again it is not right to be angry, just as it is not right to be angry at the sky when marred by the appearance in the sky of smoke and the like. So thinking, one suppresses anger (confer) *Caryāvatāra* (VI, 39–40):

> If the bare nature of foolish men is to do harm to others, it is as improper for me to be angry at them, as at the fire which has the nature of burning.
>
> But if this fault is adventitious, and the beings are inherently good, in such a case, anger at them is not right, any more than it is, at the atmosphere with the disagreeable smoke.

In terms of examining the harm directly or indirectly, the impropriety is as follows: If one is angry at the harm-doing that works harm directly, he should be angry at the club as at the person; and if one is angry at the harm-doer indirectly — since the person is impelled by hatred to do harm with a club—one should be angry at hatred; (confer) VI, 41:

> If one is going to be angry, not at the immediate entity, the club and so on, but at the one who sets it in motion; then best I hate the hatred, for he [with the club] was set in motion by hatred.

Thus, if one is not angry at the club, neither is it right to be angry at the one who used it. If one is angry at the one who used it, then it is right to be angry at the hatred; and when one does not accept it so, his mind goes astray in a wrong path. Therefore, one should be certain that the logic is the same in every case; and one should direct his mind to not be angry at a person as it would not be at the club. Besides, this non-distinguishing of the club and its wielder by way of attributing or, not attributing ill-will, one may understand by the previously explained logic exposing the non-independence.

In terms of examining the cause which urges the harm-doing, the impropriety of anger is as follows: The experience of suffering brought about by harm-doing does not arise without a cause or from a non-conforming cause. Hence, it arises from a conforming cause; and since there was prior unvirtuous *karma*, this urges the harm-doing by dint of one's own *karma* and without independence (or, own-control). For that reason, one should think, "I have reprimanded myself; it is not right to be angry at another!" and having thus found the reprimand in himself, he should quash every kind of anger. For example, the sentient beings by their own sinful acts generate the "guardians" of the infernal regions which ("guardians") then inflict harm upon them (confer VI, 42):

> I myself, on a former occasion, did just such harm to sentient beings; so it is right that I should endure harm to the same extent from the sentient beings.

And (VI, 45–47):

> Like a fool I hate the suffering and love the cause of
> suffering. Since the suffering comes from one's own
> sin, why be angry at another?

> For example, the guardians of the infernal regions and the forest of dagger leaves are generated by my own deeds. Well, then, at what should one be angry?
>
> Urged on by my own action, arisen are the doers of harm to me. By that, they go lovingly to the hell beings. It is not for me to hurt them.

Also it was heard from Śa-bo-pa: At the time I don't admit the reprimand, it means there's not even a drop of Dharma to work (on). So I teach.

2. *the impropriety of anger, upon consideration, in regard to the subject*. The generation of anger at the harm-doing is the non-forbearance of suffering. If there is this (non-forbearance) it is a mistake, because through not forbearing a slight suffering of the present time, one generates pressingly the cause of unfathomable suffering in bad destinies. Hence one should think, "I am (behaving like) a great fool," and should himself be ashamed and endeavor that anger not trespass in his mind (confer VI, 73):

> If one is unable to endure this slight suffering of today, then, given that anger is the cause of hell's pain, why does one not ward off [that anger]?

In this regard, the suffering generated by harm is the fruit of former evil action; hence, through experiencing it (i.e. the suffering), the former evil action is consumed; and if one behaves with forbearance, he does not collect sins anew, but greatly expands his merit. Therefore, one should look with kindness upon the harm-doer such as the one who, without noticing the damage to one's own Dharma, engages in purifying our own sins. This is the message of the *Jātakamālā* (No. 33, Story of the Buffalo, k. 15):

> When someone, not noticing the damage to his own Dharma, proceeds to purify my sins, who else than I would be ungrateful if I did not use forbearance toward him?

Besides, the *(Madhyamaka-)Avatāra* (III, 5) puts it this way:

> Given the fruit of unvirtuous *karma* formerly done and which is the very thing we claim to call destroyer [of the unvirtuous *karma*],

> how could one, by reason of anger, harm another person and guide that very seed [i.e. of the harm] toward [even more intense later] suffering?

Thus, just as one would endure the burning and bleeding as a means of healing a severe affliction, so also it is indeed proper to ensure a minor suffering for the sake of averting a great suffering.

3. *the impropriety of anger, upon consideration, in regard to the basis*. This examines the cause of the harm, the guilty as the blameless (confer VI, 43–44):

> His blade and my body are both the cause of pain; the blade is held by him; the body, by me. At what should one be angry?
>
> This sore in human form cannot tolerate a touch and is pained; I clasping it am thirsty and blind. At what anguish here should one be angry?

And (VI, 67):

> Some, through delusion, are offensive; others, deluded, are angry. Among those, which person acts blamelessly? Which one is guilty?

The examination of what was pledged by oneself is the thinking: "If it is not right for the Śrāvaka—who engages for the sake of himself alone — to be angry, namely with non-forbearance; how much more (is it not right to be angry) for me, who has taken the pledge, from the time of generating the Mind (of Enlightenment), to accomplish the benefit and happiness of all sentient beings; and who, having engaged in the aim of others, is assisting all the sentient beings"; and having so thought, one generates the sufferance consisting in forbearance.

Furthermore, it was heard from Po-to-ba: According to the teaching of the Buddha (as some claim), when (someone) commits no sin, but a little harm occurs to him, then without cultivating forbearance he subverts the very foundation of the teaching. But the one adopting such a course condemns his vow. We no longer have the general teaching (of the Buddha). If our own vow is lost, everything is lost. So he said.

And (it was heard from him): Because the yak on whom the saddle was being fitted was loose, the saddle hit his leg. Because it was loose, rearing with his rear legs the leg-halter fell off. (The yak) felt at ease (comfortable). The harm-doer should be at ease; otherwise, oneself becoming his opponent, cannot be at ease (i.e. comfortable).

(b) *teaching the propriety of engaging in good will.* One should think, "As all the sentient beings have been in the cyclical flow from time immemorial, there is no one who has not been my friend or relative as father, mother, etc. Being impermanent, they were parted from life and suffered with the three pains. A person deranged by the demon of defilement destroys one's own aims in the present and future lives. I must apply good will. How can it be right to be angry and to retaliate?" So thinking, one wills this from the bottom of one's heart.

2) *not encouraging anyone to hinder with respect or anyone to commit the three, contempt, and so on.* This has two parts; and of these, (1) not to encourage anyone to hinder with the three, beginning with praise, has three parts: resolving that praise, etc. are essentially devoid of good quality, resolving that they are essentially faulty, hence being glad to oppose those.

1. *resolving that praise, etc. are essentially devoid of good quality.* He should think, "When another person praises oneself and one's fame is widespread, there are still neither of the two aims — that of this life, to live long, be free from illness, etc., and that of the future life, to acquire merit, etc. There is no joy when those things are lost. Thus, whatever requirement of a building is not fulfilled, it crumbles like a house of sand; and then I am not different from the little children who weep." Having thus castigated himself, he can act unattached (confer VI, 90–91a–b):

> The respect consisting in praise and fame neither serves for merit nor for long life; neither for the aim of power, nor for freedom from illness, nor for bodily pleasure.
>
> The wise man, knowing his own aim, will have his own aim, such as it be.

And (VI, 93):

> The child weeps piteously when that one's sand house crumbles. Likewise, when praise and fame are lost, my own mind is like that one's.

2. *resolving that praise, etc. are essentially faulty*. One should think, "Praise and so forth distract the mind to useless purposes and destroy dispassion; they produce jealousy of the virtuous man, and decrease virtuous deeds." Having so thought, one should get the mind that shrinks from those (confer VI, 98):

> Praise and the like upset my peace and ardor. They make me envious of the virtuous man, and destroy my accomplishments.

3. *hence being glad to oppose those*. One should think, "That being the case, to lose praises and fame, good and honor—protects against going to bad destinies, cuts the bonds of craving, blocks the desire-door for entrance to suffering, and is tantamount to the spiritual support by the Buddha." Having so thought, one eradicates anger from the very bottom of the heart, and arouses joy (confer VI, 90–101):

> Hence, these persons coming upon the scene to destroy my reputation, and so on—it seems are operating to save me from falling into bad destiny.
>
> Goods and honor are a bondage for me who aspires to liberation. How could I hate those who free me from that bond?
>
> How could I hate those who, in the manner of the Buddha's spiritual support, have come to block me wanting to enter suffering?

(b) *not blaming anyone who has committed the three, contempt, and so on*. One should think, "The mind is incorporeal. Therefore, another has no way to directly harm it; but there is harm to the mind indirectly from direct harm to the body. Now, there is no way for contempt, and so on, to harm the body. And since (those three) do not harm (my) body or mind, I may be glad." Having so thought, one dispels the brooding on a wrong, because if this is closed off, hatred does not arise; so also (VI, 52–53):

> Because it is incorporeal, the mind cannot be assailed by anyone, anywhere. But because it is attached to the body, it is harmed by the body's suffering.

> This host of words, contemptuous, harsh, and inglorious, harms not the body. Well, then, O mind, why are you furious?"

It was heard from Śa-ra-ba. As much as one calls to the ear of Kham-lung-pa, Sne'u-zur-pa, and Grub-pa, it is no different from talking to a stone of the earth, so they are happy. Later ones will be unhappy due to oversensitivity of hearing. So he said. Someone reported to Gshen-ston what others said: Even the king has criticism behind his back. (Gshen-ston replied:) Confess what slander you have committed! Someone reported to the yogi Shes-rab-rdo-rje: People are saying that even the subordinates (*'gab ma*) are more well-known than we (are). And Shes-rab-rdo-rje answered: Your honor, gossip should stay with the subordinates, not go to someone else. Stop all your slander!

Now, another person dislikes anyone who uses contempt, and so on, toward him. Suppose one thinks: "For that reason he dislikes me." And "because another dislikes me, it harms me." It (the dislike) is true. But it doesn't harm. So give up the brooding! (confer VI, 54):

> Whoever among others dislikes me, this one would not drain me in this or in another life. Why should not that be wished by me?

Suppose one thinks, "Because they dislike me, even if not to the extent of harming me, on the basis of that (dislike) there would occur interruption in the obtaining of any goods from them; hence I am angry at the contemptuous, reviling, and ugly words." But even if one has obtained goods, one must leave them here (in this world), while the sin of anger follows after this one. Hence, of the two possibilities—dying quickly with no goods, or living a long life of sin—the former is the better one. Even if one obtains goods and lives for a long time, this one must die because not emancipated from death. At the time of death, whether it be that one had previously lived happily for a hundred years, or lived happily for only one year, alike both come to an end in only the domain of memory, because at that time there is no distinction at all of happiness and unhappiness. For example, both the experience in dream of happiness for a hundred years, or of happiness for a single moment, are not distinguished at all in the happiness and unhappiness at the time of waking. So thinking, when one wards off the attachment to goods and honor, then contemptuous and ugly words do not bring about a brooding on wrongs; because whether one accomplishes for one's self the special thing of the aim of others, or whether one does not (so) accomplish by reason of no directed effort, one does not ward off the joyous mind; so also VI, 55–59:

> If that is not wished by me, it is because it interrupts the goods. My goods come to nothing here, but my sins will stay firm.
>
> Better I die today than live long in sin. For even if I remained a long time, the suffering of death would be exactly that way for me.
>
> Someone enjoys happiness of a hundred years in dream and awakes; another enjoys happiness [in dream] for a moment and awakes. When both these persons awakened, their happiness is not turned off. Just so at death is the long-lived one and the short-lived one. And even when I have obtained many goods, and enjoyed pleasures for a long time, I shall go empty handed, naked, as though robbed [at the time of death].

a–2) *suppression of dissatisfaction at an enemy's wealth and satisfaction at his downfall*. One should think, "Having generated the Mind of Enlightenment for the sake of accomplishing the benefit and happiness of the sentient beings, that I have been angry at the sentient beings who attain happiness by themselves; and having resolved that all sentient beings should become Buddhas, that I have been dissatisfied with gaining merely trivial goods and honor; — such are great contradictions." Thus, one must shed the envy toward the wealth of others, whoever they may be; and generate gladness tied to resolve. Otherwise, the Mind of Enlightenment and the accomplishment of benefit and happiness of the sentient beings, are only words (confer VI, 80–84):

> Now why are you angry at the sentient beings who today
> have obtained their own happiness, when you have

generated the Mind of Enlightenment through desire
for the happiness of all sentient beings?

Did you not desire for the sentient beings the Buddhahood
honoured in the three worlds? Why, then are you
depressed when seeing their evanescent honours?

The one who nourishes those whom you should nourish—
that one only give to you! Having obtained a benefactor
for your family, you don't rejoice but are angry!

What does that one not wish for the sentient beings, when
that one wishes their enlightenment? How could
someone have the Mind of Enlightenment when angry
at another's good fortune?

If one did not receive it, or it stayed in the patron's house,
in any case, it is not yours. What does it matter whether
it was given or not?

Again, whether it be a case of evil resolves, exulting in the downfall of the enemy or thinking of that one's death, with so much one does not harm the enemy but merely torments oneself. If it be a case of harming that one, one should think of the disadvantage—the disaster to oneself and the other; and should suppress those completely (confer VI, 87–89):

Granted your ill-will for an enemy, but how could that
happen by your preference? Since it is only your
wishful thinking, and will not occur in the absence of a
cause.

And suppose it could be accomplished by your wish. Do
you take pleasure in that one's suffering? O, you are
satisfied! How does that compare with your coming
disaster?

A terrifying fish hook is cast by the defilement-fisherman.
Having caught you with that, the hell wardens will
cook you in their pots.

Accordingly, when one views the hindrance to what oneself and friends want, the workings of the disliked side, the success of one's enemy, as disliked aspects in one set, one broods on wrongs; as this develops, one generates hatred. On the other hand, by turning off the dislike that is in the one set, one wards off the brooding on wrongs; and turning that off, hatred does not arise. Thus, by the previously explained principles one should ward off those disliked images in the single set and should suppress anger by the various avenues, because the disadvantage (the possible penalty) is very great.

The precepts of suppression are the principles which the Buddha and the children of the Conqueror (Bodhisattvas) have previously taught, namely one inquires into and gets answers regarding one's defilement, and turns this off within. These are the methods of conquering anger, which is the great enemy. Thus, having well examined by discriminative insight, one suppresses it through many avenues of principles. The blocking, with many principles, of the inner set of anger, arises through many avenues of forbearance. The experience arisen from the profound level of understanding is obtained by the pure principle, which is the right meaning of scripture. Therefore, the disposition is very steadfast.

Those who cast aside the examination-cultivation by discriminative insight reject all the great magnanimous practices of the Bodhisattvas consisting in those (principles) and others. One may understand this (rejection) as the incomparable hindrance to receiving the essence of the favorable basis (i.e. fortunate birth) of oneself and others; so one should avoid (that course) like poison.

b) *the resignation to suffering*. The generation of forbearance consisting in the resignation to suffering, has three parts: the reason, i.e. certainty requirement, for resignation to suffering; the means of generating it; the extensive explanation by way of basis.

b–1) *the reason, i.e. certainty requirement, for resignation to suffering*. It is just as is said in the *Caryāvatāra* (VI, 12a–b):

> There is scarcely a cause of happiness; suffering multi-caused [stays without effort].

Thus, suffering, of whatever its kind, happens to us in continuity. Therefore, it is compulsory to have recognition (of suffering) to carry along on the path; because, if that is not present, then, as the *Śikṣāsamuccaya* states, either one gets hatred, or one is subject to alternate enthusiasm and timidity toward cultivating the path, and this interrupts one's practice in virtue. Furthermore, some sufferings are brought about by others; some arise from what is done and not done in endeavor along the path; and some are produced by former *karma*. Some, as will be explained below, occur during the performance of virtue, and do not occur otherwise. Accordingly, by dint of former *karma* and an immediate condition, those (sufferings) certainly arise, i.e. there is virtually no ability to avert them; so one must be resigned to them. If one is not (resigned), then on top of the suffering which was already there, is added the suffering of mental punishment generated by one's imagination (or, constructive thought), and it becomes very difficult to forbear. On the other hand, if there is resignation, then, while not turning off the remaining basic suffering, one pays attention to it and definitely avoids the suffering of mental punishment consisting of brooding on (imagined) wrongs; because one gets the means of carrying that other (i.e. the natural) suffering along the path, and whether it be an intense or minor suffering, one is able to forbear it. Hence, generating the forbearance consisting in the resignation to suffering, is a great essential.

b – 2) *the means of generating it*. This has two parts: (1) suppressing the adherence to brooding singly impelled regarding the occurrence of pain; (2) teaching the worthiness of resignation to suffering.

(1) *suppressing the adherence to brooding singly impelled regarding the occurrence of pain*. If one resorts to a remedy after pain occurs, there is no need to perform brooding; while if a remedy is not feasible, still there is no benefit in brooding; indeed, it is even harmful and is a disadvantage; because when there is great sensitivity, a slight pain is hard to tolerate; and when there is insensitivity, a great pain can be tolerated (confer VI, 10):

> If there were a remedy, what would be the use of brooding? And even when there is no remedy, what would be the use of brooding?

And (VI, 16):

> When there is cold, heat, rain, wind, illness, [prison] chains, and blows, I should not brood the pain. Otherwise, the harm grows.

(2) *teaching the worthiness of resignation to suffering*. This has three parts: resolve that suffering has its own virtue; resolve that the austerity of suffering is the virtue of forbearance; the easiness after familiarization from small beginnings.

(a) *resolve that suffering has its own virtue*. Here the virtues are five:

1. If there were no suffering, there would be no desire for escape (from *saṃsāra*); so it is the virtue of exhorting the mind to liberation.
2. When one is overtaken by suffering, one's haughtiness through pride is destroyed; so it is the virtue of dispelling pride.
3. When one experiences strong pangs, they arise from non-virtue; and if one does not like that result, one must turn it off at the cause; so it is the virtue of shrinking from sin.
4. When one is downcast by suffering, one desires happiness; and if this is needed, then one needs to do good which is its cause; so it is the virtue of being glad to do good.
5. When it has penetrated one's own heart, one may think, "Suffering like this occurs also to other sentient beings," and so one gets compassion for those who wander in cyclical flow (*saṃsāra*).

One may figure out for oneself other virtues from those (five) and what is suggested by them; and should again and again bend his mind to think, "This suffering is a desirable state" (confer VI, 12cd):

> Only by reason of suffering is there the escape. Therefore, O mind, be firm!

And (VI, 21):

> Besides, a virtue of suffering is that through agitation there is a humbling of pride. It is the compassion toward those in *saṃsāra;* it shrinks from sin; it is the devotion to the Lord.

(b) *Resolve that the austerity of suffering is the virtue of forbearance.* This has two parts: resolve that it is the benefit of great purpose, i.e. of liberation, etc.: resolve that it is the benefit of warding off fathomless suffering.

1. *resolve that it is the benefit of great purpose, i.e. of liberation, etc.* One should think, "Formerly, at the time I was revolving in cyclical flow, I recognized the source of suffering on account of each trifling desire, i.e. inferior need. Also I was oblivious of many sufferings, the cause of my experiencing unfathomable suffering in the future, and was resigned to the many purposeless sufferings. Now I have engaged in the virtue which makes the unfathomable benefit and happiness for myself and others. Being aware of this, I have to be resigned to the suffering myriad times more than the former ones. Hence, it is needless to speak of small sufferings! And one should again and again firm one's mind (by so thinking). It is also as said in the *Caryāvatāra* (VI, 74–75):

> Just for the sake of passion, I have been rendered thousands of times into the hells [hot and cold]; and yet performed no aims, whether of myself or others.
>
> Not so [i.e. not aimless], this suffering that accomplishes the great aim. Here is right just the joy in the suffering that dispels the suffering of the whole world.

Accordingly, one should think, "Formerly I gave heed to doing only those difficult practices which accomplished no aims, whether of myself or of others; now why should I not forbear the suffering which accomplishes the great aim? Hence, let there be the suffering, and let me act that way. I shall well achieve!" So thinking, one generates an exalted state of mind. Furthermore, one thinks that, deceived by bad associates one also practiced forbearance in the mortification of jumping onto the trident and standing upon the five fires, even on a bad, purposeless path; and pushed one's tolerance in numerous sufferings while struggling with agriculture and commerce for the sake of inferior requirements of the world. So one should arouse fearlessness by austerities (in matters of higher purpose).

2. *resolve that it is the benefit of warding off fathomless suffering.* One should think, "A man condemned to death would be very joyful if only a finger of his hand is cut off and then he is released from the death sentence. In the same way, it would be a fine thing if by means of such a slight pain as this human austerity I am able to ward off the continual suffering of evil destinies of numberless cycles of life in general, and of the hells in particular." And well thinking of special ones among the two kinds of suffering—the immediate and the long-time—one generates the heart force of fearlessness in austerity (confer, VI, 72):

> A man is to be killed, but his hand is cut off, and he is released. How could that be unfortunate? To be freed from the hells by the sufferings of the human condition—how could that be unfortunate?

The non-difficulty if one makes it part of one's nature starting from small beginnings, is what is stated (confer VI, 14):

> There is no given thing whatever that does not become easy when it is made part of one's nature. Hence, by the repeated practice of minor hardships, one may endure even a great hardship.

(c) *Easiness after familiarization.*

Accordingly, when one attires himself in the armor of resolve to be resigned to suffering and exposes himself to the minor steps of suffering, the power of resignation to suffering will grow ever greater. Also, the *Śikṣāsamuccaya* states:

> There, given a prior repeated practice of small pains, the repeated practice accomplishes the more and more severe. For example, by dint of repeated practice, all sentient beings have the idea that the difficult is easy. In the same way, for all cases of suffering arising there is the idea that they are happiness. By repeated practice placed near-by, the idea that it is happy [or, easy] stands near-by.

Those (precepts) also come in the *Ugradattaparipṛcchā:*

> Be free of the mind that is like cotton-wool!

Moreover, the *Gaṇḍavyūha* puts it this way:

> Girl, for destroying all defilement you should generate the mind hard to withstand.

As that says, given the requirement of heart force on the level of very firm mind, it does not work with weak thought.

Hence, if from the outset one generates a large heart-force, it supports even great suffering. For example when a hero enters a battle and sees his own blood, this causes the arousal of heart-force. If one had not heard this from the outset, or if he had heard it, thinking, "That would not work for me," then even though it be a time of small suffering (for him), it becomes a condition that diverts him from the path. It is like the example of some timid persons seeing the blood of another, and fainting (confer VI,17–18ab):

> There are soldiers who are filled with extraordinary courage upon seeing their own blood; and there are those who faint upon seeing the blood of others. The former go forth through their firmness of mind, and [the latter] through their timidity.

b – 3) *the extensive explanation by way of basis*. One should think, "If I must be resigned to the suffering that arises, of which arisings are the sufferings to which I am to be resigned?" (In reply,) there are eight:

(1) *based on site*. These are the sites which enhance the pure life (*brahmacarya*) — religious garb, alms, bedding, seat, remedy for sickness, utensils. When these are poor, received in meager amount, not respected by others, given only after long delay; moreover, unpleasant or boring — one should be resigned to the suffering arising from them.

(2) *based on perishable natures*. These are the nine perishable natures (*loka-dharma*), all of which dissolve and die — the non-receipt, the condemnation, blame, and the painful; the natures of dissolution, exhaustion, old age, sickness, and death. Having individually examined the sufferings based on each and all of them, one is resigned.

(3) *based on posture*. There are four postures (*īryāpatha*): walking, standing, sitting, lying down. While one is purifying

the mind during day and night from obscurations (*āvaraṇa*) by means of the first and third of them (i.e. walking and sitting), since one is resigned to the discomfort occasioned thereby, one does not lie on one side at the wrong time on a couch, bedstead, carpet of roots, or carpet of leaves.

(4) *based on embrace of the Dharma.* There are seven ways to embrace the Dharma: 1. praising and honouring the Three Jewels; 2. praising and honouring the *guru;* 3. retaining the doctrines; 4. teaching extensively to others those which one has retained; 5. reciting in a clear voice; 6. taking up a solitary abode, reflecting on proper subjects; 7. cultivating calming and discerning that is governed by the mental orientation of yoga. While engaged in those, one is resigned to any pains that arise.

(5) *based on living by alms.* There are seven acts to living by alms: 1. being resigned to the loss of good looks due to having hair shaven; 2. being resigned to the discarded and poor-looking clothing; 3. dwelling in a condition where all worldly practices are suppressed and other standards are met; 4. abandoning agriculture, and so on, as one who depends on others for living by receiving (food, etc.) from them; 5. not collecting goods, but seeking religious garb and so on from others for the duration of this livelihood; 6. abandoning impure practices, and turning away from mundane desires for as long as one lives; 7. abandoning dance, jest, and so forth, and for the sake of shedding family ties, affections, consort, and so forth, and entertainments — turning away from mundane sports for as long as one lives. While based on those, one is resigned to any pains that arise.

(6) *based on weariness due to endeavour.* This is the weariness and disturbance of body and mind during endeavour in the virtuous direction. One is resigned to pains arising on those grounds.

(7) *based on performing the aims of sentient beings.* There a eleven aims to be accomplished, and one is resigned to the suffering arising thereby.[82]

(8) *based on the act of separation.* The act of separation means entering the religious life, involving the alms bowl, religious garb, and so on. The separation from home is also from the sinless agriculture, as well as from commerce, revenue to the king, etc. One is resigned to the suffering arising therefrom.

Accordingly, whatever the sufferings arising, also successively as the case may be, from the eight (foregoing) bases, one does not give up his respective strivings; he engages toward enlightenment, and having engaged, there is no hindrance that turns him aside; and he engages without mental dislikes.

c) *forbearance with certitude toward the Dharma*. For generating the forbearance of conviction (*adhimukti*), i.e. certitude toward the Dharma, there are eight objects of conviction:

(1) object of pure trust is the good qualities of the Three Jewels.

(2) object of realization is the reality of the two selflessnesses (*nairātmya*).

(3) object of desire is the great power of the Buddhas and Bodhisattva; moreover, it is threefold — the power of supernormal faculty (*abhijñā*), the power of the six perfections (*pāramitā*), co-natal power (*sahaja*).

(4–5) object of accepting and rejecting is taken as two by the respective cause, i.e. good practice and evil practice, and their desirable and undesirable fruit.

(6–7) object of cultivation (*bhāvanā*) is taken as two, as the enlightenment which is the goal to be attained, and the means of attaining it, which is all the path of instruction by the Bodhisattvas.

(8) object to be practiced by hearing and pondering is the domain (*gocara*) of the knowable. Gro-luṅ-pa believed that this is impermanence, and so forth.

The chapter Balagotra (of the *Bodhisattvabhūmi*) mentions eight kinds for the Illustrious Doctrine (*saddharma*) such as the twelve branches of scripture, so I opine one must take it accordingly. The method of conviction is according to those objects; and having gained certainty, then avoiding anything inconsistent therewith, one gives volitional thought to them again and again.

The two sets — resignation to suffering and the eight certitudes regarding the Dharma — are the formulation stated in the *Bodhisattvabhūmi*, which presents extensively especially the certitudes toward the Dharma.

4) *how one acts at the time of their practice*. When one is performing whatever forbearance be the case, one does it in possession of the six lustres and with the complete six perfections. This

has already been explained, except for mentioning that to install another in forbearance is the giving of forbearance.

5) *summarizing their goal*. The recollection and cultivation, i.e. the generation of the Mind (of Enlightenment), which is the basis of the (Bodhisattva) practice, is the root of desiring to install all the sentient beings in the forbearance that exhausts the fluxes. Hence, one should make that (root) grow, and take as one's object of aspiration even the forbearances of the high stage. One attends to the things to be learned in the beginner's forbearance, and studies this methodically. If one has transgressed the bounds, as previously explained, one must endeavour to make amends. But if at the time of those path-procedures, one neglects and abandons them, one is continually defiled with many great sins; and also in other lives it will be especially difficult to have the path-procedures in the glorious practices of the Bodhisattva. Thus, one should observe the sublime essentials of the path; and those who are able, should from now on work at it; while those who are unable should purify their resolve. As said in the *Subāhuparipṛcchā*, at the time of small troubles and minor suffering, one may bring to fulfillment the perfection of forbearance.

Perfection of Striving

There are five parts to the instruction in the Perfection of Striving. 1) the actuality of striving; 2) the means of entering its practice; 3 varieties of striving; 4) how one acts at the time of their practice; 5) summarizing their goal.

1) *the actuality of striving*. Focussing (the mind) on a virtuous meditative object, one perseveres in the (mental) image, as is said in the *Caryāvatāra* (VII, 2a): "What is striving? The perseverance in virtue."[83] The *Bodhisattvabhūmi* explains it as the sinless mental perseverence for amassing virtue and performing for the sake of sentient beings; and also as the *karma*-motion of the three doors (i.e. body, speech, and mind) incited thereby.

2) *the means of entering into practice*. One frequently thinks of the benefit in engaging the striving, and of the disadvantage in not engaging it, because when one repeatedly thinks about it striving is generated. Here, the benefit is stated in the *Adhyāśayasañcodana:*

All the Buddhas always extol the continuous recourse to noble striving which dispels all suffering and the darkness [of mind] and which is the basis for avoiding evil destiny.

Whatever the designs there be in this world, and whatever the designs there be in the world beyond, the one who engages in striving has no difficulty in gaining them. So whoever are wise will use themselves with the force of striving.

Those who work for the enlightenment of the Buddhas, having observed the faults in torpor and sleepiness, should continually engage themselves in striving. This is my exhortation to them.

The *Sūtrālaṃkāra* (XVI, 65, 66, 70) states:

Striving is chief among the virtuous *dharmas* because based on it [striving] there is subsequent attainment of all those [virtuous *dharmas*]. By striving there is promptly a very pleasant dwelling and success both mundane and supramundane. Through striving one achieves the desired enjoyment in life. By striving those [virtues] get intense purity. By striving those [bodhisattvas] transcend reification and are liberated, fully awakened to the supreme enlightenment.

The striving person is not overcome by enjoyments; not overcome by defilement; not overcome by weariness;[84] not overcome by [small] receipts.

Also, the *Bodhisattvabhūmi* explains:

Nothing else but striving is the chief and best cause for maturing that way all the virtuous *dharmas* that bring about [the bodhisattva's] enlightenment. For that reason the Tathāgatas point to striving for the incomparable rightly completed enlightenment.

The *Pāramitāsamāsa* (IV, 2c–d, 41c–d, 42) puts it this way:

By a bold advance unacquainted with weariness there is no form whatsoever that cannot be obtained.

There is even the arising of assistance to the non-humans, and the obtaining of [all] kinds of *samādhis;* the fact that while activities go on day and night, one suffers no loss of virtues but prospers;[85] and that one is like a full-blown lotus by reason of one's virtues whose purposes surpass human duty.

The disadvantage (of not having it) is as told in the *Sāgara-mati-paripṛcchā:*

> But far away is the enlightenment of lazy men. The lazy man has no giving, and so on, up to, no insight.[86] The lazy man does not have the aim of others.

And also as in the *Smṛtyupasthāna* (*Dharmasamuccaya*, XXX, 58a–b; 59a–b):

> The sole basis of defilements is anyone's laziness. Whoever has a single [bit of] laziness, has no *dharma*.

Thus, in the absence of striving, one passes into the dominion of laziness and becomes destitute of all 'virtuous *dharma*.' So one loses all human aims of temporary states and the final goal.

3) *varieties of striving*. There are two: fundamental varieties and the means of generating striving.

The fundamental varieties are three: armored striving, striving which amasses virtuous natures, and striving which serves the aim of sentient beings.

a) *armored striving*. When the Bodhisattvas engage in striving, they attire themselves as though with armor, a preliminary resolve—an enthusiasm of mind through former exertion, i.e. he thinks, "I shall not abandon my entrance into striving, for a hundred million of three uncountable eons accumulated in days and nights that are as long as a thousand great *kalpas*, to endeavor to dispel the suffering of a single sentient being; and [to endeavor] to consummate enlightenment, being joyful if even a being now dwelling in hell were to become a Buddha — not to speak of a briefer length of time or of whether the suffering is very small." Such (a resolve) is armored striving. Whatever bodhisattva generates just the conviction and just the faith in such a striving, these are very firm — not to speak of his being possessed of that striving if he nourishes the unfathomable cause, the engaging in striving for the incomparable enlightenment! The *Bodhisattva-bhūmi* mentions that there is no difficulty whatsoever in doing what is necessary of difficult practice that the mind might dread, when the action is for (one's own) enlightenment and for another's sake. If one habituates in such a resolve as this, it will be the certainty cause of awakening to the capacity in the Mahāyāna family. Therefore, one should practice (like this).

Besides, the *Pāramitāsamāsa* (IV, 5, 6, 8) has this:

> If for years made up of days that were as long as both limits of *saṃsāra,* and for *kalpas* that were longer due to the piling up of those [years] and equal in number to the drops of water in the ocean, I were to generate one single thought of enlightenment by this bold advance, even so, I would collect the remaining equipment, again dispelling the [discouraging] weariness [by compassion].[87] [5, 6]
>
> By disregarding his own suffering in *saṃsāra,* and developing inconceivable hardness of armor—they say this is the first right acceptance of the avowed heroes with compassionate nature. [8]

That is also armored striving.

Moreover, the *Akṣayamatinirdeśa* has set forth the non-dreading armor and the inexhaustible armor. He should think: "If the elapsed time from beginningless *saṃsāra* to the present were made into a day; and thirty of these into a month; twelve of these into a year; then in a thousand (of these years), may I generate one thought of enlightenment, may I see one Buddha; and by a single such (thought of enlightenment, or seeing a Buddha) equal in number (of such thoughts or seeing) to the sands of the Ganges, may I know the thought and conduct of a single sentient being; and in such manner, may I know the thought and conduct of all sentient beings."[88] This is the armored striving without a superior.

In short, if one is able to generate a single resolve of such kind he easily consummates a limitless collection (of merit) and purifies a bottomless obscuration; and it becomes the best cause for irreversibility (of the bodhisattva).[89] Delighting in such a long space of time, in just that (delight) one quickly becomes enlightened. But when there is no enthusiasm at all for limitless practice or for such matters as the long time, the one who desires to become a Buddha in a short time takes a very long time to become a Buddha, because one has a barrier to production of the wondrous heart force (*sñiṅ stobs*) of the children of the Jina.

Having donned armor of such kind, for what purpose one engages striving is twofold:

b) *striving which amasses virtuous natures.* Because one should rightly accomplish the six perfections, one operates in those.

c) *striving that performs the aim of sentient beings.* It is the striving which operates in the eleven (kinds of) helping.[90]

The means of generating striving. As previously explained, the production, stabilization, and flourishing of all the virtuous natures of the two collections (of merit and knowledge) is dependent upon this; consequently, the procedure of generating this is of great importance. Moreover, it is easy to understand and pleasant to practice according to the text of the great sage Śāntideva, and therefore I shall explain it in his manner. Here, there are four parts: eliminating the unfavorable conditions that hinder striving; amassing a collection of favorable conditions; having taken recourse to those two, the application that engages striving; through that, the method of creating bodily and mental serviceability.[91]

a) *eliminating the unfavorable conditions that hinder striving.* This has two parts—determination of the adversary, and relying on the means of eliminating it.

a–1) *determination of the adversary.* There are two ways to not enter the path. Even seeing that one is able to accomplish, and then not entering; or thinking, "How could I accomplish such a thing," and through timidity, not entering. Besides, there is no accomplishment when one does not direct his mind to his capacity or incapacity, but this does not deserve a treatment since our explanations are meant for the one who aims at liberation.

The first (able to, but not entering) is of two kinds: the lazy man who thinks, "There is still time," and postpones; and, although lacking that (laziness), the man of inferior deeds, who is overcome by attachment to vulgar deeds. So also the *Caryāvatāra* (in VII, 2):

> What is its adversary is said to be — laziness, attachment to vulgarity, discouragement, and self-reproach.

The causes of laziness are: negligence, attachment to the taste of low pleasures, hankering for the pleasure of sleep, and being unbothered by *saṃsāra*. (So, VII, 3):

> Laziness arises because of the craving based on negligence, savoring of pleasure, and sleep; and from lack of unease amidst the sufferings of *saṃsāra*.

Some persons maintain that the first two lines (i.e. "because of the craving based on negligence, savoring of pleasure, and sleep") show the form in which it (i.e. laziness) arises.

a–2) *relying on the means of eliminating it* is threefold.

(1) Opposing the laziness that consists of postponement has three parts:

One contemplates that this body that has been obtained will soon disintegrate and die; that subsequently one will fall into evil destinies; and that later it will be difficult to obtain this favorable (birth) basis.

Then one supposes the laziness which holds that there is time to spare.

Thereupon one generates in his consciousness-stream (the conclusion) that there is no time to spare.

Those three parts have already been explained in the section of the lesser person.

(2) Opposing the attachment to vile deeds is as follows: One observes and contemplates that the sublime doctrine (*saddharma*) engenders limitless joy in this one and in a future life; that profitless chatter, the distractions of jest, and so on, cause the great purpose of this life to be lost; and that one has a purposeless situation of a future life which generates many sufferings; so one should oppose (the vile deeds). (Again, VII, 15):

> You have abandoned this finest joy of Dharma, endless chain of joy. Why do you rejoice in the cause of suffering — distraction, jokes, and so forth?

(3) Opposing discouragement and self-reproach is as follows: When one has in that way opposed the craving for post-

ponement and vile deeds, and has aroused an enthusiasm for the sublime doctrine, this alone does not suffice, for it is necessary to practice the Great Vehicle (*mahāyāna*). Hence, if one shrinks, thinking, "A person like myself cannot practice it," one should dispel that (discouragement). There are three parts to this: opposing the discouragement regarding the attainable, opposing the discouragement regarding the means of attaining it, opposing the timidity regarding the place where one accomplishes after being there placed.

(a) *Opposing the discouragement regarding the attainable.* Should there be an on-going timidity, whereby he thinks, "Since the Buddhahood to be attained involves the exhaustion of all faults and the consummation of all virtues, and since I find it most difficult to accomplish every kind of virtue and to eliminate every kind of fault, then how can a person like myself be able to attain a fruit like that?" this has a great disadvantage because it abandons the generation of the mind (of enlightenment); even if it is not (on-going), from the outset one must oppose that alternative. The method of opposing is this: One thinks, "The truthful Bhagavat and speaker of the genuine—that authoritative person (*pramāṇa-puruṣa*) who does not speak the false or the wayward, has stated that even insects and so forth attain enlightenment; now I having been born as a human have the power of intellect to examine what is to be accepted and what rejected in this fortunate basis, so if I do not abandon my striving, why should I not achieve it," and thus raises his spirit. (VII, 17–19):

> I should not discourage myself, thinking, "How could enlightenment be mine?" For the truth-telling Tathāgata has spoken this truth:
> "There are insects, flies, bees, and likewise worms, by whom the supreme enlightenment difficult to attain has been attained through the power of striving." But I, having been born a human, am able to know the beneficial and the harmful; why, through not abandoning the proper conduct for omniscience, would I not attain enlightenment?

Also, one thinks, "In the past there were the former Buddhas, in the present there are the Buddhas dwelling, in the future there will be those becoming Buddhas; it is not that the path was consummated by a single Buddha. So even a person like myself, proceeding upward ever higher, may pass into Buddhahood," and so contemplating opposes one's timidity. This is the message of the *Ratnamegha:*

> The bodhisattva should allow himself to think this way: "Whoever the Tathāgata-Arhat-Samyaksaṃbuddhas that were manifestly awakened [in the past], that are being manifestly awakened [in the present]. or that will be manifestly awakened [in the future], they were manifestly awakened, are being manifestly awakened, and will be manifestly awakened, by a like means, by a like path, by a like striving, until they are Tathāgatas manifestly awakened. So I too will exert myself that way, will endeavor that way, by a striving shared by all sentient beings, by a striving that supports all sentient beings, to become manifestly awakened to the incomparable right complete enlightenment."

Besides, the *Guṇāparyantastotra* has this:

> By certain [practices] you [formerly] attained the rank of Sugata, and by this [practice] you have fallen into this very vile state. On that account, at the time you have descended into this stricken state you do not disparage yourself. It is not right to disparage oneself because it makes even developing persons timid.[92]

Indeed, that timidity arises by understanding that Buddhahood is a fruit amounting to limitless merits following upon the cause, so at the time of the path it was required to accomplish the merits in limitless ways and to oppose faults in limitless ways. Then, taking oneself into account, the timidity arises. But one should think, "Those limitless merits of the Buddha were accomplished by practicing successively and incisively each tiny portion of the merits in the time of the [path] procedure"; if one thus avoids a faulty understanding of the path, at least for the time being one's timidity will not usually occur. However, someone may respond that one, lacking the good marks, has not acquired certainty in the method of proceeding on the path, or one's understanding of it being sporadic one has not taken it in hand, so it is obscured by a seeming easiness. (To this we say:) when one encounters the (path) procedure it is only required that one be taught just so much of the complete body of the path as arranges its rough steps from the beginning to the end. If we need this much, who can do such (a practice), saying, "One gives it up easily."?

Moreover, it was heard from Śa-ra-ba:[93] Not all the practice of the Bodhisattva is engaged in (Bodhisattva) practice, (like) the easiness to see the arrow in flight. Similarly we don't have the complete (Bodhisattva) practice, so we are not in the state of both timidity and self-deprecation.[94] When we do have the complete (Bodhisattva) practice, there will be a great chance to have both timidity and self-deprecation. That is positively correct. So said Śa-ra-ba.

(b) *Opposing the discouragement regarding the means of attaining it*. If one thinks, "For accomplishing Buddhahood, one must give up feet, hands, and so forth, but I am incapable of such things," one must forbear that much suffering. When one does not engage in the (Bodhisattva) practices, but sticks to self-indulgence, as one cycles in the cycle of life one endures such sufferings as having one's body cut, torn apart, put an end to, and burned; and in these experiences—too numerous to list—even so, one does not accomplish one's own aim. As to the sufferings of difficult practices for the purpose of enlightenment, there is not just the part of the previously mentioned sufferings, but also the part requiring that both one's own aim and the aim of others be accomplished. (So, also, *Caryāvatāra*, VII, 20–23):

> What you say, "I would have to give up hands, feet, and so on," is my fear. It is mine through not examining the confusion between heavy and light. I shall be mutilated, torn apart, burnt, and dispatched not just once, but for uncountable myriads of eons, and yet enlightenment will not occur (on that account). So I have assessed the suffering that consummates enlightenment: it is like the removal of the painful thorn.
>
> All medicines produce their cures through discomfitures! Then, to assail the host of pains, you should forbear a minor one.

As to giving the body, at first, being the time of fearfulness, one does not give it up. But when one trains gradually in the giving, one may turn away the attachment to one's body; and at the time when the power of great compassion flourishes, when there is a great purpose to it, by giving away at the proper time for giving away, there is no difficulty. (Again, VII, 24–26):

> The supreme healer did not provide this possible remedy, although customary. By a gentle procedure he cured the great afflictions.
>
> The guide directs an initial gift of vegetables, and so on. One does that gradually, so that finally one gives away even one's own flesh.
>
> At the time an insight arises that takes one's own flesh as the vegetable, at that time how can there be any difficulty for that one in the donation of flesh and bone!

Granted that some persons are disheartened by the requirement in the Vehicle of Perfections (Mahāyāna) to give away the life of body. What they say, to wit, "It is a path hard to perform," seems well refuted by this text; because as long as one has the idea, "It is hard to perform," one does not give away. But when it is as easy as the donating of vegetables, and the like, one may give away.

(c) *Opposing the timidity regarding the place where one practices, after being there placed*. One may think, "For accomplishing Buddhahood I must perform in the course of innumerable lives in cyclical flow (*saṃsāra*) and during that time be subject to the sufferings of cyclical flow. I just cannot do that." But one should contemplate that the bodhisattva does not experience the fruitional feeling of suffering because one has averted its cause by eliminating sin; and that there is no suffering in one's mind because one steadfastly comprehends that the cyclical flow, being without self-existence, is like an illusion; and that as one flourishes with corporeal and mental joy, even staying in the cyclical flow, one's weariness is pointless. (*Caryāvatāra,* VII, 27–28):

> Because one has eliminated sin, one doesn't suffer; because one is wise, one is not sad. Thus, by deviant imagination and sin, there is harm to mind and body.
>
> The body is happy because of merit; the mind is happy because of wisdom. When one remains in the cyclical flow for the sake of others, what can weary the compassionate person!

And (VII, 30):

> Having thus mounted the chariot of enlightenment-mind that chases away all weariness; and travelling from pleasure to pleasure, what sensible person would be discouraged!

Likewise, the fact that there is staying (in cyclical flow) for immeasurable time does not (itself) give discouragement, because even in a long time there would be no cause for weariness. And because in this (Bodhisattva) way, in the event of a very severe suffering, one would be weary only briefly; while in the event of being free from suffering and being joyful, one would not be weary even in a long time. So says the *Ratnāvalī* (III, 25–27):[95]

> It is hard to forbear pain for even a short time. How much more would it be for a long time! As long as one is free from suffering and is happy, how could one be harmed even in infinite time?
> In one without suffering of body, how is there suffering of mind? One by reason of compassion, mourns the world; and for that reason stays long [in cyclical flow].
> Therefore, do not be discouraged, thinking that Buddhahood is far off. Always endeavor in this—ending faults, and for gaining virtues.

Moreover, one should not be timid, thinking, "For becoming a Buddha one must consummate an infinite collection (of merit and knowledge); as that is very difficult, I cannot do it." Rather one should think, "I have been aroused with longing to attain the infinite merits of the attainable Buddha for the sake of an infinity of deserving sentient beings; and I shall consummate an infinite collection with a view to remaining for immeasurable time [for the purpose," and takes this pledge. Because as long as there is this pledge, whose merit is equal to the sky, in all (situations), whether sleeping or not sleeping, or whether the mind strays or does not stray,—it is not difficult to consummate an infinite collection by constantly collecting. So says the same work (*Ratnāvalī*, III, 15–20):

Just as space, earth, water, fire, and wind, are infinite in all directions, so also, we claim, suffering beings are infinite.

The Bodhisattva, because of compassion for those unlimited sentient beings, decides to draw them out of their sufferings and install them in Buddhahood.

He remaining steadfast that way, rightly taking and holding [the pledge], whether sleeping or not sleeping, and even when careless.

For the sake of the infinite sentient beings, he always collects merit as infinite as the sentient beings. Because of that infinity, it is not difficult for him to attain the Buddha infinity.

Whoever remains for time immeasurable, desiring the immeasurable enlightenment for the sake of the immeasurable embodied beings, performs immeasurable virtue.

For that very reason, even though enlightenment is immeasurable, how would one not attain it, and without delay, by these four immeasurable collections?[96]

Now, if one thinks, "By moving the mind through a most intense love, compassion, and mind of enlightenment, I would attain in brief time Buddhahood for the sake of sentient beings," while this is wonderful (in itself), as long as one is not in their directions, it will take a very long time (for Buddhahood). And if one thinks, "Observing the requirement to learn an infinity of practices and the requirement for numerous difficult practices, who is capable of proceeding like that?" and announces the seeking of a 'near path,' this is an indirect harm to the aspiration mind, and is an on-going i.e. direct harm to the entrance mind (of the bodhisattva). Thus one's capacity in the Great-Vehicle family declines more and more, and it takes even longer to become a Buddha, because one directly contradicts the method of expanding ever more the power of enlightenment mind, and (contradicts) the purport of the Buddha as laid down by Nāgārjuna and

Asaṅga. That being the case, the one who postpones through timidity and who may also be involving oneself in the unbeneficial and ever greater timidity, should properly learn the means of accomplishing enlightenment and raise the spirit of one's discrimination, so that the accomplishment of the aims be as though in one's hand. So the *Jātakamālā* (Story of Supāraga, 10–11):

> Discouragement does not help for getting out of distress. Therefore, enough of your enclosure in low spirits! But by constancy[97] those who are wise in the doing of the requirement surmount difficulties without difficulty. Well then, shake off the discouragement and distress! Resort by action to the opportunity of a requirement, for the spirit (*tejas*) of a wise man, kindled by constancy, is the hand in which one grasps the success of all aims.

Āryāsaṅga states again and again that one must possess both non-timidity while well knowing the methods of practicing in breadth, and non-contentment with merely inferior virtues. In the beginning, persons think they have carved out a large section of the path when what has arisen is a character of virtue that amounts to a semblance of virtue; or even if it be a right one, is one-sided, and they are self-satisfied with their progress. But a person who is learned in both scripture and logic for practicing the essentials of the path, points out that those persons ("self-satisfied"), with only so much, go nowhere. Then, when they understand this, it seems to cause much timidity. The requirement is to seek ever higher without being satisfied with one-sided virtue, and to practice the unlimited points of instruction. But a lack of timidity appears to be extremely rare.

b) *Amassing a collection of favorable conditions*. This has four parts—generating the power of conviction, of constancy, of joy, and of suspension.

b–1) *generating the power of conviction*. Since longing is said to serve as basis of striving, here 'conviction' is longing. The requirement to generate it is as stated (*Caryāvatāra*, VII, 39–40a–b):

> Because I lacked conviction in [longing for] the Dharma in former lives and in the present one, such distress as this happened to me. Who [then] should abandon conviction [longing] in the Dharma!

> The *muni* declared that conviction [longing] is the basis of all the virtues.

How conviction is generated is as stated (VII, 40c–d):

> Moreover, its root is continually the cultivation of a fruit which is [*karma*'s] maturation.[98]

This explains the cultivation as the method giving rise to pleasant and unpleasant fruit from good and bad action (*karma*). Faith (*śraddha*) is said to serve as the basis of longing, because by means of two trusting faiths one generates the two desiderata, to reject and to accept. Furthermore, one should think of the generality of cause and effect and especially the benefit of the Bodhisattva practices and of the disadvantage of transgressing those (bodhisattva practices); this is known from a (previous) section.

Thus after conviction toward the Great Vehicle the entrance through its gateway is a vow to get rid of all one's own and others' faults and to perfect all the virtues. One should think, "If it is required to cultivate a good many eons to purify each fault and its habit-energy as well, and to enhance to its ultimate state each virtue, then even should I not have each fraction of striving that (respectively) gets rid of, or perfects those, I should not allow my fortunate birth to be purposeless," and so contemplating one must personally exhort oneself. (*Caryāvatāra*, VII, 33–36):

> I shall have to destroy immeasurable faults, my own and others'; and it would take a myriad of eons to destroy the faults one by one.
>
> As to the enterprise that eradicates faults, even though one cannot see in me even its fraction, why should not my heart tremble at the dwelling of immeasurable suffering!
>
> Many are the virtues I ought repeat in myself and others; and would not a staying on each virtue among them require a myriad eons?
>
> Never have I stayed repeating even a particle of the virtue. It is amazing that I should render the birth, somehow obtained, to be purposeless!

b–2) *generating the power of constancy.* In whatever one has engaged the striving, one should continue to its conclusion without turning away from it. Moreover, first one should well examine whether it is feasible without involving oneself in the sense of feasibility (already determined); one should get involved if one's capability is apparent; and not get involved if one's capability is not (apparent). It is better to not engage than to discard it in some phase after embarking upon it. The reason is that if one abandons in the middle what one pledged, and repeats this, it becomes an addicted cause to abandon the pledges of training also in another life, thus to increase sin in that life and to increase its fruit, i.e. suffering, in other lives; because when one contemplated doing it formerly, the other virtue was not accomplished; when one turned away from it formerly, its fruit was inferior; and when one did not complete that thing formerly, one did not bring it to perfection. In short, whoever has taken a vow to do something, and does not keep going after starting, creates a hindrance for accomplishing other things. Thus, by reason of the addicted cause, given one's previous pledge, when one (then) takes a vow it is not constant. This is also said (*Caryāvatāra*, VII, 47–48):

> First I should examine the whole thing: Should one start it or not start it? For it is better to not start than to turn back after starting.
>
> Repeating the practice [of breaking the pledge] promotes sin and suffering[99] in another life. Besides, the resultative-time is inferior; and it [the project] was not perfected.

Now, the one who desires to bring one's vow to fulfillment should cultivate three prides (VII, 49a–b):

> The action [to be done], the defilement [to be eliminated], and the capability [to succeed], about these three one should have pride.

Among them, the *pride about action* is as follows: No matter who else is a companion while accomplishing one's own path, one does not depend on him, but accomplishes it entirely by one's self (VII, 49c–d):

> Thinking, "I shall do it just by myself,"—this is the pride about action.

And it is just as said in the *Friendly Epistle* (from verse 52):

> Liberation depends on one's self. It cannot happen that this be done by another as companion.

One should think, "I must accomplish this by myself alone, without hoping for somebody else"; and since this is comparable to pride, it is so (metaphorically) designated here.

The *pride about capability* is as follows: One thinks, "Since the living beings are in the dominion of defilement, they are incapable of accomplishing even their own aim, how much less the aim of others! I am capable of accomplishing my own and others' aim!" (VII, 50):

> This world, dominated by defilement, is not able to fulfill its own aim. I am not incapable like worldly people are. Hence, I shall do this.

Moreover, one should think, "Even though these persons do not stop their pursuance of vile acts, why should I not perform the acts which bring about the excellent fruit?" and having so contemplated, he accomplishes. (VII, 51a–b):

> Another performs a vile act. Why should it also stay in me?

However, when one accomplishes those two (the power of conviction and the power of constancy), one should not accomplish with pride in oneself through deprecation of another, but should regard that one in a kindly way and not mixed with pride (VII, 51c–d):

> If this does not work with pride, then better my pride perish!

Thinking another cannot do it while oneself can do it, is similar to pride. Therefore, it is designated "pride."

The *pride against defilement* is as follows: Thinking, through deprecating all kinds of defilement, "I am victorious over these; and these will never defeat me"; one creates constancy by generating the mental courage to defeat the opposing side (i.e. the defilements) (*Caryāvatāra*, VII, 55):

> I shall triumph over all; none shall defeat me. Such is my pride: Am I not the son of the Victors, the Lions?

When one does not do it like that, one's power declines and even a minor opponent can injure that one (VII, 52; 53a–b):

> Even a crow, upon encountering a dead snake, can act like a Garuḍa-bird. If my mind is weak, even a little temptation will bring it low. When a man is insolent and inactive, are not temptations easily acted [upon]?

It was heard from Śa-ra-ba: Whatever the happiness in abandoning the Dharma, it is not better than previous happiness. If one rejects Dharma in this life, then, starting next life, one will experience endless suffering. One should think like that. If one does not make effort, even the defilements have no compassion for that one. You cannot cultivate the adversary. But you say: "I will finish it by myself." That won't work. Even the Buddhas and Bodhisattvas cannot protect. —Śa-ra-ba said.

If one creates the aforementioned pride, even a great opponent is unable to interrupt it; hence one should generate that pride (*Caryāvatāra*, VII, 53cd; 54ab):

> But when one generates the energetic pride, even a great [temptation] could not defeat it. Therefore, with a steadfast mind I shall destroy the temptations.

Otherwise the practitioner is defeated by temptation; and if one claims to be victorious over the defilements of the three realms, wise persons are ashamed of it (VII, 54cd):

> For me defeated by temptation, the desire to be victorious over the three worlds is a joke!

This concerns the "pride against defilement" because of the claim to defeat defilement when one (merely) criticizes (it). While some commentators explain in a different way from this, we would rather accept the former good wording of the texts. Accordingly, having prevented the expectation toward others, one should don the armour to do it by oneself alone. However, one should think "another person cannot do it, but I can do it," so one should have confidence and determination, such that at the time of performance one contemplates the disadvantage of abandoning the effort in the interval, and overcomes the defilement on that side; while it (the defilement) cannot defeat in one's own direction. Having well considered this, as long as one has not achieved constancy of mind wishing to succeed in all the pledges executed for doing it, one should exert (in that direction).

b – 3) *generating the power of joy*. One generates the striving, so far not arisen, by the power of conviction consisting of keen longing of that sort; and when arisen, so as not to turn away from it, one arouses the power of constancy or the power of pride. Since at the time when one initially engages one engages joyfully; and at the time when one has already engaged, not wishing to cut off the extension of that action, one should generate it with the power of joy which is an unsatiated resolve. Here, as to how one generates in the unsatiated way, it is as stated (*Caryāvatāra*, VII, 62):

> Like one wishing play as a pleasurable result, whatever be the action one should perform, one should be devoted to it, one's joy of doing it unsatiated.

Thus, children engage in playful activity without satiation; and one should work at the arising of such a mental arising. Furthermore, given unsatiation with the fruitional pleasure, one must also not be satiated with the activity which is its cause. This is because how may one speak of certainty that the fruitional pleasure will arise when one practices any activity? [Indeed,] ordinary persons engage in the application with doubt as to whether they will or will not attain the fruitional pleasure (VII, 63):

> Even though one performs a deed for the sake of pleasure, it is unknown whether the pleasure will or will not occur for whom the deed itself is pleasure. How is one happy who does not perform the deed?

Also, for this reason it is not right to be satiated (VII, 64):

> If one is unsatiated with [sense] desires in cyclical flow that are like [tasting] honey on a razor's edge, why be satiated with the [ambrosial] merit that has sweet maturation and is mild?

According to this (verse), if there is no satiation even when practicing the attractive qualities of (sense) desires that have temporary small pleasure while giving much great suffering, like the honey on a sharp razor's edge that serves for a small amount of sweet taste while the tongue licking it gets cut — one should think, why is it right to be satiated with the collection that grants unlimited pleasure during a space of time with the sinless state? and (so) one should generate unsatiated resolve.

Hence, for fully accomplishing the virtuous deeds in whatever one is engaged, when one engages in those one should work at it until one has the mind which is like the elephant oppressed by the sun and which at noontime plunges into a pleasing lotus lake (VII, 65):

> Hence, for finishing a work, [at the outset] one should plunge into the work like an elephant, oppressed at noontime, upon encountering a lake would there [plunge] into the lake.

b – 4) *generating the power of suspension.* Whoever enterprises striving and becomes tired in body and mind, should for a while take rest; because, otherwise, one's fatigue and weariness would later become an interruption to the striving. Also, given that one rested, and then that one's previous striving has culminated, one should not be satisfied with just that, but should apply one's striving to something else that is higher (VII, 66):

> When there is obstruction of weak strength, one should suspend further action; and when one has well completed [the project], one should release it by a desire ever higher.

This "higher" is of great importance, because if one is satisfied with each previous merit, it becomes a great obstacle to attaining the many higher excellences. This teaches the manner of engaging in striving, to wit, when one is over-confident one's application may be tense or over-relaxed; one should avoid both these and be like an elongated river. Thus *śrīmat* Mātṛceṭa (his *Śatapañcāśatka*, II, 21) says:

> The upward movement of your excellences was never relaxed [or over-intensified]; hence in you the increase by degrees of excellences was not differentiated [into either side].

Furthermore, it was heard from Po-to-ba: It is like when told to watch out for a robbery. The watchman of Se-mo-gru-pa took it easy (i.e. was over-relaxed); while the watchman of Byang pa, going for the purpose, preceded [the robbery] (i.e. was tense); and they later told of the robbery. And for example, a louse going for the purpose, not waiting for (the host-prey) to arrive, goes quickly to the goal. A flea comes out, jumps up a while, staying (in the same place, both tense and over-relaxed), so does not go (anywhere). It is like that, he said.

Thus, having determined the three opponent conditions to striving, one should rely upon the adversaries (to those three) and should generate the power of joy that when the overturning (of those three) has not arisen, to be convinced about the conditions consistent with the arising; that when engagement has taken place, to be firm in the cause of no turning away (or, backsliding); that when one has entered upon the activity, to shun an interruption to its continuation. And when one is skilled in the manner of engaging the striving by the power of suspension, it is required to generate the power of exclusive application to striving, so this will be explained.

c) *the application that engages striving*. As to this, how one acts at the time one engages the striving to eliminate what should be eliminated, is as stated (VII, 67):

> Like a man who has entered a sword fight with a trained ["seasoned veteran," "old pro"] enemy, one should guard against the blows of defilement and should resolutely smite the defilements.

For example, during the contending-sword, etc., — with the enemy — the "old pro," which is the skill of repetition in the activity

—one should not plan solely the defeat of the opponent. That is to say, one should perform both acts of skill, namely, defending oneself against the befalling of weapon harm, and in the defeat of the opponent. Accordingly, it is required to engage upon gaining skill in both, namely, 1) during the performer's fight with defilement, the protection against or avoiding defilement's wounding of consciousness in one's direction; and 2) defeat of the opponent through recourse to its adversary. Because, otherwise, say, opposing with an adversary the agency of a single part of defilement, some other defilements could rob some virtuous part, or much sin might spring up in the mind; so it would be difficult to have a progress of virtuous praxis that goes with the two as (mutually) even. Having taken that as example, some people think that for understanding the Dharma, to practice is important. Then they hold only the understanding as essential. While studying, the ignorance of not understanding was removed, but they are defiled by many bad acts and the stream of consciousness becomes spoiled. Some others think that taming the mind is more important than understanding; make meditation the important thing—thus do not care about the adversary to nescience, so do not study the Dharma, and are much deluded about engagement and disengagement and are continually defeated by transgressions.

Accordingly, during the fight with defilement, at the time of contending in battle, if the sword falls from one's hand, one has fear, dread of being slain. Thus, without relaxing, one would at once take hold (of the sword). In the same way, if one loses the mindfulness-weapon that does not forget the meditative supports of engagement and disengagement for what is to be rejected and what accepted, one would fear a falling into evil destiny (*durgati*), so at once one must take recourse to mindfulness (VII, 68):

> Should one drop the sword, being fearful, one would quickly take hold of it. In the same way, should one lose the mindfulness-weapon, fearfully remembering about hell, one should take hold of it.

Nātha Nāgārjuna also speaks of the overriding importance of mindfulness (*Friendly Epistle*, k. 54):

> O lord, the Sugata declared mindfulness regarding the body to be the solitary path [to liberation]. Since the loss of mindfulness will destroy all [virtuous] natures, guard it well by holding it fast.

On whatever object one places mindfulness, one should also well analyze it with insight, while holding it with mindfulness; but mindfulness has no motive to analyze the object independently. Whatever the thing required to be analyzed by insight, one should complete the procedure by using mindfulness and awareness, in general with all cases of engagement and avoidance as explained in the scriptures, and in particular with the individual things to be rejected or accepted according to pledge taken. But one gets nowhere by just using mindfulness and awareness on a single tying of the mind to a meditative object.

According to the illustration: One would endeavor from the outset not to drop the sword in battle; and should it drop—it might happen!—one would at once pick it up, being in a state of genuine fear, the dread of being killed. In the same way, the one cultivating the path should from the outset dread losing the mindfulness that does not forget what it is to be rejected and what accepted; and when one loses it, should at once resort (to it), one's stream of consciousness during the loss of mindfulness being with genuine fear of falling into bad destiny as the fruit of being tainted by transgressions.

Moreover, those who do not bear in mind, "For us to plumb the depths of *karma* and fruit, relying upon guarding—those are profound precepts," may cut off the root of the virtues that delight those skilled in the sublime essence of the path.

Now suppose one thinks: why is it required to observe fearfully even a minor fault and to oppose it immediately without allowing it any continuance? For example, when a poisoned arrow creates only a slight wound on the body, on that account, before long the poison spreads throughout the body; and so it is necessary to extract (the poison) through cutting the wound. Along the same lines, even though a sin does not loom much as a wound in the mind, when one neglects it, quickly it spreads through the mind. Hence, it does not subside, but becomes great. Thus, from the outset one must oppose it so that it does not arise; and should it arise, must immediately cut it out (VII, 69):

> When poison penetrates to the blood, it spreads throughout the body. In the same way, when a fault finds a chink, it spreads throughout the mind.

Well, how does one desirous of defeating the defilement-warrior use mindfulness and awareness? (VII, 70):

> As [in the legend] a man is carrying a vase full of oil; soldiers bearing swords approach him; the least spill will be fatal. Just as he would be fearful, so should be the avowed one [i.e. the Bodhisattva].[100]

According to that (verse), it is required to hold fast (not stumble); this may be known from what is told in the story about Avanti concerning Kātyāyana.[101] When holding fast in that manner, if there should happen to occur, in general, sinful conduct, or, in particular, sleepiness or languor; not giving in to them, one must ward them off at their beginning (VII, 71):

> As when a serpent comes onto the lap, one would get up without delay, so also when sleepiness and languor occur, one should ward them off without delay.

At the mere continuance (of sleepiness, etc.) one should arouse dissatisfaction in that fault. So he should reflect: "Because this happened before, I have wandered in *saṃsāra*; and in particular, having taken the Bodhisattva vow, to stay in the opposing side to what should be learned for it, is staying in detestable manner;" and should reflect: "I resolve that from this time on, this fault will by no means occur;" and afterwards many times apply these two castings of his vow (VII, 72):

> At each occurrence of a fault, one should intensely detest oneself and reflect: "How shall I do it so that this will not happen to me again?"

One should endeavor to deepen such a root, the cause of possessing mindfulness in continuity, namely, one should associate with illustrious guides and illustrious companions; and one should rely on the acts of much hearing, etc. — which are the cause of that (continuity). Along the same lines (VII, 73):

> Thinking, "In what circumstances does the habituation of mindfulness occur?" as its cause one should seek [proper] association or valid acts.

Accordingly, in short, it is of great importance to not mistake the striving stage by the requirement to engage striving, 1) by learning the right analysis of aims, i.e. what is to be rejected and what accepted in the instruction of the Bodhisattva; and 2) by relying with continuous mindfulness on those cognitive objects and in every behavior.

d) *as a consequence of this, the method of bodily and mental serviceability*. This is the power of mastery. Moreover, as was explained in the Awareness Chapter (i.e. *Bodhicaryāvatāra*, Chap. V), there is the requirement-manner which requires the instruction in what the Bodhisattva is supposed to practice; and there is the seeing-manner which takes the vow and does not practice, [wrongly] (seeing) the great disadvantage and the defilement as the enemy. At that time, one should not carry austerity as a burden, but look at it as an ornament. Those are the methods of generating the power of mind. So one first cultivates the engagement therein; then one can ward off all the hesitations that keep one from enabling the virtues of body and mind; then renders (himself) light, rising to the instruction in the Bodhisattva practice (VII, 74):

> Remembering the sermon on heedfulness, one renders oneself light [i.e. rising]; one operates advisedly in everything, even before commencing the act.

Now, what sort of striving will arise by reason of endeavoring that way? As a cotton ball goes that way and comes this way, commanded by the wind; so also one's own body and mind perseveres in virtue, commanded by the impetus of the enthusiasm. Upon following that, striving is well consummated. When this occurs, then the entire aggregate attains felicity (VII, 75):

> As a piece of cotton would go, impelled by the wind for going and coming, so also would one go, impelled by enthusiasm. In this way, magical faculty is consummated.

Even if deeds of such sort be difficult, it is not proper to abandon them, but one must endeavor. Thus *śrīmat* Mātṛceṭa (his *Śatapañcāśatka*, II, 20) says:

> The rank hard to reach is not gained without deeds hard to perform; so thinking, you fostered striving without regard for self.

4) *how one acts at the time of their practice*. Moreover, whoever engages striving must act in possession of the six lustres and proceed in association with the six perfections. Thus, the giving (*dāna*) of striving means to install others in the very state in which oneself is abiding; and the remaining (perfections) are as already explained.

5) *summarizing their goal*. The basis of the praxis, i.e. the remembrance and cultivation of the enlightenment-mind, is the exhortation to train so as to install all sentient beings in striving. Hence one has as scope of aspiration the promoting ever higher and the manner of engaging the striving of the high rank, and works at this. One endeavors in a way comparable to the capacity the beginner has in the manners of training in striving. In particular, one well opposes the timidity which is to be rejected for the unshared striving (i.e. unshared with the beginner). One accomplishes joy for the attainable enlightenment and for all the sentient beings (who are candidates) of the high goal and dispells their suffering. Through the resolve of armored striving, one has enthusiasm in long ages for incalculable collections (of merits) and for unfathomable austerities. And the *Subāhuparipṛcchā* states that with such a magnificent resolve alone one collects

magnificent merits. Hence, one should endeavor that way; for otherwise, one's capacity of the family does not grow at all, and one is continually defiled with many sins; even in other lives it will be very difficult to train in the Bodhisattva practice. But when one understands those matters, even if one does not adopt the procedures exactly, one's mind should take that direction and engage in striving with whatever ability at hand; because, as the *Subāhuparipṛcchā* states, in other lives one will quickly accomplish striving without pain with a short time of troubles.

Perfection of Meditation

There are five parts to the instruction in the perfection of meditation. 1) the actuality of meditation; 2) the means of beginning its cultivation; 3) varieties of meditation; 4) how one acts at the time of its practice; 5) summarizing their goal.

1) *the actuality of meditation*. This is the virtue of a single area of thought that stays on the meditative object without straying elsewhere, as the *Bodhisattvabhumi* states:

> The fixation of thought consisting in a virtuous single area of thought of the Bodhisattvas that is mundane or supramundane, and preceded by hearing and pondering of the *bodhisattva-piṭaka*; and whether it [the fixation of thought] is in the category of calming, the category of discerning, or the category of both of them, i.e. the path proceeding pairwise—this is the actuality of the Bodhisattvas' meditation.

Besides, the *Caryāvatara* (VIII, 1a–b) says:

> When one has in that way developed striving, one should fix one's mind in *samādhi*.

2) *the means of beginning its cultivation*. It will be explained in the section on Calming (the Mind) that one thinks of the benefit of cultivating meditation and the disadvantage of not cultivating it.

3) *varieties*. When one variegates by way of actuality as was previously cited (i.e. *Bodhisattvabhumi*), there are the two—the

mundane kind and the kind transcending it, and a third by categories; to wit, when one variegates by way of function, there is the meditation that creates a pleasant state of body and mind in the present life; the meditation that accomplishes distinct powers;[102] and the meditation that performs the aim of sentient beings. Among them, the first one is the meditations that, given an equipoise on something, generate the cathartic of body and mind.[103] The second is the meditations that accomplish distinct powers in common with Śrāvakas, i.e. the supernormal faculties, the liberations, the totalities, the masteries, etc. The third is the meditation that accomplishes the aims of the eleven (kinds of) help.

4) *how one acts*. Whatever the virtuous *samādhi* one is practicing, one performs it in accompaniment of the six sublimities, and one accomplishes it in union with the six perfections. After some one has stayed in one's own meditation, one's installation of other persons in that (kind) is the gift of meditation; and except for that, they are to be understood as previously explained.

5) *summarizing the goal*. The cultivation, keeping in mind the previous generation of the mind (of enlightenment) which is the basis of the practice, is to encourage all sentient beings toward the non-fluxional meditation, thus exhorting them to the practice. Therefore, having steadily developed that (Thought of Enlightenment), one should make even the higher meditations the object of aspiration, and practice them. When one is unable to perfect such meditations, it is necessary to endeavor time after time in the *samādhi* of single-area thought, and with whatever one's ability, to not abandon the application of practice. If one does not do it that way, one is continually tainted by faults that violate what is to be practiced; and also in other lives finds it enormously difficult to study what is to be practiced, i.e. that engages the many doors of Bodhisattva *samādhis*. While if one does it that way, even in the present life the mind ever less strays elsewhere, while in future lives one has great strength for accumulations of virtue, as is stated in the (scripture) *Subāhuparipṛcchā*; because it is easy to fulfill the Perfection of Meditation when one has pleasure of body and mind and has mental pleasure. Since this is expounded extensively in the section Calming (the Mind), here it is not (further) treated.

Perfection of Insight

There are five parts to the instruction in the perfection of insight. 1) the actuality of insight; 2) the means of beginning its generation; 3) varieties of insight; 4) how one acts at the time of its practice; 5) summarizing their goal.

1) *the actuality of insight*. Generally, insight is the supernal analysis of the features (*dharma*) in the on-going thing being examined. In the present context, it is the insight with skill in the five sciences, and so on. This is told in the *Bodhisattvabhūmi*:

> Whatever supernal analysis of features takes place for understanding any knowable; and, when one has understood any knowable, involves the five sciences, to wit, inner science, logic, medicine, grammar, and the arts — this is the actuality of the Bodhisattva's insight.

The insight which is about to enter is the one before attaining the stage; and the one already entered is the one after attaining the stage.

2) *the means of beginning its generation*. This is thinking about the benefit of generating insight and the disadvantage of not generating it. Moreover, the benefit and disadvantage of whether there is or is not the insight of non-self as it really is, will be explained in the section on Discerning (the Real), so here will be dealt with only briefly matters not treated (there). First, for showing the benefit—it is the root of all virtues of this and later lives, as *nātha* Nāgārjuna sets forth:

> Insight is the root of all virtues, whether visible or not visible. Accordingly, so as to accomplish both, one should embrace insight. It is the great clear realization (*vidyā*), the source of the Dharma ["visible" of the present life], the desired aims ["not visible" of the future life], and liberation. Accordingly, at the outset with devotion one should embrace the great mother Insight.

Insight is like an eye for the five (perfections) giving, etc., according to the *Saṃcaya* (VII, 2):

> Within the time-span one is governed by Insight, the eye is obtained, and its name conferred. For example, a portrait is well nigh

> finished, except for the eye. As long as the eye is not drawn, the fee is not awarded.

As to the way it is required for other merits, for example, ornaments made from gold become superior when studded with sapphire and other gems and are more ravishing than previously; so also, the gold ornaments of the five (perfections) from giving to meditation become more wondrous when inset with the insight capable of deciding between the right and wrong principle; because with this, one renders the five of giving, etc. more pure; like mind-cognition, having decided between fault and merit in the sense objects of the five senses, eye, and so forth, makes them go toward (the meritorious ones) and turn away from (the faulty ones). This is Ārya-Śūra's message (*Pāramitāsamāsa*, VI, 1–2):

> These merits, beginning with giving, shine more with insight as their mistress,[104] like golden ornaments shine with the light of inset gems.
>
> For on behalf of these [five perfections], which have a clear sequence, just insight renders the far-ranging merit suitable to their possible acitivity [*kriyā*], like on behalf of the sense organs, the mind-stream [renders it suitable] to the respective function of their objects.

Likewise, insight is the chief one for the other faculties of faith and so on; and when insight is the mistress, on behalf of giving, faith, etc., one well knows the merits as well as the faults of avarice, etc., and has skill in the means of ending defilement and of promoting merits (*Pāramitāsamāsa*, VI, 4):

> Also, insight is the chief one among the faculties that begin with faith, as is the intellect among the sense organs, for one with that as his mistress knows merit and fault, and so becomes skillful in destroying defilement.

Even though the Bodhisattva give away his flesh to one who asks for it, like taking from a healing tree, he does not alter by reason of discursive thought of pride, timidity, and so on—it is through realizing reality by insight. By insight that observes the trouble of phenomenal life and of quiescence, he purifies morality with a morality that works for the aim of others. Having comprehended with insight the fault of no forbearance and the merit of forbearance, and having tamed his mind, he is not carried away by deviant working or by suffering. Well knowing by insight in what is the point to start striving, there is a great success of the path by engaging therein. The insight based on the method of the principle prepares the best joy and pleasure of meditation that dwells on the meaning of reality. Hence, one depends on insight to purify the five (perfections), giving, and so on (*Pāramitāsamāsa*, VI, 6, 12, 14–15ab, 17):

> But Bodhisattvas with the wide-open eye of insight, having given away their own flesh, experience neither haughtiness nor depression, being without discursive thought like the healing trees.

And,

> But the morality of the wise man, who has seen the fault of phenomenal life's prisons, is not for his own aim. Then, when he desires to eject the whole world, how is it for the aim of others!
>
> But the harm done by others to those endowed with insight become merits of forbearance and create steadfastness, like the many special work-impositions on good-natured elephants [develop forbearance].
>
> Also striving, when alone, ends in fatigue, but in the attending of one whose mistress is insight there arises the great success.

And,

> Since those medications have the best joy and pleasure, how will they be entered by the minds of the ignoble? Those minds are coarse with great accumulations of faults and take the wrong road to insight as though [the wrong road were] the principle.

Even when a Bodhisattva is a king who exercises dominion over the four continents; equipped with the insight of two virtues, given violations he desists from violations, being empowered by the insight-minister to not pass into the dominion of (tempting) sense objects. Likewise, even when he has fervent love upon observing gratifying sentient beings he does not mix that with the slightest passion. Even when a long time in fervent compassion toward the intolerable suffering of sentient beings, while having been pained (in empathy) he avoids the lassitude unenthusiastic toward virtue. Even with boundless sympathetic joy he has no swaying (*ya ya po*) whereby his mind would stray from the (proper) meditative object. Staying a long time in great equanimity (or, impartiality) he is not attracted, even for a moment, to a worldly object. Namely, when he acts with insight, because he opposes with insight the hindrance that renders those (opponents) of equal power (to the four boundless states). That is the message (of *Pāramitāsamāsa*, VI, 43–45):

> For Bodhisattvas, even when powerful kings, do not change their nature to an unnatural state on account of sense objects rivalling those of the gods, given that insight is the mistress as the minister for the merits, to wit: Love (or, friendliness), which has the single taste of service to others, avoiding the colouring of passion; compassion given over to the sufferings of others and that does not get lassitude through the burden of sorrow; not scattering when their mind is sympathetically joyful; and equanimity not attracted to worldly illusion. These and those virtues appear even more lovely when their course of adversaries is blocked by insight.

Moreover, it is as told in the *Varṇārhavarṇe stotra* (V, 23ab):

> [Your speech] does not abandon the true nature, and yet is consistent with convention.

Thus, one need not abandon the true nature where is the great certainty that the focussings that posit sign-sources do not prove even an atom; and one can be consistent, i.e. not contradict convention, where is the deeply held certainty that from the inner and outer causes and conditions severally arise the results. While another may take it as a great contradiction, for a wise person there is no contradiction — they are consistent. Besides, it is as told in the same work (V, 7):

In permitting and prohibiting, Your promulation is sometimes definite, sometimes indefinite. And yet there is no mutual contradiction.

Thus, there are numerous different permissions and prohibitions in the higher and lower vehicles and in the *sūtras* and the *tantras*; and while both of these can be taken into experience by a single person, for a confused person of no discriminative power to search the purport of the far-ranging scripture, there is contradiction; for a wise person, as the result of insight, there is no contradiction. In this way, there are many contradictions to the unwise person that are not contradictions to the wise person. There are many establishments of the two truths, and there are many permissions and prohibitions in the scriptures; but when the uncontradictory purport is analyzed by insight, this is the incomparable praise of insight. In short, all merits arise from insight (*Pāramitāsamāsa*, VI, 39cd 40–42):

What a marvel in this case that this perfection should arise from a mother [i.e. insight] who loves her offspring [i.e. Buddhas and Bodhisattvas]! When just from that as basis should arise the ten superior powers of the *munis*, as well as the other one of unshared beauty, the uncountable jewel heap of virtues.

The *śāstras* that are like an eye in the world, the best treasury of the special arts [*kalā*], various incantations for protection, the separate special establishments of Dharma, the many terms for the path to liberation, and this and that means of benefit for the world that the Bodhisattvas reveal—they all arise through the power of insight.

For the trouble of lacking insight, (the teaching that) giving, etc. (the five Perfections), in the absence of insight are like the lack of an eye, is in the *Saṃcaya* (VII, 1):

Those without guides among the myriads of creatures blind from birth, how can they, ignorant of the path, enter the city? Lacking insight, the five perfections lack the eye; and without a guide they are unable to contact enlightenment.

Therefore, (the five) giving, etc. do not become pure, and one does not acquire the right view (as stated in *Pāramitāsamāsa*, VI, 5, 11, 13, 16, 18a):

> Since they lack insight, the seekers of the fruit have no purity of giving by itself, for they say the gift is for the sake of others, but it remains a design for the sake of profit.

And,

> How can there be purity of morality of one whose darkness has not been dispelled by [the light of] insight; for usually moral rules become defiled by faults of imagination due to lacking insight.

And,

> How can the virtue of forbearance stay in it, when the mind is deluded by wrong insight? It is like fame in a demeritorious king who is reluctant to examine merit and demerit.

And,

> There is no lack of insight on the straight path of mind, which is praised by wise men — there is nothing more subtle than this, when it is not obscured by the faults of lust.

And,

> For the view [i.e. meditation] of the mind that does not persevere with insight is not pure.

In those verses, "fame in a king" means fame in a demeritorious king, i.e. happened at one time, but then is lost. Thus, also, delusion, i.e. the "darkness" of the confused person is not averted as long as the great light of insight does not arise; and is averted when it arises. Hence, it is necessary to endeavor with whatever be one's ability and power to generate insight (as is said, *Pāramitāsamāsa*, VI, 25, 28cd):

> The cognitions of the world which the darknesses cover even at the arising of the thousand-rayed sun, those, when the powerful light of insight arises, are all dispelled, except for their names.

And,

> Therefore, having assembled all his forces, he should advance in the way of insight.

The cause of confusion is: —reliance on bad companions, sloth and indolence, much sleeping, no delight in the respective inquiry-ponderings, so faith in the far-ranging, not knowing but having the pride of thinking that one knows, given to wayward views, and not liking to rely on learned men through fear that such as oneself is incapable (as is said, *Pāramitāsamāsa*, VI, 52–53):

> The cause of delusion is: —slothful and indolent mind, ignoble companions, domination by sleep, a non-reflecting nature, domination by no faith in the wisdom of the *muni*, questions that are held back by false pride; shirking wise men because of a discouragement brought about by personal sorrow, false views with the poison of wayward imagination.

Hence (*Pāramitāsamāsa*, VI, 47ab):

> In order to obtain it [i.e. insight], having approached respectfully a guru as a resort, he should search for the hearing (*śruta*).

According to that passage, having relied upon a learned person, it is necessary to do each hearing (*śruta*) consistent with ability. If not, there would not arise the insight consisting of hearing and the one consisting of pondering. And if so, because one does not know (at the outset) what be the cultivation, and if one has done the hearing, one ponders the meaning of that, so the insight consisting of pondering arises, and because from that grows the insight consisting of cultivation. Besides, *śrimat* Śūra writes (*Pāramitāsamāsa*, VI, 48):

> Like a blind man, one of little hearing does not know the path of cultivation. And what is there for that one to ponder, who lacks that [hearing]? Therefore, one should strive to hear, for insight, with that as basis, grows through pondering and cultivation.

Besides, according to the Venerable Maitreya (*Uttaratantra*, V, 14–15):

> We claim that the discursive thought of the three spheres is the hindrance of the knowable. We claim that the discursive thought of miserliness, and so on, is the hindrance of defilement.[105] Other than insight, there is not another cause of eliminating [the two hindrances]. Therefore, insight is best; and since its basis is hearing, hearing is best.

Also, the *Śikṣāsamuccaya* states (k. 20a–c):

> Be forbearing, seek hearing, then reside in the forest, strive to equipoise [the mind].

And its self-commentary (by Śāntideva) remarks:

> For when at the outset a person lacks forbearance one cannot tolerate weariness and so one's striving is lost. And the one who does not hear does not know the means of *samādhi*, or the means of purifying defilement. Therefore, without weariness, seek the hearing!

Furthermore, the *Nārāyaṇaparipṛcchā* declares:

> Thus, son of the family, insight comes to him that hears. Defilement ends in him with insight. Māra [the temptor] has no opportunity for him devoid of defilement.

Accordingly, for those wishing to practice the Dharma methodically, it is necessary to generate the insight with thorough analysis of the Dharma that is the sublime life of the path; and as its basis, to hear much the incomparable, faultless scriptures and *śāstras*. That being so, it was proved by way of scripture and logic, but some persons do not think these are necessary. Accordingly, they do not attain certainty about the necessity of examining-cultivation of discriminative insight at the time of the practice. The thought that those are not necessary has the fault of deviant certainty. So if one wishes well for oneself, one should reject such an attitude as though it were poison.

It was heard from the Great Yogin: "O Jo-bo-pa, for accomplishing Buddhahood that knows all the aspects (of the world), one needs the equivalent of a zo-load of books.[106] Then, without doing that, just to hold up your hand with closed fist—whatever you have hid (there), that gets you nowhere!"

Phu-chung-ba said: Some persons open large texts and put them on their pillow and say—"We should study [them], but have not even viewed [them]." He said: "If you practice the Dharma without knowing it, how do you do it?"

A monk of Spyan-snga was going with Po-to-ba to see him off (on his journey). Po-to-ba said three times: "You are happy," (and continued:) "You are relying on my spiritual friend [*kalyāṇamitra*], who is like the sky [by far-ranging virtues] which covers the earth, so your mouth doesn't get watery. You don't need to go through the root texts and their commentaries, so you have little work to do. You don't contemplate cause and effect, so your mind is at ease. You think that with a mantra you will accomplish the purpose: Many are satisfied with just that."

It was heard from Śa-ra-ba: "There is no end to training-application as long as one is not fully enlightened; but when one is fully enlightened, there is the end [of training]."[107]

It was heard from Ka-ma-pa: Some people say that when one practices the Dharma, then why do we need to know it? Such attitudes make one slip backwards. This is close to happening to ourselves who study little. We might say: "If we are disciplined, why do we need to know?" But when we practice the Dharma with discipline, we need to know it. We cannot finish in this short life. Therefore, we should not confuse the members of the favorable states. Therefore, we should bear in mind to study continuously. You may think that a meditator is not necessary, and an explainer is necessary; but when the explainer chances to move in sin, only the meditator is necessary. He said.

Thus, it is not proper to lack the insight for the practice or the hearing as its basis, and the requirement is to gain great certainty (about this). Indeed, if one does not gain certainty in the requirement of examining-cultivation at the time of the practice, he has exceeding difficulty to succeed. A person who (merely) retains the scripture with "I am" pride does not take the preliminary steps to the practice and to the real instruction, but takes it like the opposite side of a mountain. For this reason, some people say: In order to speedily attain Buddhahood, one needs to practice; but to benefit the teaching of the Buddha, one needs to study. In this way, they make two separate things out of it—the practice, and the need to study. Thus they speak with contradiction and with great silliness. However, there are no more than two teachings of the Buddha. The former makes known the manner of doing the practice; the latter is putting into practice, after having known. Therefore, if one does errorless practice, one is an excellent doctrine-holder. Then, in order to hold the doctrine of practice without mistake, it depends on the errorless understanding of the scripture.

Given that one first learns many doctrines. Therefore, it is not right to forget them while practicing, and one should put their meaning into application. On the other hand, when at the beginning one does not know the doctrines, one should not be timid. One should strive for either big or small studies according to one's mental capacity. One should not make a different topic of study and practice, because it is necessary to study the topic which one practices. Therefore, one should avoid being one-sided in study or practice. Thus, the one practicing must be certain about the procedure of the beginning Bodhisattva who has the complete path. If there is small force of mind, one should practice that much. If there is already great force of mind, or a small force has been enlarged through development of that step of the path, one proceeds through associating with all the faultless scripture and authoritative commentary. Therefore, it is not necessary to search a study separately.

Therefore, when the precepts are errorless and complete, even if compressed, they have the complete essential for going to all the teaching. When they are elucidated extensively, they complete all the passageways of the path of *sūtras* and *tantras* and of the upper and lower vehicles. Now, as long as such as that is not achieved, it is possible to gain eagerness in just a single side of the practice, but it is not possible to gain certainty in the essential points of the practice that fully completes the body of the teaching. So one should rely upon illustrious friends and companions, listen again and again to precepts that mainly deal with moral rules to espouse, guard the meditative object by dividing into four sessions, fervently implore the gods and gurus. Then one should endeavor in each complete portion of cause for entering by many gateways for amassing the collections (of merit and knowledge) and for purifying obscurations. Thereupon arises the station of deep certainty that increases higher and higher in a distinguished way in the mind.

Also, it was heard from the illustrious ancients: Having caused the previously heard doctrines to exist gracefully in the mind, it is required to again and again give thought to them, judge them, imagine them. In the event of forgetting the doctrines, even though one practices to one-pointedness of mind, one has no success. When the great contemplation is superior, let the teaching be superior; when the great contemplation is middling, let the teaching be middling. As much as is the contemplation, that much should be the knowledge of Dharma; and a movement ever greater is the requirement. Now, a sinful companion may say, "By contemplating that way, when one is firm in certainty knowledge, the thinking in terms of virtue and non-virtue is all discursive thought (*vikalpa*), so it should be rejected," but beneficial friends (*kalyāṇamitra*), who accord with the Dharma, do not talk that way. May one not heed such an opinion and not obey its commandment. Otherwise, faith goes like the beginning of running water (led here and there). If you have not the insight of extensive hearing, you would cry when others cry and laugh when others laugh. Having thought it to be true, where such guidance leads, you would go to that place!

3) *Varieties of insight*. There are three: the insight comprehending *paramārtha* (the ultimate), comprehending *saṃvṛti* (convention), and comprehending what to do for the aim of sentient beings.

The insight comprehending the ultimate is the appraising by way of the generality of the non-self reality, and is the appraising by way of realizing directly. *The insight comprehending convention* is the insight learned in the five sciences, as the *Sūtrālaṃkāra* (XI, 60) states:

> The highest saint, if one has not applied oneself to the five kinds of science would positively not arrive at omniscience. Therefore.

> for vanquishing as well as for assisting others, or for one's own aim of mastery one applies oneself to those [five]

Thus, there is the particular requirement for one to apply oneself to the sciences of grammar and logic for vanquishing disbelievers in the teaching, to the sciences of arts and medicine for assisting the believers, and to inner science (i.e. Buddhist doctrine) for one's own mastery; and even all of them are not a particular (requirement) when applying oneself for attaining Buddhahood.

The insight comprehending what to do for the aim of sentient beings knows the method of sinless accomplishment of the aim of sentient beings in their present and future lives.

4) *How one performs at the time of the practice.* At the time of generating those three insights, one performs while full of the six sublimities and while associated with the six perfections. After oneself is planted therein, the disposing of others in insight is the gift of insight. The other (*pāramitā*-s) were explained in a previous context.

5) *Summarizing their goal.* Even when there is the insight directly realizing voidness, if there is no mind of enlightenment the Bodhisattva practice does not occur. Hence, one should manage to heighten the basis of the practice—the generation of the mind (of enlightenment). Then one may practice even the perfections of the high-level insight by making them the object of aspiration; and may generate the three insights that are the means of perfecting the ultimate great collection of knowledge. One should endeavor from this very time, and it is required to seek hearing; for otherwise, one violates the main thing of training, and is defeated by falling into sin, and even in other lives will take no pleasure in much hearing with consequent lack of ability to study the Bodhisattva's points of instruction. On the other hand, if one endeavors in the various means of generating insight at this time, it prevents the fall into non-application in the present life, and in another life as well, because according to the *Subāhuparipṛcchā* it is the ability to finish happily and easily the perfection of insight.

Nowadays, of the six perfections which are the central element of both the *sūtras* and the *tantras*, the steps of practice going with meditation appear in small measure, while the steps of practice in the other five have disappeared. Therefore, I have briefly expounded the condensed essentials of their practice and the means of generating certainty knowledge. Given this, I shall teach below the extended meaning drawn from the great texts of the steps of practicing calming (the mind) which is the actual meaning of meditation and the steps of practicing discerning (the real) which is the actual meaning of insight — that have as their support-object a noumenon or a phenomenon.

As to how the Bodhisattvas come to enlightenment, they are all enlightened by reliance on the six perfections, as the *Bodhisattvabhūmi* carefully mentions at the end of each of the six perfections. So one should recognize that the Bodhisattvas of past, present, and future have this path of a single passageway. These six are the great ocean of all the virtuous natures (*śukladharma*), whereby they are the incomparable comprisal of the essential points of the practice. This is told in the *Bodhisattvabhūmi:*

> By these six perfections the bodhisattvas rightly attain the incomparable right enlightenment. They are said to be the great stream of virtuous natures, to be the great ocean of virtuous natures. They are said to be the great gift-flow of jewels that cause for all sentient beings the perfection of all the aspects. Thus, moreover, there is nothing else comparable to their fruit, the incomparable right enlightenment — [the fruit] of the unfathomable fulfillment of the merit-knowledge collections.

Study of the Four Persuasions which Mature the Mental Series of Others

There are five sections: the actual meaning of the four persuasions; the reason for positing four; causative agency of the four persuasions; the requirement to rely on them because they persuade the assembly; explaining in some expansion.

1) *the actual meaning of the four persuasions*. *Giving* is the same as was previously explained in the section on the perfections. *Pleasant speech* is what teaches the perfections to the candidate. *Aim inducement* is what induces the candidate to perform the acts, or induces him to rightly adopt those aims in the way explained. *Common pursuits* means that whatever the aims to which others

apply, oneself being stationed therein practices in conformity with those (others). Cf. *Sūtrālaṃkāra* (XVI, 72):

> *Giving* is the same [as "perfection of giving"]. *Pleasant speech* is the teaching of those [perfections]. *Aim inducement* is the inducing [of the candidate to performance]. *Common pursuits* is one's own conformity.[108]

2) *the reason for positing four.* Why is it certain that the persuasions are four? In order that the assembly apply to virtue, at first persuasion must please it; and besides, *giving* of material things relates to benefitting the body. Having pleased it (i.e. the assembly) that way, that it apply to the path, at the outset it must know the way to do it, and one should explain the Dharma by *pleasant speech;* because it (the assembly) should be induced to hold in errorless manner the aim, having abandoned ignorance and doubt. When it knows that way, *aim inducement* induces it to perform virtue. Now, if it were declared, "Though oneself has not practiced, the other person must do this way the engagement and avoidance," (the other) would say, "If you have not practiced that pursuit yourself, why do you ask another to practice it?" and should the reply be, "You must now be corrected by another," (being urged that way) that person would not listen to the practice (advice). And when there is a practice by oneself, (the other) may think, "Whatever the virtue we have taken inside, in that (virtue) both you and myself are made to dwell; hence, by practicing it, it is certain we will have benefit and happiness." In this case, those who have newly entered, and those who have already entered, will be steadfast in not backsliding. So this is the reason for requiring *common pursuits;* cf. *Sūtrālaṃkāra* (XVI, 73):

> A means to assist, to make take hold, to make apply, to work in accordance with, [so] one may know the four persuasions.

3) *the causative agency of the four persuasions.* As to the question, how is the candidate by reason of these four persuasions?—*Giving* renders that one a suitable vessel for hearing the Dharma, because it makes that one pleased with the explainer. *Pleasant speech* gives that one faith in the Dharma to be explained, because

it makes that one know that meaning in particular and dispels that one's doubt. *Aim inducement* makes that one practice according to the Teaching. *Common pursuits* install that one, because they make that one practice for a long time without turning back; cf. XVI, 74:

> By the first, one becomes a fit vessel. By the second, one has faith. By the third, one practices. By the fourth, one applies.

4) *the requirement to rely on them because they persuade the assembly.* The Buddhas explained that they (the persuasions) fulfill the aims of all the candidates and are the good means. Therefore, the persuaders must resort to these; cf. XVI, 77:

> This is the means resorted to by those engaged in attracting the assembly in fulfillment of all the aims of all [candidates]; and is proclaimed "good means."

5) *explaining in some expansion. Pleasant speech* is of two kinds: a) *Pleasant speech equipped with rules of the world* is as follows: Starting out with clear, smiling face free from anger wrinkles, one pleases sentient beings by worldly rules of inquiring as to their health, etc. b) *Pleasant speech endowed with teaching of the genuine Dharma,* is as follows: Starting with generation of faith, morality, hearing, giving away, and insight, for benefit and happiness, one teaches the Dharma to sentient beings.

The gates of *pleasant speech* are as follows: One speaks beneficial words with an untroubled mind even to the enemy who harms him. Without being discouraged, and without getting tired of it, one must tell Dharma stories to persons of dullest faculties so those persons will adopt virtue. When shifty, crafty beings deceive teachers and disciples, etc., one should not hate them, but use helpful and pleasant speech; and one practices even though it is difficult. One teaches the Dharma by telling first of all stories of giving and morality to immature persons so they may eliminate obscuration and be reborn in a good destiny. When beings have a mature stream of consciousness free from obscuration and who are possessed of a happy mental state, the genuine, excellent Dharma to teach them is the four Noble

Truths. When householders and monastery-dwellers are heedless, one preaches the Dharma urging that they be heedful, and gives holy sermons dispelling their doubts.

Aim inducement is of two kinds: maturing those who are not mature, and giving to those that are mature.

Of three kinds, *arranging that they adopt the aim of the present life* is arranging in practice consistent with Dharma the means of gaining, protecting, and promoting the possessions. *Arranging that they adopt the aim of the next life* is installing them among the monastery-dwellers who live by aims after having abandoned their possessions. This gives certainty of happiness in the next life; but it does not give much certainty in the present life. *Arranging that they adopt the aim of both the present and the next life* is arranging that the householders and the monastery-dwellers adopt the mundane and the supramundane non-clinging; because in the present life it generates the corporeal and the mental cathartic; and in the next life one gains right views and Nirvāṇa.

To mention some particular difficulties of *aim inducement:* There is the difficulty of arranging those who have not previously collected virtuous roots to adopt virtue; the difficulty for persons who have a great endowment of possessions, since they are in a situation making them prone to heedlessness; and the difficulty of aim inducement for persons who have repeatedly dwelt in adversary views, since these foolish persons, disdaining this Teaching, do not understand (right) principles.

As to the sequence of *aim inducement:* At first one uses easy precepts for those with immature insight; afterwards, when they are of middling discrimination, one uses middling precepts; and when their insight has become great, one can use the profound Dharma and subtle precepts.

Common pursuits. To whatever (religious purpose) one would turn the other person, oneself should be likewise in it or even more so. If it is that way, one is required, when considering how to perform the aim of sentient beings, to have a resolve not lacking the other's aim; and required to discipline oneself by application to it; cf. *Guṇāparyantastotra:*

> Some persons, not themselves tamed, speak words evincing principles [of engagement and avoidance]. Since they violate their own

> words, they are declared incapable of taming others. Since You have noticed this, and turned your [compassionate] Mind to all the living beings of that time, not tamed by yourself, you strove to tame yourself.

The four persuasions are grouped into persuading by material things, and persuading by Dharma. The first one is the giving of material things; and the remaining three are grouped as persuasion of Dharma. Moreover, they are the *dharma* of consciousness-support (*ālambana*), the *dharma* of practice, and the *dharma* of applying; cf. (*Sūtrālaṃkāra*) XVI, 75:

> The four persuasions go into two groups, by material things and by *dharma;* and by *dharma*, the consciousness-support, etc.

That is the rule for all the Bodhisattvas of the three times when performing the aim of others. Therefore, it is the solitary path (*ekayānamārga*); cf. XVI, 78:

> All those who have been persuaded, will be persuaded, or are now being persuaded are "thus" [*evam*]. Hence, it is the path for maturing the sentient beings.

Now, while the Bodhisattva practice in general is endless, the great summary is the perfections and the four persuasions; because the Bodhisattva should mature the collection (of merit and knowledge) which is the cause of his own Buddhahood, and should mature the mental series of the sentient beings; (because) outside of those two there is nothing (he should do), and those two are accomplished by the perfections and the persuasions. Consistently, the *Bodhisattvabhūmi* states:

> In short, by the perfections one matures the Buddha *dharmas* for oneself; and by the persuasions one matures all the sentient beings. One should understand this as the Bodhisattva's acting of the virtuous natures.

Consequently, here also those two are formulated; and if one wishes to know this extensively he should search it out in the *Bodhisattvabhūmi*.

The rule for how one performs those in equipoise (*samāpatti*) and afterward is stated by the Great Jo-bo:[109]

> The Bodhisattva's practice is the magnanimous six perfections, etc. The yogin should resolutely practice the path of collection, both in equipoise and afterward.

According to that, the beginner Bodhisattva who takes the vow of the Jinaputra while staying on the path of collection is limited to the six perfections, whichever of the two — in equipoise, or subsequent to equipoise — he practices. He will carry on some of the six perfections in equipoise, and will carry on some in subsequent attainment. Calming, which is the character of meditation (*dhyāna*), and Discerning, which is the character of insight (*prajñā*), are cultivated in equipoise. The first three perfections, also some part of meditation and some part of insight, should be carried on in subsequent attainment. Striving occurs in both equipoise and subsequent attainment. Some part of forbearance, i.e. the deep thought (*nidhyapti*) on the profound *dharma*, also occurs in equipoise. The great Jo-bo tells this:

> At the times of equipoise and after-attainment, having cultivated the view of all dharmas, e.g. by the eight similes of illusion, he should mainly purify constructive thought. In subsequent attainment, one should mainly purify constructive thought and practice the [skillful] means. At the time of equipoise, one should cultivate Calming and Discerning in equal parts and in continuity.

Such a practice is wondrous and difficult to do. When those who have not exercised their discrimination hear of it, they become dejected in mind. Even Bodhisattvas are unable to take it into experience in the beginning. Having been informed of it, they contemplate to the extent of fervent aspiration, and later disregard the endeavor and practice according to their habits. So the cultivation is very important; because when they see that they are unable to actually engage, they abandon also the cultivation that exercises discrimination, and very much postpone the pure path; cf. *Guṇāparyantastotra:*

> What practices did You not practice and cultivate for a long time when you adopted bodies? Having heard which, these worldlings get discouraged, and in time practice according to their habits. On that account, they do not cultivate those [attainable] virtues, and it is difficult to expand them.

For that reason, given those who have taken the vow of Bodhisattva, it is compulsory that they engage in the praxis. While given those who have not taken the entrance thought ritually, they should endeavor in the desire for the (Bodhisattva) practice. If one promotes the urging of eagerness and takes the vow, he would then endeavor in very steadfast manner.

From the steps of the path of the great person, finished are the steps of practicing the exercise of the aspiration mind and the general practice of the Jinaputra (Bodhisattva).

Notes

Introduction

1. The original 1978 edition was published by Columbia University Press, New York. In 1979, Motilal Banarsidass, Delhi, put out an Indian edition of the same. Hereafter: *Calming the Mind.*

2. Carol Meadows, *Ārya-Śūra's Compendium of the Perfections: Text, Translation and Analysis of the Pāramitāsamāsa,* Indica et Tibetica 8, ed. by Michael Hahn (Bonn, 1986).

3. Wayman, *Calming the Mind,* p. 9.

4. In the Tashilunpo edition of the *Lam rim chen mo,* the passage occurs at fol. 98b–3.

5. This scripture was apparently important in Sino-Japanese Buddhism, especially for *karma* theory as applied to taking life; cf. the lengthy citations from this text in the Japanese classic, *The Kyogyoshinsho,* translated and annotated by Kosho Yamamoto (Tokyo, 1958).

6. For example, the very first page in the translation of the Bodhisattva section herein has the remark: "there is a one-sidedness of ending of faults and gaining of merit."

7. This commentary has been translated: Mark Tatz, tr., *Asanga's Chapter on Ethics, With the Commentary of Tsong-Kha-Pa* (The Edwin Mellen Press, Lewiston/Queenston, 1986).

8. Various works deal with the two periods of Tibetan Buddhism. One may consult George N. Roerich, *The Blue Annals,* Part One (Royal Asiatic Society of Bengal, Calcutta, 1949), the first two 'books' (i.e. chapters).

9. Cf. A. Wayman, "A Report on the *Akṣayamatinirdeśa-sūtra* (Buddhist Doctrinal History, Study 2)," *Studies in Indo-Asian Art and Culture,* Vol. 6, ed. by Lokesh Chandra (International Academy of Indian Culture, New Delhi, Oct. 1980), pp. 211–232.

10. The writer observed this structure of the *Bodhisattvapiṭaka-sūtra* in the edition of the Peking Tibetan canon (the Japanese photo. edn., abbrev. PTT).

11. For these three periods of Nāgārjuna's life, cf. A. Wayman, "Nāgārjuna: Moralist Reformer of Buddhism," *Studia Missionalia,* Vol. 34, 1985, pp. 63–95.

12. R. Thurman, ed., *Life & Teachings of Tsong Khapa* (Dharamsala, 1982).

13. Cf. *Rgyan-drug mchog-gnyis* (Namgyal Institute of Tibetology, Gangtok, Sikkim, 1962).

14. E. Steinkellner, "*Tshad Ma'i Skyes Bu*. Meaning and Historical Significance of the Term," *Contributions on Tibetan and Buddhist Religion and Philosophy* (Wien 1983), p. 279.

15. A. Wayman's article, "Received Teachings of Tibet and Analysis of the Tantric Canon," was first published in *Indo-Asian Studies,* Part I (1962), ed. by Lokesh Chandra; reprinted in A. Wayman, *The Buddhist Tantras; Light on Indo-Tibetan Esotericism* (Samuel Weiser, New York, 1973); cf. here, p. 236, n. 20.

16. A. Wayman, *Yoga of the Guhyasamājatantra* (Motilal Banarsidass, Delhi, 1977), pp. 116–7, for the six alternatives and the four ways.

17. The rendition 'consignment' for the Tibetan equivalent to the Sanskrit *pariṇāmana* is based on Tsong-kha-pa's explanations in the Bodhisattva section of the *Lam rim chen mo.* Other translators frequently render it 'transference' or 'dedication.'

18. For this deity, cf. the references in Rene de Nebesky-Wojkowitz, *Oracles and Demons of Tibet* ('S-Gravenhage, 1956), especially Chap. XI on this deity. The deity's characteristic hat of white felt accounts for this part of the name, Phying dkar ba. However, the hat of white felt is usually called Phying zhva; this is worn by some Tibetan tribes living at the foot of the mountain Rma-chen-spom-ra, in Amdo. The learned lama Geshe Rabten, who died some

years ago at Vevey, Switzerland, once in a conversation with the present translator explained that this deity was a mountain spirit of Amdo; and that when Tsong-kha-pa in his youth left Amdo for Lhasa, this spirit went along with him, so it became a special protective spirit of the new Gelugpa order (when Tsong-kha-pa started that new order). This may help explain a curious feature in the earlier life of Tsong-kha-pa, as the present writer reported in the biographical sketch included in the work *Calming the Mind and Discerning the Real:* that when Tsong-kha-pa left his native place he never turned back to look. Besides, when Ven. Rizong Rinpoche (Abbot of Drepung Loseling Monastery) visited N.Y. June 7, 1990, he informed this translator of a legend that Tsong-kha-pa recited verses of the *Mañjuśrī-nāma-saṃgīti* as he left Amdo.

Translation

1. Tsong-kha-pa alludes to his two previous sections on the lesser and middling persons (cf. the three kinds of persons depicted in Atīśa's *Bodhipathapradīpa* in our Introduction) and the instruction for them.

2. The three instructions are of Morality (*śīla*), Mind Training (*samādhi*), and Insight (*prajñā*). The celebrated classic of Pāli Buddhism, Buddhaghosa's *Visuddhimagga,* devotes its three parts to the three instructions in that order. For Asaṅga's school, cf. "Asaṅga's Treatise on the Three Instructions of Buddhism," *Buddhist Insight; Essays by Alex Wayman,* ed. by George R. Elder (Delhi, 1984), pp. 353–365.

3. Cf. *Nagarjuna's Letter to King Gautamiputra,* tr. by Lozang Jamspal, Ngawang Samten Chophel, and Peter Della Santino (Delhi, 1978), pp. 40–1 (k. 69): "Having become *Indra,* deserving the reverence [of] the world, [one] will again fall to the earth on account of the force of [previous] deeds; . . ." This topic is expounded by Tsong-kha-pa in the instruction to the lesser person.

4. *Mchan* (BA), Kha, 251a-1: i.e. does not achieve the Dharmakāya.

5. The term *tejas* here can mean that there is light emanating from the person.

6. The sentence involves an important point which *Mchan,* Kha, f. 253a, discusses at length. One does not neglect the "own-aim" of accomplishing the Dharmakāya by engaging in "others' aim." In

fact, it is through pursuing "others' aim" that at the time of becoming a Buddha one is 'omniscient." This is part of the argument against those who claimed that Enlightenment is internal and independent of externally oriented conduct.

7. In Buddhist texts after the time of Dignāga it is usual to interpret the term 'logic' as intending 'direct perception' (*pratyakṣa*) and 'inference' (*anumāna*).

8. The intention of placing here this passage from an important Tantra of the Caryā-tantra class is to show the requirement of having the Bodhisattva vow before there can be a birth of the Mantra vow. As to the restriction showing of the *maṇḍala*, the *Vairocanābhisambodhitantra* — the most important one of the Caryā-tantra class — would agree when it is a matter of the 'Secret Maṇḍala" of the Mind, but allow the viewing of the 'Body Maṇḍala,' the *Karuṇāgarbhodbhava-maṇḍala*, by anyone, and restrict the initiation into it to those with the Bodhisattva vow. Cf. A. Wayman and R. Tajima, *The Enlightenment of Vairocana* (forthcoming from Motilal Banarsidass).

9. The theory of three enlightenments is expounded in the *Abhisamayālaṃkāra* literature. The three are of the Śrāvaka, the Pratyekabuddha, and the Bodhisattva.

10. *Mchan* (BA), Kha, f. 256a–3, 4, has a comparable illustration from the Vajrayāna, where someone lacks the Generation and Completion (stages) of the non-two Deep and Bright (*zab gsal gnyis med*), and just recites (*bzlas pa tsam*) and just stays in the Prajñāpāramitā thought (*phar phyin gyi sems gnas tsam*). For "each tiny part of the path"—e.g. giving (*dāna*). Thus, Tsong-kha-pa refers to a person who forgets the Thought of Enlightenment when he is asleep, and just repeats the words at the beginning of a session; and so it is implied that his practices of giving, etc. are not genuine Mahāyāna practices, just as in the *Mchan* example, the Tantra was not genuine.

11. The three generations are for the three kinds of enlightenment; cf. n. 9, above.

12. For Dharmakāya as one's own aim, cf. n. 6, above.

13. By the "two Arhats" the author apparently refers to the Śrāvakas and Pratyekabuddhas at the culmination of their respective paths.

14. Using the information in Ratnākaraśānti's *Śrī-sarvarahasya-nibandha-rahasya-pradīpa-nāma*, PTT, Vol. 76, p. 12 – 2— "Because they take the sentient beings as object, the four boundless states (*apramāṇa*) of friendliness, etc. are called 'boundless.' When they take as object the sentient beings involved with the realm of desire, they are called the 'pure abodes' (*brahma-vihāra*)." The four are friendliness (*maitrī*), compassion (*karuṇā*), sympathetic joy (*anumodanā*), and impartiality (*upekṣā*). Of the two kinds of the fourth one mentioned by Tsong-kha-pa, the first kind is what Ratnākaraśānti refers to by the frequent terminology of Brahmavihāra. Thus, the second kind, intended in the present context, is not identified with Brahmavihāras.

15. The Sanskrit is mostly available from the *Śrāvakabhūmi* (cf. Appendix of Sanskrit passages). Tsong-kha-pa may have combined two passages from Asaṅga's *Yogācārabhuūmi*, and so referred to '*Bhūmivastu*'.

16. The commentary in the Tanjur on the *Akṣayamatinirdeśa-sūtra* (Derge, *Mdo-'grel*, Vol. Ci, 3b – 5f.) states that the Devaputramara was defeated by the *samādhi* of love (*maitrī*) beneath the Tree of Enlightenment (*bodhivṛkṣa*).

17. The differentiation of persons in Buddhist Abhidharma as to being with flux or without flux ('flux': *āsrava*) is complicated. Speaking generally, while not yet an Arhat, one has 'flux'; when an Arhat, one is 'without flux.' One may consult Vasubandhu's *Abhidharmakośa* for more information.

18. Asaṅga (*Viniścayasaṃgrahaṇī* on *Cintāmayī bhūmi*, PTT, Vol. 111, p. 28 – 3, 4) identifies them with the three standard feelings, painful, pleasurable, and neither painful nor pleasurable. The first one is the misery of suffering (*duḥkha*), and as the painful kind of feeling, it is the misery experienced and acknowledged in the world. The second misery is the misery of change (*vipariṇāma*), and as the pleasurable kind of feeling it is not recognized as misery by ordinary persons. The third misery is the misery of motivations (*saṃskāra*), and as the feeling that is neither painful nor pleasurable, it is also not recognized as misery by ordinary persons.

19. É. Lamotte, *La Somme du Grand Véhicule*, tr. of Asaṅga's *Mahāyānasaṃgraha*, Tome II (Louvain, 1939), pp. 210 – 1, informs that 1. 'good power' means the Bodhisattva has the power of roots of merit (*kuśalamūla-bala*); 2. 'aspired power' means the Bodhisattva has the power of great aspiration (*mahāpraṇidhāna-bala*); 3. 'stead-

fast mind' and 'distinguished going' means the Bodhisattva never abandons the Thought of Enlightenment; cultivates virtuous natures (*kuśaladharma*) exclusively, and so on.

20. Cf. *The Dharma-Samgraha* (New Delhi, 1981), list XIV, *Saptavidhān-uttarapūjā*, praise (*vandanā*), offering (*pūjanā*), confession of sins (*pāpadeśanā*), sympathetic joy (*anumodanā*), asking for instruction (*adhyesanā*), arousing the Thought of Enlightenment (*bodhicittotpāda*), and consignment (to others) (*pariṇāmanā*).

21. Tsong-kha-pa's allusion to a work here does not refer to the *Prajñāpāramitopadeśa* of Ratnākaraśānti, which does not contain the data about twenty-two generations of the Thought [cf. also Shoryu Katsura, "A Synopsis of the Prajñāpāramitopadeśa of Ratnākaraśānti," *JIBS* (Japan), XXV, No. 1, Dec. 1976, pp. 484–7]. However, *Mchan* (NGA), Kha, 273b–2, states that the work is actually the *Munimatālaṃkāra* (Tib. title: *Thub pa dgongs brgyan*), which is by Abhayākaragupta.

22. The twenty-two generations of the Thought of Enlightenment follow the order of the eighty *akṣaya*-s of the *Akṣayamatinirdeśasūtra*, as is pointed out by Alex Wayman, "A Report on the *Akṣayamatinirdeśasūtra*," *Studies in Indo-Asian Art and Culture*, ed. by Lokesh Chandra, Vol. 6 (New Delhi, 1980), pp. 216–7. The first ten generations are the first ten *akṣaya*-s, namely, 1. generating the mind (of enlightenment); 2. resolve (*āśaya*); 3. praxis (*prayoga*); 4. aspiration (*adhyāśaya*); 5–10. the six perfections (*pāramitā*); 11. the four immeasurables (*apramāṇa*) of friendliness, etc.; 12. the five supernormal faculties (*abhijñā*) of divine eye, etc.; 13. the four persuasions (*saṃgrahavastūni*) of giving, etc.; 14. the four special knowledges (*pratisaṃvid*), namely, of meaning (*artha*), of natures (*dharma*), of languages (*nirukti*), of eloquence (*pratibhāna*); 15. the four final resorts (*pratisaraṇa*), namely, on meaning rather than word, on knowledge (*jñāna*) rather than perception (*vijñāna*), on final meaning (*nītārtha*) rather than provisional meaning (*neyārtha*) scriptures, on true nature (*dharma*) rather than a person (*pudgala*); 16. collection of merit and collection of knowledge; 17. the 37 *bodhipaksyadharma*-s, namely, the four stations of mindfulness, and so on; 18. calming (*samatha*), and discerning (*vipaśyanā*); 19. memory (*dhāraṇī*) and eloquence (*pratibhāna*); 20. the four epitomes of the Dharma, *viz.*, "All *saṃskāras* are impermanent," "All *saṃskāras* are suffering," "All *dharmas* are non-self," "Nirvāṇa is quiescent"; 21. the solitary path (*ekayānamārga*); 22. the means (*upāya*).

23. This is verse 42 in the text which Mark Tatz translates with title "Praise in Confession." Its original Sanskrit title is *Deśana-stava*. Cf. *Difficult Beginnings; Three Works on the Bodhisattva Path; Candragomin* (Boston, 1985), p. 45.

24. Mchan, Kha, 279a – 6, 7, does not clarify whether this title is the true title of an actual work, or perhaps a nickname for a different title.

25. Verses 76–80 according to Chr. Lindtner, *Nagarjuniana* (Delhi edition, 1987), pp. 206–9. *Mchan*, Kha, 279a–7, f. was consulted.

26. Verses 82B–84 according to Lindtner, pp. 208–9. *Mchan*, Kha, 280a –4, f. was consulted.

27. Verses 85 – 87A according to Lindtner, pp. 208 – 11. *Mchan*, Kha, 280b–3, f. was consulted.

28. According to *Mchan*, Kha, 283a–6, the human methods can be occupations; and the annotation cites from a commentary these eighteen: 1. merchant (*tshong pa*), 2. potter (*rdza mkhan*), 3. seller of flower garlands (*'phreng rgyud mkhan*), 4. woman selling wine (*chang ma*), 5. shepherd (*phyugs rdzi*), 6. barber (*'breg mkhan*), 7. printer (*'bru mar mkhan*), 8. fortune teller (*phya mkhan*), 9. blacksmith (*mgar ba*), 10. teacher (*śod mkhan*), 11. holder of reins, horserider (*thag pa*), 12. tanner (*ko lpags mkhan*), 13. fisherman (*nya pa*), 14. washerman, dyer (*btso blag mkhan*), 15. worker in bamboo (*smyug ma mkhan*), 16. boatman (*śan pa*), 17. executioner (*gśed ma*), 18. charioteer (*śing rta mkhan*). Another list of eighteen covers human activities, e.g. listening, memorizing, and so on.

29. *Mchan* (NGA), Kha, 284a–7, presents a theory this annotator has heard that the human method is the method of protecting kinsfolk (*gnyen skyong ba'i thabs*) and that the horse method is the method of taming enemies (*dgra 'dul ba'i thabs*). The rationale of this theory seems to be that the human, by already having in his stream of consciousness an attitude of protection, can expand this beyond his kinsfolk to other sentient beings. In contrast, the horse, while able to compete with and dominate others, is unable to tame itself and never will.

30. However, Tsong-kha-pa's own explanation seems to be that the human method is to benefit other sentient beings, while the horse method is to have self-serving thoughts. Thus, it is not just a mat-

ter of looking human or looking like a horse; because the implication is that one could look human and behave as a horse, or worse.

31. This is a scripture included in the Ratnakūṭa collection as no. 9; the Tibetan Kanjur gives the title as *Ārya-daśadharmaka-nāma-mahāyāna-sūtra*.

32. The five cow products (*ba byung lnga*) are presented in the three-volume Tibetan dictionary published in China, the *Bod rgya tshig mdzod chen mo*, p. 1802. They are the five not yet fallen upon the ground: 1. urine, 2. dung, 3. milk, 4. butter, 5. curds.

33. According to *Mchan*, (JA), Kha, 286a – 5, this is to represent the Buddha among the Three Jewels.

34. *Mchan* (JA), Kha, 286a – 6, this is to represent the Dharma among the Three Jewels.

35. *Mchan*, Kha, 286b–2: "seven members" of the *Bhadracaryā*. The Tibetan Tanjur has five commentaries on this celebrated verse work, namely, by Nāgārjuna, Dignāga, Śākyamitra, Bhadrāpana, and Vasubandhu. Using the commentary by Lcang-skya Khutukhtu Lalitavajra, ed. with an intro. by Lokesh Chandra (Namgyal Institute of Tibetology, Gangtok, Sikkim, 1963), we find the list on p. 18, in agreement with the seven given above (n. 20), with slightly different wording, to wit, no. 4, 'sympathetic joy' is with the merits (of others); no. 5, 'asking for instruction' is here 'exhorting that the Wheel of the Doctrine be set in motion'; no. 6, 'arousing the Thought of Enlightenment' is here 'imploring (the Buddha) not to pass away into Nirvāṇa'; and no. 7, 'consignment (to others)' is here 'consignment of the roots of virtue' (*kuśalamūla-parināmanā*). The alternate statement of no. 6, which removes the explicit mention of arousing the Thought of Enlightenment, apparently goes with the position in Tsong-kha-pa's text that all seven members precede the generation of the Thought of Enlightenment, and are aimed at that generation.

36. Also the term for the vow, *saṃvara* (Tib. *sdom pa*) means 'firm,' 'holding together,' thus not falling apart in the stream of consciousness.

37. *Mchan* (JA), Kha, 290a – 5, possibly explains the 'doubling' as the guardian Vajrapāṇi and his thousand-guardian retinue. The king who turns the wheel, i.e. has in subjection all the creatures, may

well be the demonic being who in representations of the 'Tibetan Wheel of Life' is shown as holding the wheel. Or JA's comment might mean that for each inimical force there is a guardian to counter, so the 'doubling.'

38. Of these two spirits, the *yakṣa* (male) is understood as malevolent — the female form tempting; and the *kinnāra* is a composite spirit, usually with animal head and human body. For the first, cf. Ram Nath Misra, *Yaksha Cult and Iconography* (Delhi, 1979). For the second, cf. *Gandharvas & Kinnaras in Indian Iconography* (Dharwar, 1951).

39. Here 'incantations' (S. *mantra*) goes with the male deities, 'charms' (S. *vidyā*) goes with the goddesses. In the present context, the *mantra* could be credited with protective power, the *vidyā* with curative power; cf. A. Wayman, "The Significance of Mantras . . . ," in *Buddhist Insight; Essays by Alex Wayman*, ed. G. R. Elder (Delhi, 1984).

40. Cf. Ferdinand D. Lessing and Alex Wayman, trs., *Mkhas grub rje's Fundamentals of the Buddhist Tantras* (The Hague, 1968), p. 201, for the set of three rites for siddhis, the Appeasing, Prosperity, and Terrible rites (*karma*).

41. Cf. Lessing and Wayman, *Mkhas grub rje's*, pp. 201–2, for the various *siddhis*. Here, the term 'shared' would mean shared with all the Buddhist Tantras, of which there are four classes.

42. "Bodhisattva family": *byang sems rigs*, with *byang sems* taken as abbreviation of *byang chub sems dpa'* (S. Bodhisattva).

43. Cf. Wayman, *Calming the Mind . . .* , p. 83, "Here 'contamination' is the habit-energy [*vāsanā*] abiding in the stream of consciousness that is capable of generating ever higher subjective illusion; . . . " And Tsong-kha-pa there cites Ratnākaraśānti's *Prajñāpāramitopadeśa* that this 'contamination' is eliminated by 'discerning' (*vipaśyanā*).

44. Cf. Wayman, *Calming the Mind . . .* , p. 150. "The contamination of body and mind is the uselessness for service exactly as desired in accomplishing virtuous deeds of body and mind." Its opponent is declared to be the 'cathartic' (*praśrabdhi*) of body and mind.

45. The bad destinies (*durgati*) are usually stated as three in number — of animals, hungry ghosts (*preta*), and hell beings. Tsong-kha-pa has discussed the various sufferings of these destinies in his

foregoing section on the 'middling person,' e.g. at f. 138a – 1, he cites Vasubandhu's *Saṃbhāraparikathā* on this matter. For a further class of bad destiny, that of the 'not-gods' (*asura*) he cites Nāgārjuna's *Suhṛllekha,* k. 102, namely, at f. 138a–4, that they have mental pain by hating the gods.

46. The expression 'cyclical flow' is to render the Sanskrit term *saṃsāra*. At f. 124a – 3, Tsong-kha-pa cites Candragomin's *Śiṣyalekha,* k. 18, starting *saṃsāracakram,* i.e. "wheel of cyclical flow." Soon, at f. 131a – 6, the author cites the *Lalitavistara* (Lefmann ed., p. 175.7f.): "Dying [here] and moving [beyond], [and again] the act of dying and transmigrating, always separated from the beloved, precious folk, . . ."

47. Cf. Lessing and Wayman, *Mkhas grub rje's,* p. 193, for the times of the watches for rites. The three day periods are as follows: "The morning interval is from the moment when half of the sun disk emerges until it casts a man-sized shadow. Noon is the eighth or ninth *chu tshod* (approx. forty-five minute period, one-quarter of a watch). The afternoon interval is from the moment when there remains a man-sized shadow until half of the sun disk is submerged." The three of the night apparently go by the same system, creating two adjacent periods at dawn and at dusk.

48. *Mchan* (JA), Kha, f. 295a – 3, explains the place as where Tsong-kha-pa teaches in brief the "gate of strong *karma*" (*stobs ldan las kyi sgo*). In fact, this happens in the section on the 'middling person' in the part when treating the theory of *karma*. After the explanation of what is called "path of act" (*karmapatha*), namely the ten acts, three of body, four of speech, and three of mind, the author treats the important topic of the good and bad acts that are not included in the traditional "path of act." This topic is found in the *Abhidharmakośa* in Chap. IV, after verse 66. *The Mchan* edition of the *Lam rim chen mo* has this passage at Kha, 151b–5: *stobs ldan gyi las kyi sgo bsdus te bstan pa'o.*

49. The traditional source of information about prophecies to Bodhisattvas and others and withholding prophecies from some persons is found in the scripture *Śūraṃgamasamādhisūtra,* which was translated into French and richly annotated by Étienne Lamotte (Bruxelles, 1965). Cf. a selection in Wayman, "Eschatology in Buddhism," *Studia Missionalia,* Vol. 32, 1983, esp. 88–90. There were four types: (1) The prediction concerning the persons who has not yet aroused the mind of enlightenment. (2) The prediction con-

ferred on the person who has just aroused the mind of enlightenment. (3) The withheld prediction. (4) The prediction made in the presence of the one who has the forbearance toward the non-arising natures (*anutpattikadharmakṣānti*.

50. Cf. F. D. Lessing, "Miscellaneous Lamaist Notes, I: Notes on the Thanksgiving Offering," *Central Asiatic Journal*, II:1 (1956), 58–71; meant to supplement the article on the topic by Johannes Schubert, "Das Reismandala. Ein tibetischer Ritualtext, herausgegeben, übersetzt und erläutert," in *Asiatica, Festschrift Friedrich Weller* (Leipzig, 1954), pp. 584–609.

51. Cf. Mark Tatz, *Asanga's Chapter on Ethics With the Commentary of Tsong-Kha-Pa* (Lewiston/Queenston, 1986), pp. 187–190.

52. The two appear to be those the author explicitly mentions below, to wit, "the non-abandonment of aspiration thought" and "the non-abandonment of the sentient beings."

53. There is no information available to the translator about this Sūtra. Possibly it is an alternate title for some canonical work, and possibly it was cited by some canonical commentator and only known to Tibetan authors by such citation.

54. Tsong-kha-pa apparently refers to the terminology of four powers for generation of the Thought of Enlightenment, which he had discussed early in this Bodhisattva section.

55. Cf. our introduction for a brief treatment of the two kinds of the Thought of Enlightenment. There is more information in Lobsang Dargyay, "The View of Bodhicitta in Tibetan Buddhism," *The Bodhisattva Doctrine in Buddhism*, edt. and intro. by Leslie S. Kawamura (Waterloo, Ontario, Wilfrid Laurier University Press, 1981), pp. 95–109. Dargyay utilized Tsong-kha-pa's *Gser phreng*, his great commentary on the *Abhisamayālaṃkāra*, and the writings of Mipham. The reader should understand that generation of the Thought (*cittotpāda*) is the "conventional mind" because generated, and whether it is an "aspiration" or a "mind-based perception." Dargyay does not well treat the absolute kind of Thought. According to Abhayākaragupta's *Munimatālaṃkāra* (PTT, Vol. 101, p. 168.1 – 6), It "is non-fluxional insight (*anāsrava-prajñā*) that all the *dharmas* are non-arising." Hence, the absolute Thought of Enlightenment cannot be generated, or constructed, and presumably applies to the last three Bodhisattva stages when the Bodhisattva is irreversible. Tsong-kha-pa insists that one must first

generate the Thought of Enlightenment; otherwise there would not be for that person an absolute Thought of Enlightenment.

56. Tsong-kha-pa identifies the Sūtra as the *Triskandhaka*, which the *Bhāvanākrama Three* (ed. by Giuseppe Tucci, Rome 1971) cites (p. 23.6 – 10) as the *Puṇyaskandhapariṇāmanā*, with footnote *phung po gsum* which agrees with *Triskandhaka*.

57. The three spheres are the giving, the gift, and the recipient.

58. Cf. Alex Wayman, *Calming the Mind and Discerning the Real* (New York, 1978), pp. 220–221, where Tsong-kha-pa points out that one is muddle-headed when thinking there is a conflict between the two Truths.

59. To give another example of what is meant: If a person were told that when he gets up in the morning, washes, and then partakes of food—that it is just the way he imagines it but that in reality (or in absolute truth) it does not happen like he thinks it does—and then that person would say, then I shall stop doing those things!

60. For the comment on the "unconstructed" that it goes with "voidness," cf. Mchan (BA), Kha, f. 309a–4. But according to the *Vairocanābhisambodhi-sūtra* in the work, A. Wayman and R. Tajima, *The Enlightenment of Vairocana* (forthcoming Motilal Banarsidass, Delhi), citing the Tibetan Chap. XX, "Instructing the Bodhisattvas," it would be the "unconstructed morality" (*asaṃskṛta-śīla*), controlled by the 'means' (*upāya*) and 'insight' (*prajñā*). By 'means' is of course meant the first five Perfections.

61. Mchan (JA), Kha, f. 309a–6, points out that what is meant is a person lacking the 'means' (*upāya*), i.e. the first five Perfections, and would practice only 'insight' (*prajñā*).

62. The Tibetan term *kha na ma tho ba* is equivalent to the Skt. *avadyā*. According to the *Abhidharmakośa* (de La Vailee Poussin's translation, Chap. II, 170–171, the two sins would be the *ahrīkya*, a lack of conscience in the commission of sin; and the *anapatrāpya*, a lack of indignation when others commit sins. According to Th. Stcherbatsky, *The Central Conception of Buddhism* (Calcutta, 1961), p. 87, one of these is present in every unvirtuous moment of consciousness, the *akuśala-dharma*.

63. Cf. Jikido Takasaki, *A Study on the Ratnagotravibhāga* (Roma, 1966), p. 189, n., informing that this scripture is Chap. XXXII of the *Avataṃsaka*, and is also translated into Chinese as an independent Sūtra.

64. The passage seems to be a condensation of the more extended Sūtra passage; cf. Etienne Lamotte, *L'Enseignement de vimalakīrti* (Louvain, 1962), Chap. II, 12, pp. 138–140; also Robert A. F. Thurman, *The Holy Teaching of Vimalakīrti* (The Pennsylvania State University Press, 1978), pp. 22–23; also Charles Luk, *The Vimalakirti Nirdesa Sutra* (Shambala, 1972), pp. 18–19. The Tathāgata body is identified as the Dharmakāya.

65. The author means that part one goes through the present Bodhisattva section and through the subsequent two parts called "Calming the Mind" and "Discerning the Real," for which see A. Wayman, *Calming the Mind and Discerning the Real*, and its p. 425, where Tsong-kha-pa presents a brief introduction to the Vajrayāna, which is what is meant here by part two. Of course, he has written a large work, the *Sngags rim chen mo* in amplification of that part two.

66. In the Tatz translation (n. 51, above), the rite of taking the vow starts p. 139, and the discussion which Tsong-kha-pa alludes to, involves the remainder of his commentary going to p. 261 of the translation.

67. The two collections are of merit (*puṇya*) and knowledge (*jñāna*). The three instructions are of morality (*śīla*), mind training (*samādhi*), and insight (*prajñā*).

68. Cf. Har Dayal, *The Bodhisattva Doctrine in Buddhist Sanskrit Literature* (London, 1932), pp. 285–288, pointing out that the *Daśabhūmika-sūtra* teaches that the four Persuasions in their given order are respectively emphasized during the first four Bodhisattva Stages. Now, as this scripture also emphasizes the six Perfections respectively in the first six Stages, with the other Perfections represented fractionally in each of the six, it follows that this scripture finds a kind of connection between the four Persuasions and the Perfections. Of course, the first Stage, emphasizing Giving (*dāna*) immediately agrees with the first Persuasion, that of giving. The second Stage, emphasizing Morality (*śīla*) would go with the second Persuasion, that of pleasant speech. Tsong-kha-pa's remark, "Taking its point of departure in the six perfections, it instructs the candidates (*vineya*)," suggests the connection, since the term *vineya* 'to be trained' goes with the word *vinaya*, the disciplinary code of Buddhism. Thus, the Perfection Morality, with the other Perfections fractionally represented, fortifies the "pleasant

speech." The third Stage, featuring Forbearance (*kṣānti*), would go with "aim inducement" — installing others in the precepts; and this seems reasonable. Even the fourth Stage, emphasizing Striving (*vīrya*), seems to agree with the persuasion of common pursuits, since one must oneself accomplish what the other person aims at. This position apparently agrees with the Tsong-kha-pa's citation below of the *Mahāyāna-Sūtrālaṃkāra* (XVI, 3), except for the fourth Perfection, Striving. This verse takes the first three Perfections as the "aim of others," and the last two, Meditation (*dhyāna*) and Insight (*prajñā*) as "one's own aim," with Striving (*vīrya*) as the substratum of both. But Tsong-kha-pa explains that all six Perfections serve for "aim of others" and "own aim." So when he in fact classifies his exposition of the six Perfections as with one's own aim of perfecting Buddha natures, and then presents the four Persuasions as with the aim of others, it must be that this is for convenience of exposition, while not in disagreement with the other doctrines.

69. This remark means that the scriptures *Bodhisattvapiṭaka-sūtra* and *Akṣayamatinirdeśa-sūtra* fill up the contents of the six Perfections but do not show their mutual relations or how one may clsssify them in various ways. Then the *Mahāyāna-Sūtrālaṃkāra,* whose verses are attributed authorship of Maitreya in Tibetan literary tradition, shows how to classify the six in various ways.

70. *Mchan* (BA), Kha, f. 314a–4: "no pettiness" in giving material things; the morality of "no injury"; the forbearance of "bearing with injury"; the striving that "never tires of performance" in the association with sentient beings; by recourse to Meditation, the "bringing joy" to chosen persons by exhibition of supernormal faculty; by recourse to insight, "speaking good words," i.e. the Illustrious Dharma, or removing the doubts of sentient beings.

71. *Mchan* (BA), Kha, f. 314b–4: "not delighting in possessions," i.e. not seeking them with craving, and not paying attention to them; given that, by adopting morality, the "intense devotion" to protecting (sentient beings); "no weariness" after forbearing the suffering occasioned through the "two," sentient and non-sentient beings; with enthusiasm for those foregoing virtues, "the *yoga* without discursive thought" of Meditation and Insight; "this in short," i.e. so cultivating, so walking the path of those six, in short, amounts to "the Supreme Vehicle."

72. *Mchan*, Kha, f. 326b–3, simply repeats the *Lam rim chen mo* words, without comment. Lozang Jamspal suggested to the present translator that it was, for example, signs of special natural events like earthquakes, regarded as "good luck," or "virtue."

73. This is an alternate name—but invariably the title when quoted—of a Mahāyāna scripture preserved in both Tibetan and Chinese, with title in the Tibetan Kanjur, *Ārya-bodhisattva-gocara-upāya-viṣaya-vikurvāṇa-nirdeśa*. It has been translated into English as part of a doctoral dissertation by Lozang Jamspal at Columbia University, and expected to be defended by Fall 1991. In Tibetan books it is cited as *Bden pa po'i le'u*.

74. The place in the *Abhidharmakośa* in Chap. IV, k. 115, and Vasubandhu's commentary thereon.

75. These stipulations are clearly meant for the later candidates, who cannot be expected to duplicate the Viśvamtara former life of the Buddha, depicted in Sānchī. This Bodhisattva gave everything away, including his household; cf. Alfred Foucher and Jeannine Auboyer, *Les Vies anterieures du Bouddha* (Paris, 1955), pp. 328–329.

76. This is Asaṅga's exegesis of his seventeen *bhūmis*, probably the exegesis of his chapter on *Dāna-pāramitā*.

77. The seven orders of the *Prātimokṣa* are: monk (*bhikṣu*), nun (*bhikṣuṇī*), male novice (*śrāmaṇera*), female novice (*śrāmaṇerikā*), pupil monk (*śikṣamāṇā*), layman (*upāsaka*), laywoman (*upāsikā*).

78. In the Tatz translation (n. 51, above), the eleven ways of helping sentient beings occupy pp. 121–132. Tsong-kha-pa here especially follows the Vinaya author Guṇaprabha as well as Bodhibhadra. See below, n. 82.

79. *Mchan* (BA), Kha, f. 344a–6, says this means the two Bodies, hence both the Saṃbhogakāya and the Nirmāṇakāya of the Buddha.

80. The four powers are evidently those introduced toward the end of the path for the lesser person, earlier in the *Lam rim chen mo*. There, the basic terms occur in a citation of the *Ārya-Caturdharmanirdeśa*, which occurs in Śāntideva's *Śikṣāsamuccaya* — and so Sanskrit is available. The four are headed by the remark— "Maitreya, there are four *dharmas*, possessed of which, a Bodhisattva great being, overcomes the sin which had been accumulated." *Mchan* (BA), Kha, f. 172a–b, points out that the term 'Bodhisattva'

means one has realized his own aim; and 'great being' has realized the aim of others. The implication, therefore, is that the Bodhisattva here teaches the four to lesser persons ("ordinary persons"), and in the further discussion Tsong-kha-pa calls each a 'power' (*stobs*). The four from the scripture are: 1. the practice of self-reproach (*vidūṣaṇāsamudācāra*); 2. the practice of the opposite (*pratipakṣasamudācāra*); 3. the power of expiation (*pratyāpattibala*); 4. the power of a refuge (*āśrayabala*). According to Tsong-kha-pa's explanations at that place, the first of these involves confession, e.g. according to a procedure in the *Suvarṇaprabhāsottama-sūtra* (its Chapter 3) or the Confession before the thirty-five buddhas of Confession: and can have three possible results (*phala*), (Tib. *rnam smin*, S. *vipāka*), (Tib. *rgyu mthun*, S. *niṣyanda*), or (Tib. *bdag po'i*, S. *adhipati*), namely, maturation, naturally resulting, or controlling. The second power is explained as having six ways of proceeding, the first being the reading of certain scriptures, such as the *Prajñāpāramitā*. The third power seems to be a sincere revulsion from the sins committed by body, speech, and mind. The fourth power seems to be refuge—for the ordinary person; and cultivation of the Thought of Enlightenment—for the Bodhisattva.

81. The two mentioned are second and third of the 'four degrees of penetration'; cf. Alex Wayman, "Buddhism," in *Historia Religionum*; Vol. II, Religions of the Present (Leiden, 1971), pp. 437–438, where the explanations of the four are given from the *Abhidharmakośa*, from the *Abhisamayālaṃkāra* tradition, and from the subcommentary on the *Mahāyāna-Sūtrālaṃkāra*. The four are Warmth, Summits, Forbearance, Supreme Mundane Natures. Since Tsong-kha-pa mentioned the Stage of Praxis (*prayoga-mārga*), he probably intends the *Abhisamayālaṃkāra* explanations. In this case, when the reality of the external world disappears, the meditator is in Forbearance and is said to be liberated from rebirth in the three evil destinies. The point made by Tsong-kha-pa is that in being so liberated from bad destiny, the person still has not eliminated the non-virtuous seed which is a cause of bad destiny. The conclusion is that this seed is unable to sprout—presumably in the foreseeable future.

82. The Tatz translation (cf. n. 78, above) is helpful, but for the present note, to give the basic list of eleven—omitting the many subdivisions, especially of the first one—it was necessary to refer to the Sanskrit of Asaṅga's *śīla* chapter, and also to refer to the Tsong-

kha-pa precious expansion in his work found in Vol. Ka of his collected works. There is no problem about the first six, which are: 1. helping those needing help; 2. helping those deluded as to the need; 3. helping those who have already helped (the performer); 4. giving refuge to those in fearful danger; 5. relieving the suffering of those afflicted with suffering; 6. helping those who are destitute. No. 7 in Tsong-kha-pa's text at f. 22a – 3 is meant for those who want a reliance in a place (*gnas la sten par 'dod pa rnams*). The Bodhisattva assembles a group of such persons in a place where he can furnish them either material goods or confer the Dharma. He does this just with compassion, and not seeking a reward. No. 8 is meant for those who want a common mind (f. 22b – 4: *sems mthun pa 'dod pa*). For this the Bodhisattva must first recognize of persons their expectation (*bsam pa*) and basic nature, and so adapt his mind to theirs, that they live as he lives, and they practice as he practices. It seems that Nos. 7 and 8 are respectively the 1st and 4th of the four Persuasions, presented at the end of the Bodhisattva section. The remainder are: 9. helping those who have engaged rightly; 10. helping those who have engaged wrongly; 11. helping those who need to be frightened into right conduct.

83. *kiṃ vīryaṃ kusalotsāhas*. My rendition 'striving' for *vīrya* will, I believe, be fully justified by the treatment in this section devoted to *vīrya-pāramitā*. The word *vīrya* is properly translated as 'strength,' 'energy,' and the like in numerous contexts of Indian literature. But here it has a different meaning.

84. The rendition 'weariness' means being weary of the same thing. Once the Dilowa Gegen Hutuhkntu explained to me that this term (Tib. *skyo ba* for Skt. *kheda*) does not mean 'fatigue' (as it is frequently rendered) but 'tired' in the sense of being 'fed up with,' as when one eats the same food all the time.

85. This is the only place — as far as the translator knows — where the translation of the verse must depart, although not significantly, from the way it was rendered into Tibetan, something like "while fruitful activities go on day and night." Years ago when Caro Meadows was doing her dissertation on Ārya-Śūra's *Pāramitāsamāsa* at Columbia University, we discussed this verse. Now he work is published: *Ārya-Śūra's Compendium of the Perfections* (Bonn 1986). For the present rendition, I accept the reading *avadyā* (vile i.e. activities); and correct the obvious corruption *mauśalī* into feasible *pauṣṭhikam*, 'prosperous.'

86. This means one would lack all six Perfections.

87. In verse IV,6, the Tib. 'by compassion' is not in the original Skt. but adds a significant element. The Tibetan's extra words *byang chub dam pa* 'the illustrious enlightenment,' not in the Sanskrit, are a repetitive awkwardness in rendering the verse into the Tibetan language.

88. The author here summarizes the passage from the *Akṣayamatinirdeśa-sūtra* as it is cited in *Śikṣāsamuccaya* (vaidya ed., p. 149.32 to p. 150.6). Here 'inexhaustible armor' is *akṣaya-saṃnāha*, and 'non-dreading armor' *anavalīna-saṃnāha*. The term *anavalīna* has a special use; cf. Edgerton's *Buddhist Hybrid Sanskrit Dictionary* under 2 *avalīyate* (p. 74). He says the Pāli *an-olīna* means 'not shrinking, not downcast.' The Tibetan *zhum pa*, here rendered 'dreading' or 'shrinking,' I later usually render as 'timid,' to indicate the timidity, i.e. shrinking, in the face of what seems an overly difficult task.

89. The term 'irreversibility' (Skt. *avaivartika-tva*) occurs in the *Aṣṭasāhasrikā Prajñāpāramitā*, especially its Chap. 17 on the attributes, tokens, and signs of irreversibility, where it means a state reached by the Bodhisattva whereby he does not turn back from his goal of enlightenment. Later, when the theory of the ten Bodhisattva stages became widely accepted in Mahāyāna Buddhism, 'irreversibility' was ascribed to the last three of the ten stages.

90. Cf. the list of eleven in n. 82, above.

91. For the author's meaning of 'serviceability' see A. Wayman, *Calming the Mind and Discerning the Real*, pp. 150 – 151, where, in brief, 'serviceability of body' is the ease of action, and 'serviceability of mind' is the ease of mind in applying right mental orientation.

92. This work is in the Bstod (Praises) section of the Tibetan canon. The author's name is preserved in Tibetan, Dkon-mchog-'bangs, which can be Sanskritized as Ratnadāsa. The Tibetan canon preserves a commentary on this work by Dignāga.

93. Śa-ra-ba (A.D. 1070 – 1141) is an early transmitter of the stages of the path.

94. The rendition 'self deprecation' is for the phrase *khyad du gsod pa*, according to the native Tibetan dictionary *Brda dag ming tshig gsal ba* by Dge-bshes chos-kyi-grags-pa (Peking edition), p. 84, entry *khyad du bsad pa*.

95. No Sanskrit is extant for chap. III of Nāgārjuna's *Ratnāvalī*.

96. The "four immeasurable collections" are the four 'immeasurables' — love (*maitrī*), compassion (*karuṇā*), sympathetic joy (*anumodanā*), and impartiality (*upekṣā*).

97. The phrase "by constancy" (for Sanskrit *dhairyāt*) should be rendered into Tibetan *brtan byas na*. However, both the Tashilunpo edition and *Mchan* edition, Kha, f. 376b–6, have the corruption *brten byas na*.

98. *Caryāvatāra*, verse VII, 40, was earlier cited in the *Lam rim chen mo* at f. 115b–4.

99. Vidhushekhara Bhattacharya, in his Sanskrit-Tibetan edition, *Bodhicaryāvatāra* (Calcutta, 1960), points out (p. 127, n.) that the Tibetan translation, rendered "sin and suffering" (for the Skt. *papād duḥkhaṃ ca*), follows the *Pañjikā* commentary on the *Caryāvatāra*. Perhaps the Sanskrit ablative was temporal, i.e. "after sin."

100. One version of the story is in A. Wayman, *Analysis of the Śrāvakabhūmi Manuscript* (Berkeley, 1961), pp. 122–123. It is about the "belle of the land" and a crowd praising her. Then a person approaching with a full bowl of oil was threatened that he must bring that bowl of oil near the "belle of the land" and the crowd and not spill a drop lest the executioner following directly behind will cut off his head. The moral of the story is that of course this person will pay no attention to the "belle of the land" or to the crowd of people but only to the bowl of oil so that it will not spill a drop. The bowl of oil was explained as the mind itself. For some literary and oral parallels to the story, see M. B. Emeneau, *Kota Texts*, Part One, Univ. Calif. Publ. Linguistics, vol. 2, no. 1 (1944), 5–7.

101. Lozang Jamspal thinks that this is the story of Kātyāyana's plan to preach in Ujjain (which was in the state of Avanti). When informed of a danger there from ruffians, Kātyāyana said, "If they kill me, I will be liberated from this body," whereupon the Buddha said: "Then go there and preach the Dharma!" As *Mchan* (NGA), Kha, f. 385a–2, starts its version of the story, it involves a place where Buddhism had not so far penetrated.

102. The term *guṇa* of the Sanskrit language is invariably translated into Tibetan as *yon tan*, but that Sanskrit term has several meanings. In Buddhist texts it is frequently used to contrast with faults (Skt. *doṣa*), in which case it means a virtue or virtues. However,

sometimes this term means a 'virtuality' or 'distinct power.' See the evidence for this in A. Wayman, *Delvings in Logic* (Bhandarkar Oriental Research Institute, Poona, 1987), Lecture One: "The Term Guṇa—a Problem in Communication," pp. 20–23. The reason that this meaning of 'distinct power' applies to the present case is that the author will now use the Tib. term *yon tan* for the various powers that *dhyāna* is credited with yielding.

103. Cf. A. Wayman, *Calming the Mind and Discerning the Real*, index, under the word 'cathartic.'

104. I adopted the rendition 'mistress' from Carol Meadows, *Ārya-Śūra's Compendium of the Perfections*, her translation of this verse, and several others.

105. The Tashilunpo edition (f. 275a–3) and the *Mchan* edition (Kha, f. 395a – 7) for this verse agree with the reading *rnam rtog* (*vikalpa*) going with *kleśāvaraṇa*. The Sanskrit edition by E. H. Johnston of the *Ratnagotravibhāga* has the incorrect reading *vipakṣa*. *Mchan* (BHA), Kha, f. 395a–7 to 395b–1, states that there is a difference of interpretation of the "hindrance of the knowable" between the two Mādhyamika schools. The Svātantrika school claims that it is the realistic imputation of *bya byed* (i.e. of deed, *kṛtya;* and agency, *kāritra*), e.g. of gift and giving. The Prāsaṅgika claims that it is the realistic imputation of six evolving cognitions (*'jug shes drug*) and the sense objects as independently real, and the resulting 'habit-energy' (*vāsanā*). Again, the "hindrance of defilement" is said to be the basic defilements (*kleśa*) and the secondary defilements (*upakleśa*).

106. The word *zo* is written *mdzo* (in transcription). This animal is a cross between a yak and a cow.

107. *Mchan* (prob. JA), Kha, f. 396b – 3: As long as the person has not experienced the *Sūraṃgama-samādhi* (the Samadhi 'going of a hero'). This is consistent with the *Vairocanābhisambodhi-tantra*, 6th chap., where the new Buddha is called "O, hero!"; cf. A. Wayman and R. Tajima, *The Enlightenment of Vairocana*, in press, Motilal Banarsidass, Delhi.

108. Cf. n. 82, above, indicating that the nos. 7 and 8 of the eleven kinds of helping are respectively the 1st and 4th of the four Persuasions. This observation seems confirmed by the *Sūtrālaṃkāra's* concise depictions of the four Persuasions. In a different interpretation,

no. 7 is all four Persuasions. Besides, the *Bodhisattvapiṭakasūtra*, Peking ed. (PTT Vol. 23), p. 89.2–8: " 'Common pursuits' is consignment to the Mahāyāna (/ don mthun pa ni theg pa chen la bsngo ba'o /). This suggests that the Mahāyāna kind of 'consignment' (*pariṇāmana*) pertains to the 4th Persuasion.

109. "Great Jo bo" is of course Atīśa, also called Dīpaṃkara Śrī-jñāna. For much information about this celebrated teacher in Tibetan history, cf. Alaka Chattopadhyaya, *Atīśa and Tibet* (Calcutta, 1967).

Bibliography for the Sanskrit Passages

Abhisamayālaṃkāra: *Abhisamayālankāra-Prajñāpāramitā-Upadeśa-Śāstra*; the work of Bodhisattva Maitreya, ed. by Th. Stcherbatsky and E. Obermiller. *Bibliotheca Buddhica*, XXIII (reprint of 1929 edition; Osnabrück, 1970).

BK One: The Sanskrit and Tibetan Texts of the First Bhāvanākrama; Giuseppe Tucci, *Minor Buddhist Texts*, Part II (Roma: Instituto Italiano per il Medio ed Estremo Oriente, 1958), pp. 187–282.

BK Three: Third Bhāvanākrama; Giuseppe Tucci, *Minor Buddhist Texts*, Part III (Roma: Istituto Italiano per il Medio ed Estremo Oriente, 1971), pp. 1–31.

Bodhisattvabhūmi: *Bodhisattvabhūmi*, ed. by Unrai wogihara; Tokyo, 1930–6; ed. by Nalinaksha Dutt (Patna: K. P. Jayaswal Research Institute, 1966).

CA: *Bodhicaryāvatāra of Śāntideva, with the Commentary Pañjikā of Prajñākaramati*, ed. by P. L. Vaidya (Darbhanga, 1960).

Daśabhūmika-sūtra: *Daśabhūmikasūtra*, ed. by J. Rahder (Paris: Paul Geuthner, 1926).

Dharmasamuccaya, XXX: *Dharma-samuccaya*; 3e partie, chap. XIII–XXXVI, by Lin Li-kouang; revised by André Bareau, J. W. ae Jong and Paul Demieville (Paris: Adrien Maisonneuve, 1973).

Jātakamālā: The Jātaka-mālā, by Ārya-Śūra; ed. by Hendrik Kern (Harvard Oriental Series, Vol. One, 1943).

The Kāśyapa Parivarta: Cf. *Mahāyāna Texts Translated into Western Languages,* compiled by Peter Pfandt (In Kommission bei E. J. Brill, Köln, 1983), pp. 43–44.

Prajñākaramati's Commentary: *Bodhicaryāvatārapañjikā,* ed. by Louis de La Valiée Poussin, Ghent, 1902; or the Vaidya edition, cf. "CA," above.

PS: *Pāramitāsamāsa,* by Ārya-Śūra; ed. by A. Ferrari, *Annali Laterenensi* vol. X (1946), pp. 19–60; or the work of Carol Meadows, our Introduction, n. 2.

PV: *Pramāṇavārttikam* of Ācārya Dharmakīrti, with the commentary 'Vṛtti' of Ācārya Manorathanandin, ed. by Dwarikadas Shastri (Varanasi, 1968).

RA: *Nāgārjuna's Ratnāvalī,* by Michael Hahn (Bonn, 1982).

SA: *Mahāyāna-Sūtrālaṃkāra,* ed. by Sylvain Lévi (Paris, 1907).

Samādhirājasūtra: Gilgit Manuscripts, Vol. II, 3 parts, ed. by Nalinaksna Dutt (Srinagar, 1941, 1953, 1954); or as ed. by P. L. Vaidya (Darbhanga, 1961).

Samcaya (or, *Samcaya-gāthā*): *Prajñā-Pāramitā-Ratna-Guṇa-Saṃcaya-Gāthā;* Sanskrit and Tibetan Text ed. by E. Obermiller ('S-Gravenhage, 1960); or as edited by Akira Yuyama (Cambridge University Press, 1976).

Śatapañcāśatka: The Śatapañcāśatka of Mātṛceṭa, by D. R. Shackleton Bailey (Cambridge, at the University Press, 1951).

Śikṣ: Śikṣāsamuccaya of Śāntideva, ed. by P. L. Vaidya (Darbhanga, 1961).

ŚL: *Śiṣya-lekha,* by Candragomin, ed. by I. P. Minayeff, in Russkoe Arckheologicheskoe Obschchestvo; Vostochnoe Otdielenie; Zapiski, Vol. IV (1889), Publ. St. Petersburg, 1890, pp. 44–52.

Śrāvakabhūmi: Śrāvakabhūmi of Ācārya Asaṅga, ed. by Karunesha Shukla (Patna, 1973); also, cf. Alex Wayman, *Analysis of the Śrāvakabhūmi Manuscript* (Berkeley, California, 1961).

Uttaratantra: Ratnagotravibhāga Mahāyānottaratantraśāstra, ed. by E. H. Johnston (Patna, 1950).

Sanskrit Passages for the Citations in Their Order of Occurrence

/ lokārthasādhanavidhāv asamartharūpaṃ yānadvayaṃ samavadhūya sa pūrvam eva /
/ kāruṇyadeśitapatho munirājayānam ātasthivān parahitaikarasasvabhāvam // PS, VI, 65 //
/ svapnopamāni vigaṇayya sukhāsukhāni saṃmohadoṣakṛpaṇāṃ janatāṃ ca teṣu /
/ ātmārtha eva gurutaṃ katham asya yāyād vyāpārabhāram avadhūya parārtharamyam // PS, VI, 67 //
/ lokārthasādhanapare jinarājavaṃśe prajñānimīlitanayeṣu pariskhalatsu /
/ cittaṃ narasya karuṇāmṛdu kasya na syāt tanmohadoṣaśamanāya dṛḍhaṃ ca vīryam // PS, VI, 73 //
/ svayam ghāsagrāsaṃ paśur api karoty eva sulabhaṃ yadṛcchā labdhaṃ vā pibati salilaṃ gāḍhatṛṣitaḥ /
/ parasyārthaṃ kartuṃ yad iha puruṣo 'yaṃ prayatato tad asya svaṃ tejaḥ sukham idam aho pauruṣam idam // Ś., 100 //
/ yad ālokaṃ kurvan bhramati ravir aśrāntaturagaḥ sadā lokaṃ dhatte yad agaṇitabhārā vasumatī /
/ na sa svārthaḥ kaścit prakṛtir iyam eva mahatāṃ yad ete lokānāṃ hitasukharasaikāntarasikāḥ // ŚL, 101 //
/ avidyādhūmrāndhabhramaparigatavyākulagatipradīpte duḥkhāgnāu patitam avaśaṃ vīkṣya bhuvanam /
/ sphuradvahnijvālā pramathitaśiroveṣṭananibhā yātante ye 'trādbhutā iha puruṣās te sukṛtinaḥ // ŚL, 102 //
/ prajñāviśuddhikaram uttamayānam etat sarvajñatā tadudayā hi mahāmunīnāṃ /

/ lokasya yā nayanatām iva saṃprayāti dīptāṃśumaṇḍalatalotpatitā prabheva // PS, VI, 69 //

/ bhavacārakabandhano varākaḥ sugatānāṃ suta ucyate kṣaṇena /

/ . . . bhavati smodita eva bodhicitte // CA,I,9 //

/ adya buddhakule jāto buddhaputro 'smi sāṃpratam // CA, III, 25cd //

/ tad yāpi nāma kulaputra bhittam api vajraratnaṃ sarvapravisiśistaṃ suvarṇālaṃkāram abhibhavati / vajraratnanāma ca na vijahāti, sarvadāridryaṃ vinivartayati, evam iva kulaputra āśayapratipattibhinnam api sarvajñatacittotpādavajraratnaṃ sarvaśrāvakapratyekabuddhaguṇa-suvarṇālaṃkāram abhibhavati, bodhicittanāma ca na vijahāti, sarvasaṃsāradāridryaṃ vinivartayati / *Maitreyavimokṣa* in *Śikṣ*, 9.2.

/ bodhicittaṃ hi kulaputra bījabhūtaṃ sarvabuddhadharmāṇām / *Gaṇḍavyūha* in *Śikṣ*, 6.28.

/ bījaṃ yeṣām agrayānādhimuktir mātā prajñā buddhadharmaprasūtyai / *Uttaratantra*, I, 34ab.

/ na bodhisattvapraṇidhir na caryāpariṇāmanā /

/ uktāḥ śrāvakayāne 'smād bodhisattvaḥ kutas tataḥ // RA, IV, 90 //

/ prajñayā na bhave sthānaṃ kṛpayā na śame sthitiḥ / *Abhisamayālaṃkāra*, I, 10a–b.

/ sattvaratnaviśeṣo 'yam apūrvo jāyate kathaṃ /

/ yat parārthāśayo 'nyeṣāṃ na svārthe 'py upajāyate // CA, I, 25 //

/ . . . sādhus tena samaḥ kutaḥ /

/ kuto vā tādṛśaṃ mitraṃ puṇyaṃ vā tādṛśaṃ kutaḥ // CA, I, 30bcd //

/ teṣāṃ śarīrāṇi namaskaromi yatroditaṃ tad varacittaratnaṃ / CA, I, 36ab /.

/ saddharmakṣīramathanān navanītaṃ samutthitam // CA, III, 31cd //

/ . . . balaṃ tu pāpasya mahat sughoram /

/ taj jīyate 'nyena śubhena kena saṃbodhicittaṃ yadi nāma na syāt // CA, I, 6bcd //

/ yugāntakālānalavan mahānti pāpāni yan nirdahati kṣaṇena / CA, I, 14ab /

/ śiraḥśūlāni sattvānāṃ nāśayāmīti cintayan /

/ aprameyeṇa puṇyena gṛhyate sma hitāśayaḥ // CA, I, 21 //
/ kim utāpramitaṃ śūlam ekaikasya jihīrṣataḥ /
/ aprameyaguṇaṃ sattvaṃ ekaikaṃ ca cikīrṣataḥ // CA, I, 22 //
/ kadalīva phalaṃ vihāya yāti kṣayam anyat kuśalaṃ hi sarvam eva /
/ satataṃ phalati kṣayaṃ na yāti prasavaty eva tu bodhicittavṛkṣaḥ // CA, I, 12 //
/ cittotpādaḥ parārthāya samyaksaṃbodhikāmatā / *Abhisamayālaṃkāra*, I, 18ab /
/ punar aparam, bhadanta śāradvatīputra, bodhisattvānāṃ mahākaruṇāpy akṣayā / tat kasya hetoḥ / pūrvaṅgamatvāt /tad yathāpi nāma, bhadanta śāradvatīputra, āśvāsāḥ puruṣasya jīvitendriyasya pūrvaṅgamaḥ / evam eva mahāyānasamudāgamāya bodhisattvasya mahākaruṇā pūrvaṅgamā / *Akṣayamatinirdeśasūtra* cited in *BK One*, p. 187.
/ kim ārambhā mañjuśrīr bodhisattvānāṃ caryā / kim adhiṣṭhānā / mañjuśrīr āha / mahākaruṇārambhā, devaputra, bodhisattvanaṃ caryā sattvādhiṣṭhānā / *Gayāśīrṣa*, cited in *BK One*, p. 187.
/ tathā hi tayā preryamāṇā bodhisattvāḥ svātmanirapekṣā ekāntena paropakārārthatayā, atiduṣkaradīrghakālike 'pi saṃbhāropārjanapariśrame pravartante / tathā coktam āryaśraddhābalādhāne / "tatra karuṇayāpi sarvasattvaparipācanārthaṃ na tat kiṃcit sukhopādhānaṃ yan na parityajati" iti / ato 'tiduṣkare pravartamāno na cireṇaiva sambhārān paripūryāvaśyam eva sarvajñapadam adhigacchati / tato buddhadharmānāṃ karuṇaiva mūlam / *BK One*, pp. 187–188.
/ na bhagavan bodhisattvenātibahuṣu dharmeṣu śikṣitavyam / eko dharmo bhagavan bodhisattvena svārādhitaḥ supratividdhaḥ kartavyaḥ / tasya sarvabuddhadharmāḥ karatalagatā bhavanti / katham ekodharmo / yad uta mahākaruṇā / mahākaruṇayā bhagavan bodhisattvānāṃ sarvabuddhadharmāḥ karatalagatā bhavanti / tad yathā bhagavan yena rājñaś cakravartinas cakraratnaṃ gacchati / tena sarvo balakāyo gacchati / evam eva bhagavan yena bodhisattvasya mahākaruṇā gacchati / tena sarve buddhadharmā gacchanti / tad yathā bhagavan *āditye udite sattvāḥ karmakriyāsu pracurā*

bhavanti / evam eva bhagavan mahākaruṇā yatroditā bhavati tatrānyabodhikarā dharmāḥ kriyāsu pracurā bhavanti / *Dharmasaṃgīti* in *Śikṣ*, 151.15–21. (The part underlined does not agree with the Tibetan, "Just so, Bhagavat, *when the life organ is present the other organs are present.*")

/ samyaksaṃbodhibījasya cittaratnasya tasya te /
/ tvam eva vīra sārajño dūre tasyetaro janaḥ // *Śatapañcāśatka*, k. 19 //

/ śreṣṭhino gṛhapater ekaputraka iṣṭaḥ kāntaḥ priyo manāpo 'pratikūlo darśanena sa ca dārako bālabhāvena nṛtyann eva mīḍhakūpe prapateta / atha te tasya dārakasya matṛjñatayaḥ paśyeyus taṃ dārakaṃ mīḍhakūpe prapatitam / dṛṣṭvā ca gambhīraṃ niśvaseyuḥ śoceyuḥ parideveran / na punas taṃ mīḍhakūpam avaruhya taṃ dārakam adhyālamberan / atha tasya dārakasya pitā taṃ pradeśam āgacchet / sa paśyetaikaputraṃ mīḍhakūpaṃ prapatitaṃ dṛṣṭvā ca sīghrasīghraṃ tvaramāṇarūpa ekaputrakādhyāśayapremānunīto 'juguptamānas taṃ mīḍhakūpam avaruhyaikaputrakam abhyutkṣipet / iti hi sāgaramate upamaiṣa kṛta yāvad evārthasya vijñaptaye / kaḥ prabandho draṣṭavyaḥ / mīḍhakūpa iti sagaramate traidhatukasyaitad adhivacanam / ekaputraka iti sattvānām etad adhivacanam / . . . / matṛjñātaya iti śrāvakapratyekabuddhayānīyānāṃ . . . etad adhivacanaṃ ye saṃsāraprapatitān sattvān dṛṣṭvā socanti paridevante na punaḥ samarthā bhavanty abhyutkṣeptum / śreṣṭhī gṛhapatir iti bodhisattvasyaitad adhivacanaṃ . . . / The *Sāgaramati* cited in *Uttaratantra*, pp. 47–48.

/ praghātitāḥ prāk ca mamātha sarve / aham viśastā ca purā bhavadbhiḥ /
/ sarve amitrā vadhakāḥ parasya / kathaṃ tu vā jāyati rāgacittam // *Candrottarā* in *Śikṣ*, p, 47.28–29.

/ api coktaṃ bhagavatā / nāham tam sulabharūpam samanupaśyāmi / yo 'nena dīrghasyādhvanotyayān mātā vā pitā vā bhrātā vā bhaginī vā ācāryo vā upādhyāyo vā gurur vā gurusthānīyo veti / Asaṅga's *Śrāvakabhūmi;* cf. S. Shukla, p. 379; but he omits from the Bihar MS the words right after *taṃ: sa tvaṃ*, the *tvaṃ* (read *tvāṃ*) governing the *sulabharūpaṃ*. Tsong-kha-pa's citation is somewhat more ample, suggesting that it occurs elsewhere in the *Yogācārabhūmi*. Or, it may be that he is simply transmitting the citation as it occurred in earlier Tibetan 'path' literature.

/ tān ārjavaṃ javavivartanadṛṣṭanaṣṭān āvartamadhyapatitān iva vīkṣyamāṇaḥ /

/ saṃsārasagaragatān apahāya bandhūn ekaḥ prayāti yadi nāsti tataḥ kṛtaghnaḥ // ŚL, 95 //

/ aṅkasthitena śiśunā vivaśena yāsāṃ pītaḥ payodhararasaṃ praṇayānuyātaḥ /

/ tanniṣphalapracuradurlalitaikabhājaḥ ko nāma dasyur api hātum ihotsaheta // ŚL, 96 //

/ yā saṃsthitato 'yam udare 'pi kṛtāvakāśo yāḥ snehaviklavadhiyaḥ ślatham enam ūhuḥ /

/ tā duḥkhitā aśaraṇāḥ kṛpaṇā vihāya ko nāma śatrur api gantum ihotsaheta // ŚL, 97 //

/ kleśonmatto 'tha mohāndhaḥ prapātabahule pathi /

/ skhalan pade pade śocyaḥ para ātmā ca sarvadā //

/ . . . samānavyasanāj janāt / *Śikṣ*, p. 195.5–7 //

/ yāvanti pūjā bahuvidha aprameyā yā kṣetrakoṭīnayutayabimbareṣu /

/ tāṃ pūja kṛtva puruṣuvareṣu nityaṃ saṃkhyākalāpī na bhavati maitracittaḥ // *Samādhirājasūtra*, Chap. 32, k. 277 //

/ imās ca suvarṇabhāsoktā maitrīkaruṇāgarbhā gāthāḥ sarvā ādarataḥ samanavāhṛtya bhāvayitavyā antaśo vacasāpi / suvarṇabhāsottamadundubhana śāmyantu duṣkhās trisahasraloke / apāyaduṣkhā yamalokaduṣkhā dāridyaduṣkhās ca iha triloke // *Śikṣ*, p. 119.1–4 //

/ yadā ca duḥkhitabālapriyeṣv iva duḥkhoddharaṇecchākārā svarasavāhinī sarvasattveṣu samapravṛttā kṛpā bhavati / tadā sa niṣpannā bhavati / mahākaruṇāvyapadeśaṃ ca labhate / *BK One*, p. 190.

/ tasyaivaṃ kṛpābhyāsabalāt sakalasattvābhyuddharaṇapratijñayānuttarasaṃyaksaṃbodhiprārthanākāram ayatnata eva bodhicittam utpadyate / *BK One*, p. 190.

/ gantukāmasya gantuś ca yathā bhedaḥ pratīyate /

/ tatha bhedo 'nayor jñeyo yāthāsaṃkhyena paṇḍitaiḥ // CA, I, 16 //

/ sakalajagato hitāya buddho bhaveyam iti prathamataraṃ prārthanąkārā cetanā tat praṇidhicittam / yataḥ prabhṛti saṃvaragrahaṇe . . . vartamānāḥ saṃbhāreṣu dṛśyante tat prasthānacittam / *BK One*, p. 193.

/ ātm̐anaṃ cāparāṃś caiva yaḥ śighraṃ trātum icchati /
/ sa caret paramaṃ guhyaṃ parātmaparivartanam // CA, VIII, 120 //

/ ye kecid duḥkhitā loke sarve te svasukhecchayā /
/ ye kecit sukhitā loke sarve te 'nyasukhecchayā // CA, VIII, 129 //

/ bahunā vā kim uktena dṛśyatām idam antaram /
/ svārthārthinaś ca bālasya muneś cānyārthakāriṇaḥ // CA, VIII, 130 //

/ na nāma sādhyaṃ buddhatvaṃ saṃsāre 'pi kutaḥ sukham /
/ svasukhasyānyaduḥkhena parivartam akurvataḥ // CA, VIII, 131 //

/ duṣkarān na nivarteta yasmād abhyāsaśaktitaḥ /
/ yasyaiva śravaṇāt trāsaste naiva na vinā ratiḥ // CA, VIII, 119 //

/ paratvaṃ tu svakāyasya sthitam eva na duṣkaram / CA, VIII, 112cd //

/ tasmād yathānyadīyeṣu śukraśoṇitabinduṣu /
/ cakartha tvam ahaṃkāraṃ tathānyeṣv api bhāvaya // CA, VIII, 158 //

/ parātmasamatābhyāsād bodhicittaṃ dṛdhībhavet /
/ āpekṣikaṃ parātmatvaṃ pārāvāraṃ yathāmṛṣā //
/ tatkūlaṃ na svataḥ pāraṃ kim apekṣyas tv apāratā /
/ ātmatvaṃ na svataḥ siddhaṃ kim apekṣya pāro bhavet // *Śikṣ*, p. 191.25–28 //

/ anena śataśaḥ sarve saṃsāravyathitā vayam //
/ aprameyā gataḥ kalpāḥ svārthaṃ jijñāsatas tava /
/ śrameṇa mahatānena duḥkham eva tvayārjitam // CA, VIII, 154cd, 155 //

/ abhaviṣyad idaṃ karma kṛtaṃ pūrvaṃ yadi tvayā /
/ bauddhaṃ saṃpat sukhaṃ muktvā nābhaviṣyad iyaṃ daśā // CA, VIII, 157 //

/ anyasaṃbaddham asmīti niścayaṃ kuru me manaḥ /
/ sarvasattvārtham utsṛjya nānyac cintyaṃ tvayādhunā //
/ na yuktaṃ svārthadṛṣṭyādi tadīyaiś cakṣurādibhiḥ /
/ na yuktaṃ syanditum svārtham anyadīyaiḥ karādibhiḥ // CA, VIII, 137–8 /

/ kva yāsyasi mayā dṛṣṭaḥ sarvadarpān nihanmi te /
/ anyo 'sau pūrvakaḥ kālas tvayā yatrāsmi nāśitaḥ //

/ adyāpy asti mama svārtha ity āśāṃ tyaja sāṃpratam /
/ tvaṃ vikrīto mayānyeṣu bahukhedam acintayan //
/ tvāṃ sattveṣu na dāsyāmi yadi nāma pramodataḥ /
/ tvaṃ māṃ narakapāleṣu pradāsyasi na saṃśayaḥ //
/ evaṃ cānekadhā dattvā tvayāhaṃ vyathitaś ciram /
/ nihanmi svārthaceṭaṃ tvāṃ tāni vairāṇy anusmaran // CA, VIII, 169–172 //
/ sattvebhyaś ca jinebhyaś ca buddhadharmāgame same /
/ jineṣu gauravaṃ yadvan na sattveṣv iti kaḥ kramaḥ // CA, VI, 113 //
/ yo 'pi pāramitāsu sarveṇa sarvaṃ sarvathā śikṣitum asamarthah, tenāpi bodhicittam utpādanīyam eva / upāyaparigraheṇa mahāphalatvāt / *BK One*, p. 191 /.
/ bodhicittād dhi yat puṇyaṃ yac ca rūpi bhavet yadi /
/ ākāsadhātuṃ saṃpūrya bhȳuaś cottari tad bhavet // iti //
/ gaṅgāvālikasaṃkhyāni buddhakṣetrāni yo naraḥ /
/ dadyāt sadratnapūrṇāni lokanāthebhya eva hi //
/ yaś caikaḥ prāñjalir bhūtvā cittaṃ bodhāya nāmayet /
/ iyaṃ viśiṣyate pūjā yasyānto 'pi na vidyate // iti // *Vīradatta* in Prajñākaramati's commentary, 32.13–14 and 33.10–14 //
/ kalpān analpān pravicintayadbhir dṛṣṭaṃ munīndrair hitam etad eva / CA, I, 7ab /
/ yadi kalpakoṭi daśabhī kuśalaiḥ pathebhis caramaṇu pratyekarhatvaspṛhāṃ janeti /
/ tada khaṇḍaśīlu bhavate api cchidraśīlo pārājiko gurutaro ayu cittapādo // *Saṃcaya*, XXXI, 6 //
/ yadi pañcakāmaguṇa bhuñjati bodhisattvo buddhaṃ ca dharma śaraṇāgatu āryasaṃghaṃ /
/ sarvajñatā ca manasī bhaviṣyāmi buddho sthitu śīlapāramita veditavya vijño // *Saṃcaya*, XXXI, 4 //
/ manasā cintayitvāpi yo na dadyāt punar naraḥ /
/ sa preto bhavatīty uktam alpamātre 'pi vastuni //
/ kim utānuttaraṃ saukhyam uccair udghuṣya bhāvataḥ /
/ jagat sarvaṃ visaṃvādya kā gatir te bhaviṣyate // CA, IV, 5–6 //
/ andhaḥ saṃkārakūṭebhyo yathā ratnam avāpnuyāt /
/ tathā kathaṃcid apy etad bodhicittaṃ mamoditam // CA, III, 27 //

/ yo bodhisattva ayu vyākṛtu vyākṛtasmin citta pradūṣayi vivāḍu samārabheḍya /
/ yāvanti cittakṣaṇikākhiladoṣayuktās tāvanta kalpa puna sannahitatavya bhonti // *Saṃcaya*, XXIV, 5 //
/ atha tasyupadyati matīti aśobhanāti . . . /
/ pratideśayati puna āyati saṃvaraṇi apayāti vāsa iha śikṣati buddhadharme // *Saçaya*, XXIV, 6a,c,d //
/ . . . na cet /
/ vipakṣair badhyate citte prayāty atyantas ātmatām // PV, Siddhi, 129cd //
/ yasmāc ca tulyajātīyapūrvabījapravṛddhayaḥ /
/ kṛpādibuddhayas tāsāṃ satyābhyāse kutaḥ sthitiḥ // PV, Siddhi, 126 //
/ bodhicittaṃ na riñcati tena sarvāsu jātiṣu /
/ svapnāntare 'pi tac cittaṃ kiṃ punar yadi jāgrataḥ //
/ yeṣu viratisthāneṣu grāmeṣu nagareṣu vā /
/ samādāyeti 'bodhāya tena cittaṃ na riñcati // *Siṃha* in *Śikṣ*, p. 33.28–32.
/ caturbhiḥ kāśyapa dharmaiḥ samanvāgatasya bodhisattvasya sarvāsu jātiṣu jātamātrasya bodhicittam āmukhībhavati / na cāntarā muhyati yāvad bodhimaṇḍaniṣadanāt / *Śikṣ*, p. 33.17–18.
/ pratipattisārāṇāṃ bodhisattvānāṃ bodhir nāpratipattisārāṇām / *Gayā* in *BK One*, p. 193.
/ tasmāt pratipattisāro bhavisyāmi ity evaṃ tvayā kumāra śikṣitavyam / tat kasya hetoḥ / pratipattisārasya hi, kumāra, na durlabhā bhavaty anuttarā samyaksaṃbodhir / *Samādhirāja* in *BK One*, p. 193.
/ evam utpāditabodhicitto bodhisattvaḥ svayam eva dānādi dadāti pratipattau prayokṣyate / na hi svayam adāntaḥ parān damayatīti matvā /na cāpi vinā pratipattyā bodhir avāpyate / *BK One*, p. 193 /
/ dayāvān duḥkhahānārtham upāyeṣv abhiyujyate /
/ parokṣopeyataddhetos takākhyānaṃ hi duṣkaram // PV, Siddhi, 132 //
/ tad etat sarvajñajñānaṃ karuṇāmūlaṃ bodhicittahetukam upāyaparyavasānam / *Vairocana* cited in *BK One*, p. 196 /

/ ekāntasattvārthavimukhasya ekāntasaṃsārābhisaṃskaravimukhasya (nā)nuttarā samyaksaṃbodhir uktā mayā / *Saṃdhinirmocana* in *BK Three*, p. 22 /

' copāyād bhavati (saṃsāra)gamanaṃ bodhisattvānāṃ mokṣaḥ / upāyarahitā ca prajñā bandhaḥ / prajñārahitas copāyo bandhaḥ / prajñāsahita upāyo moksaḥ / upāyasahitā prajñā moksaḥ / *Vimalakīrti* cited in part in *BK Three*, p. 22 /

' dvāv imāu bodhisattvānāṃ saṃkṣiptāu mārgāu / katamāu dvāu / upāyaś ca prajñā ca / *Gayā* in *BK One*, p. 194 /

' tad yathāpi nāma kāśyapa amātyasaṃgṛhītā rājanaḥ sarvarājakāryāṇi kurvanti / evam eva kāśyapa upāyasaṃgṛhītā bodhisattvasya prajñā sarvabuddhakāryāṇi karoti / *The Kāśyapa Parivarta*, No. 42 /

' tathā maitrīsaṃnāhasaṃnaddho mahākaruṇādhiṣṭhānapratiṣṭhitaḥ / sarvākāravaropetaṃ śūnyatākārābhinirhataṃ dhyānaṃ dhyāpati / tatra katamā sarvākāravaropetā śūnyatā / yā na dānavikalā /yāvan nopāyavikalā / (Sanskrit compressed:) *Ratnacūḍa* in *Śikṣ*, p. 145.11–13 /

' lekhakā ye tadākārā dānaśīlakṣamādayaḥ /

' sarvākāravaropetā śūnyatā pratimocyate // *Uttaratantra*, 1, 92 //

' yo 'py ayaṃ maitreya ṣaṭpāramitāsamudāgamo bodhisattvānāṃ saṃbodhāya taṃ te mohapuruṣā evaṃ vakṣyanti / prajñāpāramitāyām eva bodhisattvena śikṣitavyam / kiṃ śeṣābhiḥ pāramitābhiḥ / te 'nyāṃ pāramitāṃ dūṣayitavyāṃ manyante / tat kiṃ manyase 'jita duṣprajñaḥ sa kāśirājābhūd yena kapotārthaṃ śyenāya svamāṃsāni dattāni / maitreya āha / no hīdaṃ bhagavaṇ / bhagavān āha / yāni mayā maitreya bodhisattvacaryāṃ caratā ṣaṭpāramitāpratisaṃyuktāni kuśalamūlāny upacitāni apakṛtaṃ nu taiḥ kuśalamūlaiḥ / maitreya āha / no hīdaṃ bhagavan / bhagavān āha / tvaṃ tāvad ajita ṣaṣṭiṃ kalpān dānapāramitāyāṃ ṣaṣṭiṃ kalpān śīlapāramitāyāṃ ṣaṣṭiṃ kalpān kṣantipāramitāyāṃ ṣaṣṭiṃ kalpān vīryapāramitāyāṃ ṣaṣṭiṃ kalpān dhyānapāramitāyāṃ ṣaṣṭiṃ kalpān prajñāpāramitāyāṃ samudāgataḥ / tat te mohapuruṣā evaṃ vakṣyanti / ekenayenaiva bodhir yad uta śūnyatānayeneti / te caryā supariśuddhā bhaviṣyantītyādi // *Vaipulyasaṃgraha*, cited in *Śikṣ*, p. 57.13–31.

/ tasya khalu bho jinaputra bodhisattvasyaivam imām acalāṃ bodhisattvabhūmim anugatasya pūrvapraṇidhānabalādhānasthitasya buddhā bhagavantas tasmin dharmamukhasrotasi tathāgatajñānopasaṃhāraṃ kurvanti / evam cainaṃ bruvanti / sādhu sādhu kulaputra / eṣā paramārthakṣāntir buddhadharmānugamāya / api tu khalu punaḥ kulaputra yāsmākaṃ daśabalacaturvaiśāradyabuddhadharmasamṛddhiḥ sā tava nāsti / tasyā buddhadharmasamṛddheḥ paryeṣaṇāyābhiyogaṃ kuru vīryam ārabhasva / etad eva kṣāntimukhaṃ monmokṣīḥ /

/ api tu khalu punaḥ kulaputra kim cāpi tvayaivaṃ śāntavimokṣavihāro 'nuprāpta imān punar aśāntān apraśāntān bālapṛthagjanān nānākleśa-samudācāraprāptān vividhavitarkopahatamānasān samanvāharāpekṣasva /

/ api tu khalu punaḥ kulaputra pūrvapraṇidhānam anusmara sattvārthasamprāpaṇaṃ jñanamukhācintyatāṃ ca /

/ api tu khalu punaḥ kulaputraiṣā sarvadharmāṇāṃ dharmatā / utpādād vā sthitaivaiṣā dharmatā dharmadhātusthitiḥ / (yad idaṃ sarvadharmaśūnyatā sarvadharmānupalabdhiḥ /) naitayā tathāgatā eva kevalam prabhāvyante / sarvaśrāvakapratyekabuddhā api hy etam avikalpadharmatām anuprāpnuvanti /

/ api tu khalu punaḥ kulaputra prekṣasva tāvat tvam asmakaṃ kāyā-pramāṇatāṃ ca jñānāpramāṇatāṃ ca buddhakṣetrāpramānatāṃ ca jñānābhinirharāpramāṇatāṃ ca prabhāmaṇḍalāpramāṇatāṃ ca svarāṅgaviśuddhyapramāṇatāṃ ca / tathaiva tvam apy abhinirhāram utpādaya / *Daśabhūmika-sūtra*, Eighth Stage, pp. 65–66.

/ tatraivoktaṃ dānacittābhiniveśo yāvat prajñācittābhiniveśo mārakarmeti / Unnamed *sūtra*, probably as cited in *Sūtrasamuccaya; BK Three*, p. 22 /

/ yāvatī caryā sarvā parikalpyā / niḥparikalpyā ca bodhir / *Brahma* cited in *BK Three*, p. 24 /

/ asaṃskṛtaṃ ca pratyavekṣate / saṃskṛtaiś ca kuśalaiḥ parikhidyata iti mārakarma iti / bodhimārgaṃ prajanāti pāramitāmārgaṃ ca na paryeṣata iti mārakarmeti / *Sūtrasamuccaya*, cited in *BK Three*, p. 22 /

/ na copāyakauśalarahitena bodhisattvena gambhīradharmatāyām abhiyoktavyam / *Sūtrasamuccaya*, cited in *BK Three*, p. 27 /

/ sa khalu punar eṣa tathāgatañaṃ saṃbhavo naikena kāraṇena bhavati / tat kasya hetoḥ / (samudagatais) tāvad bho jinaputrāprameyaśatasahasra(daśa)karaṇais tathāgatāḥ samudāgacchanti / katamair daśabhir yadutāprameyapuṇyajñānasaṃbhārātṛptisamudāgamakāraṇena / *Tathāgatotpattisaṃbhava*, cited in *BK Three*, p. 13 /

/ śatapuṇyanirjātāḥ sarvakuśaladharmanirjātā apramāṇakuśalamūlakarma-nirjātāḥ kāyās tathā(gatasya) / *Vimalakīrti*, cited in *BK Three*, p. 13 /

/ śīlasaṃvarasamādānaṃ ca kartukāmasya bodhisattvasya purato 'syāṃ bodhisattva(sūtra)piṭakamātṛkāyāṃ yāṃ bodhisattvasya śikṣapadāni āpattisthānāni c' ākhyātāni tāny anu ... rya prajñayā pratisaṃkhyāyotsahate / na parasamādāpanikayā nāpi paraspardhayā dhīro bodhisattvo veditavyaḥ / tena ca pratigṛhītaṃ tasya ca dātavyam etena vidhinā etac chīlasaṃvarasamādanam / *Bodhisattvabhūmi*, p. 157, Wogihara ed.

/ bhogātmabhāvasaṃpat paricārārambhasaṃpad abhyudayaḥ /
/kleśāvaśagatvam api ca kṛtyeṣu sadā viparyāsaḥ // SA, XVI, 2 //

/ sattvārtheṣu suyuktas tyāgānupadhātamarṣaṇaiḥ kurute /
/ sanidānasthitimuktyā ātmārthaṃ sarvathā carati // SA, XVI, 3 //

/ avighātair viheṭhair viheṭhasaṃmarṣaṇaiḥ kriyākhedaih /
/ āvarjanaiḥ sulapitaiḥ parārtha ātmārtha etasmāt // SA, XVI, 4 //

/ bhogeṣu cānabhiratis tīvrā gurutā dvaye akhedaś ca /
/ yogaś ca nirvikalpaḥ samastam idam uttamaṃ yānaṃ // SA, XVI, 5 //

/ viṣayeṣv asaktimārgas tadāpti(r) vikṣepasaṃyameṣv aparaḥ /
/ sattvāvisṛjanavardhana āvaraṇaviśodhaneṣv aparaḥ // SA, XVI, 6 //

/ śikṣatrayam adhikṛtya ca ṣaṭ pārmitā jinaiḥ samākhyātāḥ /
/ ādyā tisro dvedhā antyadvayatas tisṛṣv ekā // SA, XVI, 7 //

/ pūrvo 'ttaravisrayatas cotpattes tatkrameṇa nirdeśaḥ /
/ hīnotkarṣasthānād āudārikasūkṣmataś cāpi // SA, XVI, 14 //

/ kas ca dānasya svabhāvaḥ / yā cetanā sarvapariṣkārasvadehānapekṣasya bodhisattvasyālābhasahagā tatsamutthāpitaṃ ca deyavastuparityāgāya kāyavākkarmānavadyaś ca / *Bodhisattvabhūmi*, Wogihara, I, p. 114 /

/ adaridraṃ jagatkṛtvā dānapāramitā yadi /
/ jagaddaridram adyāpi sa kathaṃ pūrvatāyinām //
/ phalena saha sarvasvaṃ tyāgacittaṃ jane 'khile /
/ dānapāramitā proktā tasmāt sā cittam eva tu // CA, V, 9–10 //
/ adhyavasitā ye bālāh kāye 'smin pūtike samyag /
/ jīvite cañcale 'vaśye māyāsvapnanibhopame //
/ atiraudrāṇi karmāṇi kṛtvā mohavaśānugāḥ /
/ te yānti narakān ghorān mṛtyuyānagatābudhā // *Candrapradīpa* in *Śikṣ*, p. 14.21–24 //
/ ye kecit sattvāna bhavanti vigrahāḥ parigrahas tatra nidānamūlam /
/ tasmāt tyajed yatra bhavet tṛṣṇā / utsṛṣṭatṛṣṇasya hi dhāraṇī bhavet // *Anantamukha* in *Śiks*, p. 14.26–27.
/ pratikṣaṇaṃ hi yāty eva kāyaś cittaṃ ca me yataḥ //
/ yadi nityāpy anityena nirmalā malavāhinā /
/ bodhiḥ kāyena labhyeta nanu labdhā mayaiva sā // *Śikṣ*, p. 124.2–4 //
/ nirātmake bhedini sārahīne duḥkhe kṛtaghne satatāśucāu ca /
/ dehe parasmāy upayujyamāne na prītimānyo na vicakṣaṇaḥ saḥ // *Jātakamālā* ("Story of the Tigress," k. 22) //
/ sarvatyāgas ca nirvāṇaṃ nirvāṇārthī ca me manaḥ /
/ tyaktavyaṃ cen mayā sarvaṃ varaṃ sattveṣu dīyatām // CA, III, 11 //
/ bhogān anityān abhivīkṣamānaḥ sātmyaṃ gatāyāṃ ca tataḥ kṛpāyām /
/ sa niścayaṃ gacchati dīyate yad etan madīyaṃ na tu yad gṛhe me //
/ yad dattam asmān na bhayaṃ kadācid gehe yad asmād bhayam abhyupaiti /
/ sādhāraṇaṃ rakṣyam atarpyakaṃ ca datte tu naite prabhavanty anarthāḥ //
/ sukhaṃ paratrāpi karoti dattam ihaiva duḥkhaṃ prakaroty adattam /
/ ulkāsvabhāvaṃ hi dhanaṃ narāṇām atyajyamānaṃ vyasanaṃ dadāti //
/ adīyamānaṃ nidhanaṃ prayāti nidhānatāṃ yāti hi dīyamānam /
/ dhanasya niḥsāralaghoḥ sa sāro yad dīyate lokahitonmukhena //
/ yad dattam etad viduṣāṃ praśaṃsyaṃ bālo janas tan nicayapraśaṃsī /

/ prāyo viyogo hi parigrahebhyo dānād bhavaty abhyudayo yaśaś ca //
/ dattaṃ na tatkleśaparigrahāya kleśāya mātsaryam anāryadharmaḥ /
/ yad dīyate satpatha eṣa tasmād ato 'nyatha kā patham āhur āryāḥ // PS, I, 49–54 //
/ yad evaṃ vadataḥ puṇyaṃ yadi tan mūrtimad bhavet /
/ gaṅgāyāḥ sikatākhyeṣu na māyāl lokadhātuṣu //
/ uktam etad bhagavatā hetur apy atra dṛśyate /
/ sattvadhātor ameyasya hitā saṃjñeyam īdṛsī // RA, V, 86–87 //
/ mātsaryadoṣopacayāya yat syān na tyāgacittaṃ paribṛṃhayed vā /
/ tat tyaktum evārhati bodhisattvāḥ parigrahacchadmamayam vighātam //
/ tad bodhisattvaḥ katham ādadīna ratnaṃ dhanaṃ vā divi vāpi rājyam /
/ yat tyāgacittapratipakṣadakṣaṃ saṃbodhimārgāvaraṇaṃ karoti // PS, I, 3–4 //
/ saṃsmṛtya caryātisayaṃ munīnāṃ tadunmukhīṃ svāṃ api ca pratijñam /
/ parigrahasnehavinigrahartham kuryād imāṃś cetasi sadvitarkān //
/ yadā nisṛṣṭo jagate mayāyaṃ kāyo 'pi tattyāgakṛto 'pi dharmaḥ /
/ bāhye tadā vastuni saṃgacittaṃ na me gajasnānam ivānurūpam // PS, I, 5–6 //
/ ātmabhāvāṃs tathā bhogān sarvaṃ tryadhvagataṃ śubham /
/ nirapekṣas tyajāmy eṣa sarvasattvārthasiddhaye // CA, III, 10 //

/ yusmākam eva svam idaṃ kim arthaṃ nātmābhimāno mama kaścid atra //
/ ity adbhutā yat prabhavanty abhīkṣṇaṃ saṃbuddhabhāvānuguṇā vitarkāḥ /
/ tam bodhisattvātiśayaṃ vadanti buddha mahāsattvam acintyasattvāḥ // PS, I, 11cd–12 //
/ sattvaśvāmikais tu bhogaiḥ sattvasvāmika svātmabhāvaḥ saṃrakṣata ity adoṣaḥ / na hi dāsasya nityaṃ svāmikarmavyāvṛtasya svadravyam asti yena varteta / *Śikṣ*, p. 79.12–13 /

/ na caikāntasvāmyarthaparasya dāsya vyādhyādiviklavamateḥ svāminam ananujñāpyāpi bhuñjānasya kaścid doṣaḥ / *Śikṣ*, p. 79.15–16.

/ nāpy evaṃ kurvāṇasya bodhisattvasyāntike kasyacid viditavṛttāntasyāpy aprasādo yujyate mātsaryatyāgacittāparijñānāt / na cātra nyāye kaścit saṃdeho yuktaḥ / *Śikṣ*, p. 79–16–17 /

/ yaś ca śāriputra gṛhī bodhisattvo gaṅgānadīvālikāsamāni buddhakṣetrāni saptaratnapratipūrnāni kṛtvā tathāgatebhyor arhadbhyaḥ samyaksaṃbuddhebhyo dānaṃ dadyād / yaś ca śāriputra pravrajyāparyāpanno bodhisattva ekāṃ catuṣpadikāṃ gāthāṃ prakāśayed ayam eva tato bahutaraṃ puṇyaṃ prasavati / na śāriputra tathāgatena pravrajitasyāmiṣadānam anujñātam / *Bodhisattva* in *Śikṣ*, p. 80.13–16.

/ abhyāgate yācanake ca tena saṃbodhisaṃbhāravivṛddhihetāu /
/ tatpreṣyasaṃjñātmani saṃniveśyā kalyāṇamitrapriyatā ca tasmin // PS, I, 55 //

/ bālapṛthagjanā mañjuśrīr dānaṃ dadānā matsariṇām antike 'prasādaṃ kurvanti / te tenāprasadena pratighacittam utpādayanti / pratighakhiladoṣeṇa mahānarakeṣūpapadyante / *Karma* in *Śikṣ*, p. 53.20–21 /

/ śīlaṃ rakṣanto duḥśīlān kutsayanti paribhāṣanti / te teṣām avarṇaṃ sa bhāṣanti / te teṣāṃ doṣaṃ śrutvā bahujanasyāprasādaṃ kurvanti / te tenāprasādena durgatigāmino bhavanti / *Karma* in *Śikṣ*, p. 53.21–23 /

/ kīdṛsaṃ tadvīryam / yena khedo bhavati / yad idam alpabalasya gurukarmārambho 'tivelāyāṃ vāparipakvādhimukter vā duṣkarakarmārambhas tad yathā svamāṃsadānādiḥ / dattaś cānenātmabhāvaḥ / kiṃ tv akālaparibhogād varayati / anyathā hi tesām eva sattvānāṃ bodhisattvakhedena bodhicittabījanāsān mahataḥ phalarāśer nāśaḥ syāt / etas ca gaganagañjasūtra 'bhihitam / akālapratikāṅkṣaṇatā mārakarmeti / *Śikṣ*, p. 32.22–26 /

/ tyajen na jīvitaṃ tasmād aśuddhe karuṇāśaye /
/ tulyāśaye tu tattyājyam itthaṃ na parihīyate // CA, V, 87 //
/ saddharmasevakaṃ kāyam itarārthaṃ na pīḍayet /
/ evam eva hi sattvānām āśām āśu prapūrayet // CA, V, 86 //

/ netarārthaṃ tyajec chreṣṭhām . . . / CA, V, 83c /

/ sacet punaḥ śāriputra bodhisattvaḥ tricīvaraṃ parityajya yācanaka-guruko bhaven na tenālpecchatā āsevitā bhavet / *Bodhisattva, Śikṣ,* p. 80.21–22 /

/ durbalas tāvad asmy aparipakakuśalamūlaḥ ādikarmiko mahāyāne na cittasya vaśī parityāgāya sopādānadṛṣṭiko 'smi ahaṃkāramamakārasthitiḥ / kṣamasva satpuruṣa mā paritāpsīḥ / tathāhaṃ kariṣyāmi tathā pratipatsye / *Ugradatta* in *Śikṣ,* p. 15.24–26 /

/ sacet punar yācanake 'pi labdhe dātuṃ na śaknoty atidurbalatvāt /

/ tenānuneyo madhureṇa sāmnā sa yācakaḥ syān na yathā samanyuḥ // PS, I, 57 //

/ kāryaś ca mātsaryavinigrahāya mohaprahāṇāya ca tena yatnaḥ /

/ tathā yathā yācanakaḥ kadācid vaimukhyadīno na tato vyapaiti // PS, I, 58 // (Skt. gives *moha* instead of expected *rāga*).

/ evaṃ hi bodhisattvaḥ asatsvasaṃvidyamāneṣu bhogeṣu prajñādānasya dātā bhavati yāvad āśayaśuddhiṃ nādhigacchati / śuddhāśayas tu bodhisattvo yathaivāpāyasamatikramaṃ pratilabhate tathaivākṣaya-bhogatāṃ janmani janmani pratilabhate / *Bodhisattvabhūmi,* Dutt ed., p. 88.10–13 /

/ mūlaṃ dānasyāsya saṃbodhicittaṃ tan na tyājyaṃ ditsatā dānam īdṛk /

/ taṃ saṃbuddhās tyāginām agram āhur yo lokeṣu tyāgam ādhitsur agram // PS, I, 61 //

/ matsyādayaḥ ka nīyantāṃ mārayeyaṃ yato na tān /

/ labdhe viraticitte tu śīlapāramitā matā // CA, V, 11 //

/ saṃbuddhaśīlābharaṇābhirāmān kartuṃ janān utpatitādareṇa /

/ svam eva śīlaṃ pariśodhyam ādau śīlaṃ hi śakter balam ādadhāti // PS, II, 1 //

/ śīlacyutas tv ātmahite 'py aśaktaḥ kasmin parasyārthavidhau samarthaḥ /

/ tasmād viśeṣeṇa parārthasādhor na nyāyyam asmin śithilādaratvam // PS, II, 48 //

/ vivarjayed aṇv api varjanīyaṃ tasmād bhayaṃ tīvram avekṣamāṇaḥ / PS, II, 49ab /

/ divyābhirāmā manujeṣu saṃpat prakṛṣṭasaukhyāikarasā ca divyā /

/ śīlād yadi syāt kim ivātra citraṃ yasmāt prarohanty api buddhadharmāḥ / PS, II, 47 //
/ śīlaṃ viśeṣādhigamasya mārgo dāyādyabhūtaṃ karuṇatmakānām /
/ jñānaprakarṣasya śucisvabhāvo naṣṭoddhavā maṇḍanajātir agrā //
/ lokatrayavyāpi manojñagandhaṃ vilepanaṃ pravrajitāvirodhi /
/ tulyākṛtibhyo pi pṛthagjanebhyaḥ śīlaṃ viśeṣaṃ kurute narāṇām // PS, II, 60–61 //
/ akatthanānām api dhīrabhāvād vināpi vāgbhedapariśrameṇa /
/ atrāsanābhyāṃ natasarvalokaṃ tyaktāvalepoddhavam īśvaratvam //
/ apy aprakāsānvayasambhavānām akurvatām apy upakārasāram /
/ niṣkevale śīlavidhāu sthitānām asaṃstutānām api yan narāṇām //
/ rajāṃsi pādāśrayapāvitāni praṇāmalabdhāni samudvahanti /
/ cūḍāgralagnāni manuṣyadevāḥ śrīmattaraṃ śīlamataḥ kulebhyaḥ // PS, II, 62–64 //
/ na bodhisattvābhyucitaṃ ca śīlaṃ vikhaṇḍayed ātmasukhodayena / PS, II, 49cd /
/ svecchāgatitvāc ca bhujiṣyavṛttaṃ vidvatpraśaṃsābharaṇānavadyam /
/ samagraśikṣāpadapūraṇāc ca saṃpūrṇam āmarṣavivarjitaṃ ca // PS, II, 51cd–52ab //
/ yo lokadhātuṣv amiteṣu sattvān śīle pratiṣṭhāpayiṣuḥ samagrān /
/ niṣevate lokahitāya śīlaṃ tad ucyate pāramiteti tajjñaiḥ // PS, II, 59 //
/ tasmān na durgatibhayena na rājyahetor na svargasaṃpadabhilāṣa-samudbhavena /
/ seveta śīlam amalam na hi tat tathā syāl lokārthasiddhiparamas tu bhajeta śīlam // PS, II, 65 //
/ svargasya mokṣasya ca satpathebhyo naivoccalet karmapathebhya ebhyaḥ /
/ atra sthitānāṃ hi jagaddhitārthās cintāviseṣāḥ saphalībhavanti //
/ samāsataḥ śīlam idam vadanti yaḥ saṃvaraḥ kāyavacomanastaḥ /
/ kārtsnyena cātraiva yatas sa tasmād etān prayatnena viśodhayeś ca // PS, II, 8–9 //

/ kiyato mārayiṣyāmi durjanāṃ gaganopamān /
/ mārite krodhacitte tu māritāḥ sarvaśatravaḥ //
/ bhūmiṃ chādayituṃ sarvaṃ kutaś carma bhaviṣyati /
/ upānaccarmamātreṇa channā bhavati medinī //
/ bāhyabhāvā mayā tad vacchakyā vārayituṃ na hi /
/ svacittaṃ vārayiṣyāmi kiṃ mamānyair nivāritaiḥ // CA, V, 12–14 //

/ iha bodhisattvaḥ ādita eva kṣāntāv anuśaṃsadarśī bhavati / kṣamaḥ pudgalaḥ āyatyām avairabahulo bhavati / abhedabahulo bhavati / sukhasaumanasyabahulo bhavati / avipratisārī kālaṃ karoti / kāyasya bhedāt sugatāu svargaloke deveṣūpapadyate / iti sa evam anuśaṃsadarśī svayaṃ ca kṣamo bhavati paraṃ ca kṣāntāu samādāpayati / kṣamāyāś ca varṇaṃ bhāṣate / kṣamiṇaṃ ca pudgalaṃ dṛṣṭvā sumanasko bhavaty ānandījātaḥ / *Bodhisattvabhūmi* (Wogihara, p. 196.5–13 /

/ parārtham abhyudyatamānasānāṃ dīkṣāṃ titikṣāṃ prathamāṃ vadanti /
/ setur jalānīva hi roṣadoṣaḥ śreyāṃsi lokasya samāvṛṇoti //
/ alaṃkriyā śaktisamanvitānāṃ tapodhanānāṃ balasaṃpadagrā /
/ vyāpādadāvānalavāridhārā pretyeha ca kṣāntir anarthaśāntiḥ //
/ kṣamāmaye varmaṇi sajjanānāṃ vikuṇṭhitā durjanavākyabāṇāḥ /
/ prāyah praśaṃsākusumatvam etya tatkīrtimālāvayavā bhavanti // PS, III, 3–5 //

/ karmāntaśālā guṇaśībharasya rūpasya sallakṣaṇabhūṣaṇasya / PS, III, 8cd /

/ yaḥ krodhaṃ hanti nirbandhāt sa sukhīha paratra ca / CA, VI, 6cd /

/ sarvam etat sucaritaṃ dānaṃ sugatapūjanam /
/ kṛtaṃ kalpasahasrair yat pratighaḥ pratihanti tat // CA, VI, 1 //

/ āryasarvāstivādānāṃ ca paṭhyate / paśyadhvaṃ bhikṣava etaṃ bhikṣuṃ keśanakhastūpe sarvāṅgena praṇipatya cittam abhiprasādayantam / evaṃ bhadanta / anena bhikṣavo bhikṣuṇā yāvatī bhūmir ākrāntadharaśītiyojana-sahasrāṇi yāvat kāñcanacakram / atrāntare yāvantyo vālikās tāvantyo 'nena bhikṣuṇā cakravartirājyasahasrāni paribhoktavyāni / yāvad athāyuṣmān upālir yena bhagavan tenāñjaliṃ praṇamya bhagavantam idam avocat / yad uktaṃ bhagavatāsya bhikṣor evaṃ mahānti kuśalamūlāni / kutremāni bhagavan kuśalamūlāni tanutvaṃ parikṣayaṃ paryādānaṃ gacchanti / nāham upale evaṃ kṣatiṃ copahatim ca samanupaśyāmi / yathā sabrahmacārī sabrahmacāriṇo 'ntike duṣṭacittam utpādayati / atropāle imāni mahānti kusalamūlāni tanutvaṃ parikṣayaṃ paryādānaṃ gacchanti / tasmāt tarhy upāle evaṃ śikṣitavyaṃ yad dagdhasthūṇāyām api cittam na pradūṣayiṣyāmaḥ / prāg eva savijñanake kāya iti / *Śikṣ*, p. 82.26 to 83.2 /

/ manaḥ samaṃ na gṛhṇāti na prītisukham aśnute /
/ na nidrāṃ na dhṛtiṃ yāti dveṣaśalye hṛdi sthite //
/ pūjayaty arthamānair yānye 'pi cainaṃ samāśritāḥ /
/ te 'py enaṃ hantum icchanti svāminaṃ dveṣadurbhagam //
/ suhṛdo 'py udvijante 'amād dadāti na ca sevyate /
/ saṃkṣepān nāsti tatkiṃcit krodhano yena susthitaḥ // CA, VI, 3–5 //
/ saṃkṣepān nāsti tatkiṃcit krodhano yena susthitaḥ // CA, VI, 3–5 //
/ na bhāty alaṃkāraguṇānvito 'pi krodhāgninā saṃhṛtavarṇaśobhaḥ /
/ saroṣaśalye hṛdaye ca duḥkhaṃ mahārhaśayyāṅkagato 'pi śete //
/ vismṛtya cātmakṣamasiddhipakṣaṃ roṣāt prayāty eva tad utpathena /
/ nihīyate yena yaśorthasiddhyā tāmisrapakṣendur ivātmal abdhasyā //
/ roṣeṇa gacchaty anayaprapātaṃ nivāryamāno 'pi suhṛjjanena /

/ prāyeṇa vairasya jaḍatvam eti hitāhitavekṣaṇamandabuddhiḥ //
/ krodhāc ca sātmīkṛtapāpakarmā śocaty apāyeṣu samāśatāni /
/ ataḥ paraṃ kiṃ ripavaś ca kuryus tīvrāpakāroddhatamanyavo 'pi //
/ antaḥ sapatnaḥ kopo'yaṃ tad evaṃ viditaṃ mama /
/ tasyāvalepaprasaraṃ kaḥ pumān marṣayiṣyati // *Jātakamālā*, XXI, 29/33 //
/ na ca dveṣasamaṃ pāpaṃ na ca kṣāntisamaṃ tapaḥ /
/ tasmāt kṣāntiṃ prayatnena bhāvayed vividhair nayaiḥ // CA, VI, 2 //

/ evaṃ paravaśaṃ sarvaṃ yad vaśaṃ so 'pi cāvaśaḥ /
/ nirmāṇavad aceṣṭeṣu bhāveṣv evaṃ kva kupyate // CA, VI, 31 //
/ tasmād amitraṃ mitraṃ vā dṛṣṭvāpy anyāyakāriṇam /
/ īdṛśāḥ pratyayā asyety evaṃ matvā sukhī bhavet //
/ yadi tu khecchayā siddhiḥ sarveṣām eva dehinām /
/ na bhavet kasyacid duḥkhaṃ na duḥkhaṃ kaścad icchati // CA, VI, 33–34 /
/ yadaivaṃ kleśavaśyatvād ghnanty ātmānam api priyam /
/ tadaisaṃ parakāyeṣu parihāraḥ kathaṃ bhavet // CA, VI, 37 //
/ yadi svabhāvo bālānāṃ paropadravakāritā /
/ teṣu kopo na yukto me yathāgnau dahanātmake //
/ atha doṣo 'yam āgantuḥ sattvāḥ prakṛtipeśalāḥ /
/ tathāpy ayuktas tatkopaḥ kaṭudhūme yathāmbare // CA, VI, 39–40 //
/ mukhyaṃ daṇḍādikaṃ hitvā prerake yadi kupyate /
/ dveṣeṇa preritaḥ so 'pi dveṣe dveṣo 'stu me vara // CA, VI, 41 //
/ mayāpi ūrvaṃ sattvānām īdṛśyeva vyathā kṛtā /
/ tasmān me yuktam evaitat sattvopadravakāriṇaḥ // CA, VI, 42 //
/ duḥkhaṃ necchāmi duḥkhyasya hetum icchāmi bāliśaḥ /
/ svāparādhāgate duḥkhe kasmād anyatra kupyate //
/ asipattravanaṃ yadvad yathā nārakapakṣiṇaḥ /
/ matkarmajanitā eva tathedaṃ kutra kupyate //
/ matkarmacoditā eva jātā mayyapakāriṇaḥ /
/ yena yāsyanti narakān mayaivāmī hatā nanu // CA, VI, 45–47 //
/ yady etan mātram evādya duḥkhaṃ soḍhuṃ na pāryate /
/ tan nārakavyathāhetuḥ krodhaḥ kasmān na vāryate // CA, VI, 73 //
/ svāṃ dharmapīḍām avicintya yo 'yam matpāpaśuddhyartham iva pravṛttaḥ /
/ na cet kṣamām apy aham atra kuryāmanyaḥ kṛtaghno bata kīdṛśaḥ syāt // *Jātakamālā*, No. 33, k. 15 //
/ tacchastraṃ mama kāyaś ca dvayaṃ duḥkhasya kāraṇam /
/ tena śastraṃ mayā kāyo gṛhītaḥ kutra kupyate //
/ gaṇḍo 'yaṃ pratimākāro gṛhīto ghaṭṭanāsahaḥ /
/ tṛṣṇāndhena mayā tatra vyathāyāṃ kutra kupyate // CA, VI, 43–44 //
/ mohād eke 'parādhyanti kupyanty anye 'pi mohitāḥ /

/ brūmaḥ kam eṣu nirdoṣaṃ kaṃ vā brūmo 'parādhinam // CA, VI, 67 //
/ stutir yaśo 'tha satkāro na puṇyāya na cāyuṣe /
/ na balārthaṃ na cārogye na ca kāyasukhāya me //
/ etāvāṃs ca bhavet svārtho dhīmataḥ svārthavedinaḥ / CA, VI, 90–91ab //
/ yathā pāṃśugṛhe bhinne rodity ārtaravaṃ śiśuḥ /
/ tathā stutiyaśohānau svacittaṃ pratibhāti me // CA, VI, 93 //
/ stutyādayas ca me kṣemaṃ saṃvegaṃ nāśayanty amī /
/ guṇavatsu ca mātsaryaṃ saṃpatkopaṃ ca kurvate // CA, VI, 98 //
/ tasmāt stutyādighātāya mama ye pratyupasthitāḥ /
/ apāyapātarakṣārthaṃ pravṛttā nanu te mama //
/ muktyarthinaś cāyuktaṃ me lābhasatkārabandhanam /
/ ye mocayanti māṃ bandhād dveṣas teṣu kathaṃ mama //
/ duḥkhaṃ praveṣṭukāmasya ye kapāṭatvam āgataḥ /
/ buddhādhiṣṭhānata iva dveṣas teṣu kathaṃ mama // CA, VI, 99–101 //
/ mano hantum amūrtatvān na śakyaṃ kena cit kva cit /
/ śarīrābhiniveśāt tu kāyaduḥkhena bādyate //
/ nyakkāraḥ paruṣaṃ vākyam ayaśaś cety ayaṃ gaṇaḥ /
/ kāyaṃ na bādhate tena cetaḥ kasmāt prakupyasi // CA, VI, 52–53 //
/ mayyaprasādo yo 'nyeṣāṃ sa kiṃ māṃ bhakṣayiṣyati /
/ iha janmāntare vāpi yenāsau me 'nabhīpsitaḥ // CA, VI, 54 //
/ lābhāntarāyakāritvād yady asau me 'nabhīpsitaḥ /
/ naṅkṣyatīhaiva me lābhaḥ pāpaṃ tu sthāsyati dhruvam //
/ varam adyaiva me mṛtyur na mithyājīvitaṃ ciram /
/ yasmāc ciram api sthitvā mṛtyuduḥkhaṃ tad eva me //
/ svapne varṣaśataṃ saukhyaṃ bhuktvā yaś ca vibudhyate /
/ muhūrtam aparo yaś ca sukhī bhūtvā vibhudhyate //
/ nanu nivartate saukhyaṃ dvayor api vibuddhayoḥ /
/ saivopamā mṛtyukāle cirajīvyalpajīvinoḥ //
/ labdhvāpi ca bahūṃllābhān ciraṃ bhuktvā sukhāny api /
/ riktahastaś ca nagnaś ca yāsyāmi muṣito yathā // CA, VI, 55–59 //
/ bodhicittaṃ samutpādya sarvasattvasukhecchayā /

/ svayaṃ labdhasukheṣv adya kasmāt sattveṣu kupyasi //
/ trailokyapūjyaṃ buddhatvaṃ sattvānāṃ kila vāñchasi /
/ satkāram itvaraṃ dṛṣṭvā teṣāṃ kiṃ paridahyase //
/ puṣṇāti yas tvayā poṣyaṃ tubhyam eva dadāti saḥ /
/ kuṭumbajīvinaṃ labdhvā na hṛṣyasi prakupyasi //
/ sa kiṃ necchati sattvānāṃ yas teṣāṃ bodhim icchati /
/ bodhicittaṃ kutas tasya ye 'nya saṃpadi kupyati //
/ yadi tena na tallabdhaṃ sthitaṃ dānapater gṛhe /
/ sarvathāpi na tat te 'sti dattādattena tena kim // CA, VI, 80–84 //
/ jātaṃ ced apriyaṃ śatros tvattuṣṭyā kiṃ punar bhavet /
/ tvadāśaṃsanamātreṇa na cāhetur bhaviṣyati //
/ ata tvadicchayā siddhaṃ tadduḥkhe kiṃ sukhaṃ tava /
/ athāpy artho bhaved evam anarthaḥ ko 'nvataḥ paraḥ //
/ etad dhi baḍiśaṃ ghoraṃ kleśabāḍiśikārpitam /
/ yato narakapālās tvāṃ krītvā pakṣyanti kumbhiṣu // CA, VI, 87–89 //
/ kathaṃ cil labhyate saukhyaṃ duḥkhaṃ sthitam ayatnataḥ / CA, VI, 12ab /
/ yady asty eva pratīkāro daurmanasyena tatra kim /
/ atha nāsti pratīkāro daurmanasyena tatra kim // CA, VI, 10 //
/ śītoṣṇavṛṣṭivātādhvavyādhibandhanatāḍaṇaiḥ /
/ saukumāryaṃ na kartavyam anyathā vardhate vyathā // CA, VI, 16 //
/ duḥkhenaiva ca niḥsāraḥ cetas tasmād dṛḍhībhava / CA, VI, 12cd //
/ guṇo 'paraś ca duḥkhasya yat saṃvegān madacyutiḥ /
/ saṃsāriṣu ca kāruṇyaṃ pāpād bhītir jine spṛhā // CA, VI, 21 //
/ kopārtham evam evāhaṃ narakeṣu sahasraśaḥ /
/ kārito 'smi na cātmārthaḥ parārtho vā kṛto mayā // CA, VI, 74 //
/ na cedaṃ tādṛśaṃ duḥkhaṃ mahārthaṃ ca kariṣyati /
/ jagadduḥkhahare duḥkhe prītir evātra yujyate // CA, VI, 75 //
/ māraṇiyaḥ karaṃ chittvā muktaś cet kim abhadrakam /
/ manuṣyaduḥkhair narakān muktaś cet kim abhadrakam // CA, VI, 72 //
/ na kiṃcid asti tad vastu yad abhyāsasya duṣkaram /
/ tasmān mṛduvyathābhyāsāt soḍhavyāpi mahāvyathā // CA, VI, 14 //

/ tatrālpaduṣkhābhyāsapūrvakaṃ kaṣṭaṃ kaṣṭatarābhyāsaḥ sidhyati / yathā cābhyāsavaśāt sattvānāṃ duṣkhasukhasaṃjñā / tathā sarva-duṣkhotpādeṣu sukhasaṃjñā pratyupasthānābhyāsāt sukhasaṃjñaiva pratyupatiṣṭhate / *Śikṣ*, p. 101.15–17 /

/ apagatatūlapicūpamatā cittasya / *Ugradatta* in *Śikṣ*, p. 101.5 /

/ duryodhanaṃ cittaṃ te dārike utpādayitavyaṃ sarvakleśanirghātāya / *Gaṇḍavyūha* in *Śikṣ*, p. 101.6 /

/ kecit svasoṇitaṃ dṛṣṭvā vikramante viseṣataḥ /

/ parasoṇitam apy eke dṛṣṭvā mūrcchāṃ vrajanti yat //

/ taccittasya dṛḍhatvena kātaratvena cāgatam / CA, VI, 17–18ab //

/ kiṃ vīryaṃ kuśalotsāha . . . / CA, VII, 2a /

/ yat sarvaduṣkhasya tamasya nāśanam / apāyaparivarjanatāya mūlaṃ /

/ sarve hi buddhair hi sadā praśastaṃ / taṃ vīryam āryaṃ satataṃ bhajasva // *Śikṣ*, p. 64.15–16, appears to be the only verse of the three from the *Adhyāśayasañcodana* available in Sanskrit //

/ vīryaṃ paraṃ śuklagaṇasya madhye tanniśritas tasya yato 'nulābhaḥ /

/ vīryeṇa sadhyaḥ susukho vihāro lokottarā lokagatā ca siddhiḥ //

/ vīryād avāptaṃ bhavabhogam iṣṭaṃ vīryeṇa śuddhiṃ prabalām upetāḥ /

/ vīryeṇa satkāyam atītya muktā vīryeṇa bodhiṃ paramāṃ vibuddhāḥ // SA, XVI, 65–66 //

/ na vīryavān bhogaparājito 'sti no vīryavān kleśaparājito 'sti /

/ na vīryavān khedaparājito 'sti no vīryavān prāptiparājito 'sti // SA, XVI, 70 //

/ yataś ca sarveṣāṃ bodhikarakāṇāṃ kuśalānāṃ dharmāṇām evaṃ samudāgamāya vīryam eva pradhānaṃ śreṣṭhaṃ kāraṇaṃ na tathānyat /

/ tasmād vīryam anuttarāyai samyaksaṃbodhaye iti nirdeśanti tathāgatāḥ / *Bodhisattvabhūmi*, Dutt edition, p. 139 /

/ aprāpyarūpaṃ tu na kiñcid asti khedānabhijñena parākrameṇa / PS, IV, 2cd /

/ amānuṣebhyo 'pi parigrahodayaḥ samādhigotrapratilambha eva ca / PS, IV, 41cd /

/ vrajanty avadyā yad aharniśaṃ kriyā guṇair na hāniṃ yad upaiti mauśalī /
/ vivṛddha evotpalavac ca yad guṇair manuṣyadharmād adhikaprayojanaiḥ // PS, IV, 42 //
/ kusīdānāṃ punaḥ sudūravidūre bodhiḥ / nāsti kusīdasya dānaṃ yāvan nāsti prajnā nāsti kusīdasya parārtha iti / *Sāgaramati* in *Śikṣ*, p. 146.20–21 /
/ kleśānāṃ mūlam ekaṃ hi / kausīdyaṃ yasya vidyate /
/ kausīdyam ekam yasyāsti / tasyā dharmo na vidyate // *Dharmasamuccaya*, XXX, 58a–b; 59a–b //
/ saṃsārakoṭyor ubhayoḥ samānaiḥ prayāmasārair divasair yadi syuḥ /
/ saṃvatsarās tatpracayātidīrghaiḥ kalpaiḥ samudrodakabindutulyaiḥ //
/ utpādayeyaṃ yadi bodhicittam ekaikam etena parākrameṇa /
/ saṃbhāraśeṣaṃ cinuyāṃ tathāpi bhūyasas utsāritakhedadainyaḥ // PS, IV, 5–6 //
/ saṃsāraduḥkhaṃ svam acintayitvā saṃnāhadārḍhyaṃ yad acintyam evam /
/ ādyaṃ samādānam idam vadanti vīravratānāṃ karuṇātmakānām // PS, IV, 8 //
/ . . . tadvipakṣaḥ ka ucyate /
/ ālasyaṃ kutsitāśaktir viṣādātmāvamanyanā // CA, from VII, 2 //
/ avyāpārasukhāsvādanidrāpāśrayatṛṣṇayā /
/ saṃsāraduḥkhānudvegād ālasyam upajāyate // CA, VII, 3 //
/ muktā dharmaratiṃ śreṣṭham anantaratisaṃtatim /
/ ratir auddhatyahāsyādau duḥkhahetāu kathaṃ tava // CA, VII, 15 //
/ vaivāvasādaḥ kartavyaḥ kuto me bodhir ity ataḥ /
/ yasmāt tathāgataḥ satyaṃ satyavādīdam uktavān //
/ te 'py āsandaṃśamaśakā makṣikāḥ kṛmayas tathā /
/ yair utsāhabalotprāptā durāpā bodhir uttamā //
/ kim utāhaṃ naro jātyā śakto jñātuṃ hitāhitam /
/ sarvajñānītyanutsargād bodhiṃ kiṃ nāpnuyāmy aham // CA, VII, 17–19 //
/ bodhisattvenaivaṃ cittam utpādayitavyaṃ ye 'pi te 'bhisaṃbuddhās tathāgatā arhantaḥ samyaksaṃbuddhāḥ ye cābhisaṃbudhyante ye vā abhisaṃbhotsyante te 'pidṛśenaiva

nayena īdṛśyā pratipadā / īdṛśenaiva vīryeṇābhisaṃbuddhā abhisaṃbudhyante 'bhisaṃbhotsyante ca / yāvan na te tathāgatabhūtā evābhisaṃbuddhā / aham api tathā tathā ghaṭiṣye tathā tathā vyāyaṃsye sarvasattvasādhāraṇena vīryeṇa sarvasattvārambanena vīryeṇa yathāham anuttarāṃ samyaksaṃbodhim abhisaṃbhotsya iti / *Ratnamegha* in *Śikṣ*, p. 34.14–18 /

/ athāpi hastapādādidātavyam iti me bhayam /
/ gurulāghavamūḍhatvaṃ tan me syād avicārataḥ //
/ chettavyaś cāsmi bhettavyo dāhyaḥ pāvyo 'py anekaśaḥ /
/ kalpakoṭīr asaṃkhyeyā na ca bodhir bhaviṣyati //
/ etat tu me parimitaṃ duḥkhaṃ saṃbodhisādhanam /
/ naṣṭasalyavyathāpohe tadutpāṭanaduḥkhavat //
/ sarve 'pi vaidyāḥ kurvanti kriyāduḥkhair arogatām /
/ tasmād bahūni duḥkhāni hatuṃ soḍhavyam alpakam // CA, VII, 20–23 //

/ kriyām imam apy ucitaṃ varavaidyo na dattavān /
/ madhureṇopacāreṇa cikitsati mahāturān //
/ ādāu sākādidāne 'pi niyojayati nāyakaḥ /
/ tat karoti kramāt paścād yat svamāṃsāny api tyajet //
/ yada śakeṭhv iva prajñā svamāṃse 'py upajāyate /
/ māṃsāsthityajatas yasya tad kiṃ nāma duṣkaram // CA, VII 24–26 //

/ na duḥkhī tyaktapāpatvāt paṇḍitatvān na durmanāḥ /
/ mithyākalpanayā citte pāpāt kāye yato vyathā //
/ puṇyena kāyaḥ sukhitaḥ pāṇḍityena manaḥ sukhi /
/ tiṣṭhan parārthaṃ saṃsāre kṛpāluḥ kena khidyate // CA, VII 27–28 //

/ evaṃ sukhāt sukhaṃ gacchan ko viṣīdet sacetanaḥ /
/ bodhicittarathaṃ prāpya sarvakhedaśramāpaham // CA, VII 30 //

/ nāpatpratīkāravidhir viṣādas tasmād alaṃ dainyaparigraheṇa /
/ dhairyāt tu kāryapratipattidakṣāḥ kṛcchrāṇy akṛcchreṇa samuttiranti //
/ viṣādadainyaṃ vyavadhūya tasmāt kāryāvakāśaṃ kriyayā bhajadhvam /
/ prājnasya dhairyajvalitaṃ hi tejaḥ sarvārthasiddhigrahaṇāgrahas taḥ // *Jātakamālā*, XIV, k. 10811 //

/ dharmacchandaviyogena paurvikena mamādhunā /
/ vipattir īdṛsī jātā ko dharme chandam utsṛjet //
/ kusalānāṃ ca sarveṣāṃ chandaṃ mūlaṃ munir jagau / CA, VII, 39–40ab //
/ tasyāpi mūlaṃ satataṃ vipākaphalabhāvanā / CA, VII, 40cd /
/ aprameyā mayā doṣā hantavyāḥ svaparātmanoḥ /
/ ekaikasyāpi doṣasya yatra kalpārṇavaiḥ kṣayaḥ //
/ tatra doṣakṣayārambhe kośo 'pi mama nekṣyate /
/ aprameyavyathābhājye noraḥ spuṭati me katham //
/ guṇā mayārjanīyāś ca bahavaḥ svaparātmanoḥ /
/ tatraikaikaguṇābhāso bhavet kalpārṇavair na vā //
/ guṇaleśe 'pi nābhyāso mama jātaḥ kadā cana /
/ vṛthā nītaṃ mayā janma kathaṃ cil labdhasadbhutam // CA, VII, 33–36 //
/ pūrvaṃ nirūpya sāmagrīm ārabhen nārabhet vā /
/ anārambhe varaṃ nāma na tvārabhya nivartanam //
/ janmāntare 'pi so 'bhyāsaḥ pāpād duḥkhaṃ ca vardhate /
/ anyac ca kāryakālaṃ ca hīnaṃ tac ca na sādhitam // CA, VII, 47–48 //
/ triṣu māno vidhātavyaḥ karmopakleśaśaktiṣu / CA, VII, 49ab /
/ mayaivaikena kartavyam ity eṣā karmamānitā / CA, VII, 49cd /
/ kleśasvatantro loko 'yaṃ na kṣamaḥ svārthasādhane /
/ tasmān mayaiṣāṃ kartavyaṃ nāśakto 'haṃ yathā janaḥ // CA, VII, 50 //
/ nīcaṃ karma karoty anyaḥ kathaṃ mayy api tiṣṭhati / CA, VII, 51ab /
/ mānāc cen na karomy etan māno naśyatu me varaṃ / CA, VII, 51cd /
/ mayā hi sarvaṃ jetavyam ahaṃ jeyo na kenacit /
/ mayaiṣa māno veḍhavyo jinasiṃhasuto hy ahaṃ // CA, VII, 55 //
/ mṛtaṃ duṇḍubham āsādhya kāko 'pi garuḍāyate /
/ āpad ābādhate 'lpāpi mano me yadi durbalam //
/ viṣādakṛtaniśceṣṭe āpadaḥ sukarā nanu / CA, VII, 52–53ab //
/ vyutthitas ceṣṭamānas tu mahatām api durjayaḥ //
/ tasmād dṛḍhena cittena karomy āpadam āpadaḥ / CA, VII, 53cd–54ab //
/ trailokyavijigīṣutvaṃ hāsyam āpajjitasya me / CA, VII, 54cd /
/ yad evāpadyate karma tatkarmavyasanī bhavet /

/ tatkarmaśauṇḍo 'tṛptātmā krīḍaphalasukhepsuvat // CA, VII, 62 //
/ sukhārthaṃ kriyate karma tathāpi syān na vā sukham /
/ karmaiva tu sukhaṃ yasya niṣkarmā sa sukhī katham // CA, VII, 63 //
/ kāmair na tṛptiḥ saṃsāre kṣuradhārāmadhūpamaiḥ /
/ puṇyāmṛtaiḥ kathaṃ tṛptivipākamadhuraiḥ śivaiḥ // CA, VII, 64 //
/ tasmāt karmāvasāne 'pi nimajjet tatra karmaṇi /
/ yathā madhyāhnasaṃtapta ādāu prāptasarāḥ karī // CA, VII, 65 //
/ balanāśānubandhe tu punaḥ kartuṃ parityajet /
/susamāptaṃ ca tan muñced uttarottaratṛṣṇayā // CA, VII, 66 //
/ viśeṣotkarṣaniyamo na kadācid abhūt tava /
/ atas tvayi viśeṣānāṃ chinnas taratamakramaḥ // *Śatapañcāśatka*, II, 21 //
/ kleśaprahārān saṃrakṣet kleśāṃs ca prahared dṛḍham /
/ khadgayuddham ivāpannaḥ śikṣitenāriṇā saha // CA, VII, 67 //
/ tatra khadgaṃ yathā bhraṣṭaṃ gṛhṇīyāt sabhayas tvaram /
/ smṛtikhadgaṃ tathā bhraṣṭaṃ gṛhṇīyān narakān smaran // CA, VII, 68 //
/ viṣaṃ rudhiram āsādhya prasarpati yathā tanāu /
/ tathaiva cchidram āsādhya doṣas citte prasarpati // CA, VII, 69 //
/ tailapātradharo yadvad asihastair adhiṣṭhitaḥ /
/ skhalite maraṇatrāsāt tatparaḥ syāt tathā vratī // CA, VII, 70 //
/ tasmād utsaṅgage sarpe yathottiṣṭhati satvaram /
/ nidrālasyāgame tadvat pratikurvati satvaram // CA, VII, 71 //
/ ekaikasmiṃs chale suṣṭhu paritapya vivintayet /
/ kathaṃ karomi yenedaṃ punar me na bhaved iti // CA, VII, 72 //
/ saṃsargaṃ karma vā prāptam icched etena hetunā /
/ kathaṃ nāmāsv avasthāsu smṛtyabhyāso bhaved iti // CA, VII, 73 //
/ laghuṃ kuryāt tathātmānam apramādakathāṃ smaran /
/ karmāgamād yathā pūrvaṃ sajjaḥ sarvatra vartate // CA, VII, 74 //
/ yathāiva tūlakaṃ vāyor gamanāgamane vaśam /
/ tathotsāhavaśaṃ yāyād ṛddhis caivaṃ samṛdhyati // CA, VII, 75 //

/ nākrtvā duṣkaraṃ karma durlabhaṃ labhyate padam /
/ ity ātmanirapekṣeṇa vīryaṃ saṃvardhitaṃ tvayā // *Śatapañcāśatka*, II, 20 //
/ bodhisattvapiṭakaśravaṇacintāpūrvakaṃ yal laukikaṃ lokottaraṃ bodhisattvānāṃ kuśalaṃ cittaikagryaṃ cittasthitiḥ samathapakṣyā vā vipaśyanāpakṣyā vā yuganaddhavāhimārgaṃ tadubhayapakṣyā vā / ayaṃ bodhisattvānāṃ dhyānasvabhāvo veditayaḥ / *Bodhisattvabhūmi*, p. 207.3 – 7, Wogihara edition //
/ vardhayitvaivam utsāhaṃ samādhāu sthāpayen manaḥ /CA, VIII, 1ab /
/ sarvajñeyapraveśāya ca sarvajñeyānupraviṣṭaś ca yo dharmānāṃ pravicayaḥ pañcavidyāsthānāny ālambya pravartate adhyātmavidyāṃ hetuvidyāṃ cikitsavidyāṃ śabdavidyāṃ śilpakarmasthānavidyāṃ ca / ayaṃ bodhisattvānāṃ prajñāsvabhāvo veditavyaḥ / *Bodhisattvabhūmi*, p. 212.2 – 7, Wogihara ed. //
/ yatrāntare 'smi bhavate pragṛhītaprajñā tatu labdhu cakṣu bhavatī imu nāmadheyam /
/ yatha citrakarma pariniṣṭhita cakṣuhīno na ca tāva puṇyu labhate akaritva cakṣuḥ // *Saṃcaya*, VII, 2 //
/ puṇyāni dānaprabhṛtiny amūni prajñāsanāthāny adhikaṃ vibhānti /
/ hiraṇmayānīva vibhūṣaṇāni pratyuptaratnadyutibhāsvarāṇi //
/ kriyāsu sāmarthyaguṇaṃ hi teṣāṃ prajñaiva vistāriṇam ādadhāti /
/ svārthapravṛttāu viśadakramānāṃ yathā manaḥsaṃtatir indriyāṇām // PS, VI, 1 – 2 //
/ śraddhādikānām api cendriyānāṃ prajñāgraṇī buddhir ivendriyānām /
/ guṇāguṇān vetti hi tatsanāthaḥ kleśakṣaye naipuṇam ety ataś ca // PS, VI, 4 //
/ prajñāsamunmīlitacakṣuṣas tu dattvā svamāṃsāny api bodhisattvāḥ /
/ naivonnatiṃ nāvanatiṃ prayānti bhaiṣajyavṛkṣā iva nirvikalpāḥ // PS, VI, 6 //
/ nātmārtham apy asti tu yasya śīlaṃ prajñasya tasyāsti kathaṃ parārtham /

/ yo dṛṣṭadoṣo bhavabandhānāṃ lokān samastāṃs tata ujjihīrṣuḥ // PS, VI, 12 //
/ prajñānvitānāṃ tu parāpakārāḥ kṣamāgunāḥ sthairyakarā bhavanti /
/ bhadrātmakānām iva vāraṇānāṃ karmāśrayā naikavidhā viśeṣāḥ //
/ niṣkevalaṃ vīryam api śramāya prajñāsanāthasya tu tasya kārye / PS, VI, 14–15ab //
/ tad dhyānam ekāntasukhābhirāmaṃ katham pravekṣyanty asatāṃ manāṃsi /
/ sthūlāni doṣopacayair mahadbhiḥ prajñotpathaṃ nyāyam ivāśritāni // PS, VI, 17 //
/ divyapratispardhibhir indriyārthair narendrabhāve 'pi hi bodhisattvāḥ /
/ na yad virūpāṃ prakṛtiṃ vrajanti prajñā guṇāmātyasanāthatā sā //
/ paropakāraikarasā ca maitrī rāgoparāgaprativarjitā ca /
/ parasya duḥkheṣu parā dayā ca na śokabhārālasatāṃ gatā ca //
/ anuddhatatvaṃ mudite 'pi citte tamonirārambham upekṣitaṃ ca /
/ te ca guṇā(ś) cābhyadhikaṃ vibhānti prajñāniruddhapratipakṣamārgāḥ // PS, VI, 43- 45 //
/ ko vismayo vātra sutapriyāyā mātuḥ samīyād yad iyaṃ vibhūtiḥ /
/ daśaprakāro 'pi yadā munīnāṃ tadāśrayād eva balaprakarṣaḥ /
/ udety asādhāraṇasundaraś ca śeṣo 'py asaṃkhyo guṇaratnarāśiḥ //
/ śaṣtrāṇi cakṣuḥpratimāni loke nidhanabhūtāṃś ca kalāviśeṣān /
/ mantrān paritrāṇakṛto vicitrān dharmavyavasthāś ca pṛthagviśeṣāḥ //
/ paryāyacitraṃ ca vimokṣamārgaṃ tat tac ca lokasya hitopayādi /
/ yad bodhisattvāḥ pravidarśayanti prajñāprabhāvābhyudayaḥ sa sarvaḥ // PS, VI, 39cd–42 //
/ jātyandhakoṭiniyutāny avināyakānāṃ mārge akovidu kuto nagarapraveśe /
/ vina prajña pañca imi pāramitā acakṣuḥ avināyakā na prabhavanti spṛsetu bodhim // *Saṃcaya*, VII, 1 //
/ prajñāviyogāt phalalālasānāṃ naiva svatodānaviśuddhir asti /

/ tyāgaṃ parārthaṃ hi vadanti dānaṃ śeṣas tu vṛddhyartham iva prayogaḥ // PS, VI, 5 //
/ śīlasya śuddhiḥ kuta eva tasya yaḥ prajñayā nāpahṛtāndhakāraḥ /
/ prāyeṇa śīlāni hi tadviyogād āmarṣadoṣaiḥ kaluṣīkriyante // PS, VI, 11 //
/ prajñāvipakṣair hṛdi soparāge kṣamāguṇaḥ kena dhṛtiṃ labheta /
/ guṇāguṇāvekṣaṇakātarākṣe khyāto guṇair vīra iva kṣitīśe // PS, VI, 13 // (According to Tibetan, *khyāto 'guṇe*).
/ yasmāt paraṃ sūkṣmataraṃ na kiṃ cid yan naipuṇānāṃ paramaḥ prakarṣaḥ /
/ yat kāmadoṣādibhir āvṛtānāṃ manaḥpathaṃ naiva kadā cit eti // PS, VI, 16 //
/ prajñānirudyogamater hi dṛṣṭir nāyāti śuddhiṃ . . . / PS, VI, 18a and part of 18b //
/ sahasraraśmer udaye 'pi yāni tamāṃsi rundhanti jagadgatāni /
/ namaikaśeṣāni karoti tāni prajñāprabhāyāḥ prasaraprabhāvaḥ // PS, VI, 25 //
/ prajñābhiyuktasya yatas tato 'syām sarvābhisāreṇa parākrameta / PS, VI, 28cd /
/ ālasyajṛmbhitamatitvam asatsahāyā nidrānivṛttir aviniścayaśīlatā ca /
/ jñāne muner iva kutūhalitānivṛttir mithyābhimānaparisaṃkucitāś ca pṛcchāḥ //
/ dainyena cātmaparitāpasamudbhavena vidvajjanābhigamanādarakātaratvam /
/ mithyāvikalpapaṭutā vitathā ca dṛṣṭir mohāya tatpraśamanāya tu tadvipakṣāḥ // PS, VI, 52–53 //
/ tatprāptaye śrutam . . . saṃceyam āśrayasahaṃ gurum abhyupetya / PS, VI, 47ab; Tib. 47ab does not include rendition for Skt. *aśitivikalpacitram* ('hearing' in eighty different kinds of discursive thought) //
/ alpaśruto 'ndha iva vetti na bhāvanāyā mārgaṃ vicintayati kāni ca tadvihīnaḥ /
/ tasmāc chrutaṃ prati yateta tadāśrayā hi prajñā samudbhavati cintanabhāvanābhyām // PS, VI, 48 //

/ trimaṇḍalavikalpo yas taj jñeyāvaraṇaṃ matam /
/ mātsaryādivipakṣo yas tat kleśāvaraṇaṃ matam //
/ etat prahāṇahetuś ca nānyaḥ prajñām ṛte tataḥ /
/ śreṣṭhā prajñā śrutaṃ cāsya mūlaṃ tasmāc chrutaṃ param //
Uttaratantra, V, 14–15 //
/ kṣameta śrutam eṣeta saṃśrayeta vanaṃ tataḥ /
/ samādhānāya yujyeta . . . // *Śikṣ*, k. 20a–c /
/ akṣamasya hi ādāu vīryaṃ pratihanyate 'khedasahatvāt / aśrutavāṃś ca na samādhyupāyaṃ jānāti / nāpi kleśaśodhanopāyam / tasmād akhinnaḥ śrutam eṣeta / *Śikṣ*, p. 100.5–7 /
/ tathā hi kulaputrāḥ śrutavataḥ prajñāgamo bhavati / prajñāvataḥ kleśapraśamo bhavati / niḥkleśasya māro 'vatāraṃ na labhate / *Nārāyaṇa* in *Śikṣ*, p. 105.8–9 /
/ vidyāsthāne pañcavidhe yogam akṛtvā sarvajñatvaṃ naiti kathaṃcit paramāryaḥ /
/ ity anyeṣāṃ nigrahaṇānugrahaṇāya svājñārthaṃ vā tatra karoty eva sa yogam // SA, XI, 60 //
/ ābhiḥ ṣaḍbhiḥ pāramitābhir anuttarāyai samyaksaṃbodhaye samudāgacchanto bodhisattvā mahāśukladharmārṇavā mahāśukladharmasamudrā ity ucyante sarvasattvasarvākārasaṃpattihetumahāratnahradā ity ucyante / asya punar eṣām evam apramānasya puṇyajñānasaṃbhārasamudāgamasya nānyat phalam evam anurūpaṃ yathā 'nuttaraiva samyaksaṃbodhir iti / *Bodhisattvabhūmi*, Wogihara ed., p. 216 /
/ dānaṃ samaṃ priyākhyānam arthacaryā samārthatā /
/ taddeśanā samādāya svānuvṛttibhir iṣyate // SA, XVI, 72 //
/ upāyo 'nugrahakaro grāhako 'tha pravarthakaḥ /
/ tathānuvarthako jñéyaś catuḥsaṃgrahavastutaḥ // SA, XVI, 73 //
/ ādyena bhājanībhāvo dvitīyena adhimucyanā /
/ pratipattis tṛtīyena caturthena viśodhanā // SA, XVI, 74 //
/ parṣatkarṣaṇaprayuktair vidhir eṣa samāśritaḥ /
/ sarvārthasiddhāu sarveṣāṃ sukhopāyaś ca śasyate // SA, XVI, 77 //
/ catuḥ saṃgrahavastutvaṃ saṃgrahadvayato mataṃ /
/ āmiṣeṇāpi dharmeṇa dharmeṇālambanād api // SA, XVI, 75 //
/ saṃgṛhītā grahīṣyante saṃgṛhyante ca ye 'dhunā /
/ sarve ta evaṃ tasmāc ca vartma tat sattvapācane // SA, XVI, 78 //

Index to the Bodhisattva Section, *Lam Rim Chen Mo*

Abbreviations:
Bodhisattva: Bo.
name: n.
Thought of Enlightenment: Enl.Thought

D

E

H

I

J

K

L

M

N

O